"WHAT IS JOHN?"
READERS AND READINGS OF THE FOURTH GOSPEL

SOCIETY
OF BIBLICAL
LITERATURE

SBL

SYMPOSIUM SERIES

Gail R. O'Day, Editor

Number 3

"WHAT IS JOHN?"

READERS AND READINGS OF THE FOURTH GOSPEL

edited by
Fernando F. Segovia

Fernando F. Segovia
editor

"What Is John?"
READERS AND READINGS
OF THE FOURTH GOSPEL

Scholars Press
Atlanta, Georgia

"What Is John?"
Readers and Readings of the Fourth Gospel

edited by
Fernando F. Segovia

© 1996
The Society of Biblical Literature

Library of Congress Cataloging in Publication Data
What is John? : readers and readings of the fourth Gospel / Fernando
F. Segovia, editor.
    p. cm. — (SBL symposium series ; no. 3)
  Includes bibliographical references.
  ISBN 0-7885-0239-5 (cloth : alk. paper).—ISBN 0-7885-0240-9
(pbk. : alk. paper)
  1. Bible. N.T. John—Criticism, interpretation, etc. 2. Bible.
N.T. John—Criticism, interpretation, etc.—History—20th century.
I. Segovia, Fernando F. II. Series: Symposium series (Society of
Biblical Literature) ; no. 3.
BS2615.2.W47 1996
226.5'06—dc20   96-2495
                                    CIP

Printed in the United States of America
on acid-free paper

Contents

Preface

The idea behind the present volume goes back to an issue of the journal *Semeia* for which I served as editor along with R. Alan Culpepper entitled *The Fourth Gospel from a Literary Perspective (Semeia* 53; Atlanta: Scholars Press, 1991). As the title indicates, this issue was devoted to an analysis of the Fourth Gospel from the perspective of literary criticism, with a focus on both narrative criticism (the narrative features of the text as text) and reader-response criticism (the interaction between text and reader). The volume also contained two critical responses to the collection as a whole, both of which highlighted and critiqued the highly formalist character of the entire enterprise.

Thus, Johannes Beutler of the Philosophisch-Theologische Hochschule Sankt-Georgen, observed ("Response from an European Perspective") that, from a hermeneutical point of view, the emphasis on the "literary" dimensions of the text had resulted not only in a neglect of the social conditions of authors and readers of the Gospel but also in the lack of any type of reflection on the part of the authors with regard to themselves as subjects of interpretation. Similarly, Mary Ann Tolbert, then of Vanderbilt University and now at the Pacific School of Religion, pointed out ("A Response from a Literary Perspective") that in its use of "literary criticism" the collection had remained quite formalist in tone and mode, so that even when calling upon reader-response criticism, as many of the articles had done, the "readers" in question—that is to say, the real readers behind the different reader constructs invoked—had remained largely in hiding. She went on to point out that, despite the excellent tenor and value of the collection as a whole, there was a lot more to contemporary literary criticism "than it is presented, suggested, or even dreamt of in most of these discussions" (211). Both respondents were quite correct: the collection had remained, for the most part, an exercise in artistic or esthetic formalism, whether from the point of view of the text as text or of the interaction between reader and text.

In my introductory essay to the volume ("Towards a New Direction in Johannine Scholarship"), I responded that these comments were not only very much to the point but also called for immediate and systematic attention. In effect, real readers of the Gospel had a twofold task ahead of them: not only did they have to become critically aware of the different reading constructs and strategies employed in their approaches to and interpretations of the Gospel, but they also had to be forthcoming as well with regard to their own social location as interpreters of the text and hence with regard to themselves as real readers. I concluded by stating my own determination, in my position as incoming chair of the SBL Johannine Literature Section, to take up this twofold challenge in the section by launching an ongoing, multiyear series under the title of "Readers and Readings of the Fourth Gospel."

This series lasted three years in all, beginning with the 1991 Annual Meeting in Kansas City and ending with the 1993 Annual Meeting in Washington, D.C., and proved enormously successful. I called upon a broad variety of leading Johannine scholars in the country to offer papers on the Gospel, with a specific focus on literary criticism, broadly conceived, but above all with explicit and self-conscious attention to be given to reader constructs and strategies as well as to the real readers behind such strategies and constructs. The result was a splendid series of position papers approaching the Fourth Gospel from a number of different perspectives but with a common focus on reading as such. The present volume gathers together these papers in revised form in a first major section ("Part I: Readers and Readings of the Fourth Gospel").

Given the nature of the papers, moreover, an overall division readily suggested itself. While some papers could be readily classified as primarily literary in nature, that is, as following certain established lines of inquiry within literary criticism (Koester; Kysar; Willett Newheart; Staley), others could be seen as more theological in nature (Culpepper; Kysar; Schneiders; Smith). Consequently, I availed myself of those two categories, "Literary Approaches" and "Theological Approaches," for the division of the papers. To be sure, this distinction, like all distinctions, is artificial and porous; nevertheless, I believe it is helpful as a heuristic device, as a way of orienting readers of and within the collection itself.

As a proper climax to the series, I further organized a symposium on the Gospel around the theme of "The Fourth Gospel at the Close of the Twentieth Century," which was held as a featured session of the Section at the 1994 Annual Meeting in Chicago. Once again, I called upon a number of leading Johannine scholars to reflect, as real readers, on the significance and role of the Fourth Gospel as the century drew to a close. The result was again a splendid series of reflection papers on the Gospel from a variety of different perspectives. The present volume also brings together these papers in revised form in a second major section ("Part Two: The Fourth Gospel at the Close of the Twentieth Century").

Finally, the volume also contains a conclusion from me as editor, in which I proceed to analyze in comparative fashion the entire collection from the point of view of reading constructs and strategies, with particular emphasis on the question of real readers.

A word about the title for the volume is in order. This collection of position papers and reflection papers on John reveals the enormous diversity of contemporary approaches to the Gospel as well as the enormous range of opinion regarding not only its meaning and interpretation but also its significance and relevance. The title reflects, therefore, a bit of intertextual play with the Gospel itself via a rephrasing of Pilate's own question of Jesus in the trial narrative (18:38, "What is truth?"). This serious play, with its substitution of "John" for "truth," is meant to convey this slippery nature of the text's meaning and significance in contemporary Johannine Studies. In the narrative of contemporary Johannine scholarship, there is, I am afraid, no authoritative Jesus-character and no omniscient and reliable narrator to give us the proper answer to the question—*"What is John?";* what we find instead is a host of answers from a variety of different perspectives, methodological as well as theoretical—*Readers and Readings of the Fourth Gospel.* I would only add that, at the end of this first series of "Readers and Readings of the Fourth Gospel" and given its enormous success both in terms of the papers and reflections presented and the public in attendance at the different sessions, a second series was launched, under the same title, which would include papers not only from a broad literary perspective but also from a similarly broad sociocultural perspective, would involve Johannine scholars from abroad as well as from the United States, and would conclude with a similar symposium on the significance and role of the Gospel at the turn of the century.

At the conclusion of the project, a number of people deserve a very special word of thanks. First, all the scholars whose work is represented in these pages for their kind willingness to form part of the project. Second, Professor Gail R. O'Day, of the Candler School of Theology at Emory University, for her gracious acceptance, as editor of the SBL Symposium Series, to have the volume published as part of the series. Given the goals of the series, the fit, I believe, is an ideal one. First, the volume is a collection of essay-length studies, contributed by various scholars, which address a particular topic related to biblical literature and/or its cultural environment. Second, it consists of studies that have emerged from collaborative work within the Society's own program units. Finally, it is a collection that is best published together rather than separately. Indeed, its value for students and scholars alike should be clear in these days of focused and critical attention on the interpretive process as such. Third, the staff of Scholars Press for their invaluable help throughout the process of publication. Finally, Mr. W. Gregory Carey, of the Graduate Department of Religion at Vanderbilt University, who served as my research assistant for this project and whose editorial expertise and professionalism are evident throughout these pages.

Contributors

R. Alan Culpepper
Department of Religion
Baylor University
Waco, Texas

Gail R. O'Day
Candler School of Theology
Emory University
Atlanta, Georgia

Werner H. Kelber
Department of Religious Studies
Rice University
Houston, Texas

Craig H. Koester
Luther Seminary
St. Paul, Minnesota

Robert Kysar
Candler School of Theology
Emory University
Atlanta, Georgia

J. Ramsey Michaels
Professor Emeritus
Southwest Missouri State
University
Springfield, Missouri

Michael Willett Newheart
The School of Divinity
Howard University
Washington, D.C.

Sandra M. Schneiders
The Jesuit School of Theology
at Berkeley
Berkeley, California

Fernando F. Segovia
The Divinity School
Vanderbilt University
Nashville, Tennessee

Luise Schottroff
Gesamthochschule Kassel
Universität
Kassel, Germany

D. Moody Smith
The Divinity School
Duke University
Durham, North Carolina

Jeffrey L. Staley
Department of Religious Studies
Lewis & Clark College
Portland, Oregon

Abbreviations

AB	Anchor Bible
Apol.	Justin Martyr, *Apology*
BA	*Biblical Archaeologist*
BETL	Bibliotheca ephemeridum theologicarum lovaniensium
Bib	*Biblica*
BTB	*Biblical Theology Bulletin*
CR	*Critical Review of Books in Religion*
Eccl. Hs.	Eusebius, *Ecclesiastical History*
HTR	*Harvard Theological Review*
JAAR	*Journal of the American Academy of Religion*
JBL	*Journal of Biblical Literature*
JSNT	*Journal for the Study of the New Testament*
JSNTSup	Journal for the Study of the New Testament Supplement Series
NovTSup	Novum Testamentum, Supplements
NTS	*New Testament Studies*
RevExp	*Review & Expositor*
SBLDS	Society of Biblical Literature Dissertation Series
SBLMS	Society of Biblical Literature Monograph Series
SBLSP	Society of Biblical Literature Seminar Papers
SNTSMS	Society for New Testament Studies Monograph Series
TS	*Theological Studies*

PART I
READERS AND READINGS OF THE FOURTH GOSPEL

LITERARY APPROACHES

Chapter One

The Spectrum of Johannine Readers

CRAIG R. KOESTER

Identifying the readers of the Fourth Gospel is not a new question. Scholars have long understood that knowing something about the readers of the text was integral to appreciating the message of the text. The persistent interest in the readers of the Gospel stems, in part, from the recognition that the material presented in the narrative was selected and recounted with readers in mind. The evangelist addressed them directly at the conclusion of chap. 20, saying "These things have been written in order that *you* may believe that Jesus is the Christ, the Son of God, and that believing, *you* may have life in his name" (20:31). When the pronoun "you" is taken seriously, it becomes clear that the Fourth Gospel is an exercise in communication; it is a dynamic expression of a message intended to shape the stance of its readers.

But to whom does the "you" at the end of chap. 20 refer? At one end of the reading spectrum are the contemporary readers, that eclectic group comprised of all who read the Gospel today. Those who belong to this group usually turn to the Fourth Gospel in the hope of discovering something significant in its pages, and the perennial popularity of John's Gospel indicates that many readers do find it to be an engaging and meaningful text. The problem is that contemporary readers do not necessarily understand John's Gospel in the same way. The vigorous and extended discussions of the Gospel at both the scholarly and popular levels suggest that there are about as many read*ings* as there are read*ers*. Few, however, would want to say that the text simply means whatever a reader wants it to mean, that all readers are equally competent, or that all readings of the text are equally valid. Most contemporary readers recognize the need to distinguish readings that are more or less adequate from those that are simply mistaken.

Historical and Implied Readers

Scholars have attempted to establish some interpretive parameters by pursuing "the quest for the historical reader," that is, by attempting to reconstruct the historical context of the readers to whom the Gospel was first addressed. Special attention has been given to evidence within the text that could be compared with material from other sources that might provide glimpses into the events and intellectual currents affecting early Johannine Christianity. Attempts also have been made to delineate levels of sources and redaction within the text, in order to discern connections between particular passages and the changing circumstances of a community of faith. Behind this quest lies the conviction that the Fourth Gospel was intended to speak to the issues confronting a discrete group of readers, to shape *their* views, and to influence *their* commitments. The hope is that if we, as modern readers, can temporarily enter into the circle of those who read the Gospel in the first century, and if we can read the Gospel with their eyes and listen to it with their ears, we will better be able to understand the evangelist in his own terms, rather than "in words which we moderns merely want to hear from his mouth," as Louis Martyn has put it.[1]

Attention to the differences between our own situation and outlook and those of the Gospel's first-century readers has helped discipline many to read the text carefully. Historical research is an invaluable means of self-criticism that cautions readers against absolutizing their own perspectives, and it must continue to play a key role in our attempts to assess whether or not a way of reading John's Gospel is viable. Yet it also can or should make us profoundly aware of the limits of our ability to reconstruct and enter into the life of first-century Johannine Christianity. Martyn prefaced one of his own valuable studies of the Johannine community by suggesting that when getting up each morning, a historian would do well to say three times slowly and with emphasis, "I do not know."[2] We cannot produce a portrait of the historical reader that is so complete that it guarantees the meaning of the text, and even as we gain some clarity about the first-century context we are still confronted with questions about how the text can speak to its twentieth-century readers in a compelling way.

Studies of the "implied reader" have provided a helpful means of approaching

---

[1] J. L. Martyn, *History and Theology in the Fourth Gospel* (2nd ed. rev. and enl.; Nashville: Abingdon Press, 1979) 18.

[2] J. L. Martyn, *The Gospel of John in Christian History: Essays for Interpreters* (New York: Paulist Press, 1979) 92.

this problem. Wolfgang Iser, for example, has stressed that when considering a literary work one must take into account "not only the actual text, but also, and in equal measure, the actions involved in responding to that text." [3] If a text imparts information, it also presupposes information; if it gives something to readers, it also demands something from readers—not just the original readers, but all readers. The text informs the reader selectively, stimulating the reader to supply what is not stated.[4] The expression "implied reader" designates one who possesses what is necessary for the text to exercise its effect. The implied reader is a literary construct, not a historical one, and a portrait of such a reader is not formulated by considering realities outside the text, but by looking at the network of structures within the text that invite a response from the reader. At a basic level, we can identify the kind of reader implied by a text by observing what the text assumes the reader knows and what it takes the trouble to explain.[5] Further refinement might entail distinguishing the implied reader from that shadowy figure known as the "narratee," that is, the reader who is addressed by the narrator at selected points in the Gospel story.[6]

The original "historical" readers of John's Gospel died centuries ago and were buried under the rubble of a culture that remains quite distant for most people who read the Gospel today. The implied reader is, to some extent, more immediate, since it is a literary construct and therefore can "only 'die' when the texts in which they exist are destroyed," as Jeffrey Staley has pointed out.[7] Nevertheless, at a fundamental level the implied reader of John's Gospel is also a stranger to contemporary readers, because the most essential thing that the implied reader knows is Koine Greek. Those who glance at the Greek text of the Gospel will see a sequence of curved lines on the page, an enigmatic sequence

---

[3] W. Iser, *The Implied Reader: Patterns of Communication in Prose Fiction from Bunyan to Beckett* (Baltimore: The John Hopkins University Press, 1974) 274.

[4] Ibid., 282.

[5] R. Alan Culpepper, *Anatomy of the Fourth Gospel: A Study in Literary Design* (Philadelphia: Fortress Press, 1983) 212.

[6] Ibid., 221. Jeffrey L. Staley *(The Print's First Kiss: A Rhetorical Investigation of the Implied Reader in the Fourth Gospel* [SBLDS 82; Atlanta: Scholars Press, 1988] 47) attempts to maintain a careful distinction between the implied reader and the narratee, but recognizes that there is considerable overlap between the two in John's Gospel.

[7] Staley, *The Print's First Kiss,* 30.

of squiggles that fall into patterns too regular to be accidental, yet too foreign to be understood. Similarly, those who listen to the Greek text will hear a rushing babble of noise, something full of sound and fury, yet—to the uninitiated—signifying nothing.[8]

For the text to make sense, readers must be able to connect the sounds or an lines with known realities, and those realities are, in a fundamental way, first-century Mediterranean realities. Readers must learn, for example, that the word *artos* refers to a baked mixture of flour and water, something usually called "bread" in English. The text can be translated of course, but translations are at best approximations. For many Americans, the word "bread" refers to an airy white plastic-wrapped loaves that crowd the supermarket shelves, bread that only vaguely resembles the coarse barley loaves baked over charcoal fires in eastern Mediterranean villages. Bread also has a different function in different cultures, and this too influences an way its significance is understood. In the Greco-Roman world, bread was a staple food, but in many parts of tropical Asia rice is the staple and bread is a luxury, a substance often associated with immigrants from Europe. Jesus' claim to be "the bread of life" must be understood in an appropriate cultural context: he was not claiming to be an imported luxury item but something essential for life.

Literary and historical approaches to the question of the Gospel's readers should be used in tandem. Studies of the implied reader drive us to consider again the context in which the Gospel was composed. Although we may want to say that the implied reader lives solely within the text, it is a text that was composed in a particular social and cultural context. At the same time, an must acknowledge the Fourth Gospel's striking ability to evoke responses from readers who know virtually nothing about the Greco-Roman world, readers who live in cultures as different from each other as they are from the culture of John's earliest readers. We must also keep in mind that the scholars who pursue historical questions presumably do so because they have *already* read the text and found it to be significant and engaging.

---

[8] On this point, see Bruce J. Malina, "Reading Theory Perspective: Reading Luke-Acts," in *The Social World of Luke-Acts: Models For Interpretation* (ed. Jerome H. Neyrey; Peabody, MA: Hendrickson, 1991) 3-23.

Spectrum of Readers and Readings

Although it is common to speak of "the reader" of the text, literary and historical studies suggest that it may be better to envision a spectrum of readers when considering John's Gospel. There are important indications that the Gospel was written for readers who did not all share the same perspective. Consider again the question of the implied reader. In his pioneering literary study of the Gospel, Alan Culpepper observed that the discourses in the Gospel would have made most sense for readers familiar with the major Jewish festivals. For example, the Bread of Life discourse in John 6 is set during the Passover season and develops Jesus' identity in light of traditions concerning the manna eaten by Israel's ancestors in the wilderness. Similarly, the messianic debates at the feast of Booths in chaps. 7 and 8 invoke images of water and light that were integral to the festival celebration. The comments made by the narrator, however, assume that readers have little knowledge of these festivals. The tension between the highly informed reader presupposed by the discourses and the more uninformed reader reflected in the narrator's comments suggests that the final form of the Gospel envisions a heterogeneous readership.[9] We do well, therefore, to think of a spectrum of implied readers, rather than a single, monochrome implied reader.

Recent attempts to sketch a profile of the early readers of the Gospel also suggest that the Johannine community encompassed various sorts of people by the time the Gospel was completed. It seems clear that the Gospel and the community developed over a period of time, although neither the literary history of the text nor the social history of the community can be reconstructed with certainty at each juncture. The final form of the Gospel probably addressed a community of Christians from different backgrounds.[10] A number of studies have suggested, first, that the nucleus of the community consisted of Christians of Jewish background, including some who had apparently been expelled from the synagogue, like the blind beggar of chap. 9 (cf. 16:2). The use of the Old Testament and Jewish traditions to demonstrate that Jesus was a rabbi, prophet, Messiah, and Son of God would have been especially important for such

---

[9] Culpepper, *Anatomy of the Fourth Gospel,* 221, 225.

[10] to See generally Raymond E. Brown, *The Community of the Beloved Disciple* (New York: Paulist Press, 1979).

readers. Second, the community probably came to include some Samaritan Christians. Unlike the other Gospels, John 4 says that a Samaritan village came to believe in Jesus, and the text intimates that the episode presaged the future missionary successes of Jesus' disciples. The Gospel's attention to Samaritan topography and traditions, especially traditions concerning Moses, suggests that the Johannine communities did include at least some Samaritan members. Third, there were probably some Gentile Greeks among the Johannine Christians. Just before the passion, a group of Greeks came to see Jesus, and their arrival signaled the coming of the hour when Jesus would be lifted up in death to draw all people to himself (12:20-22, 32). The Greeks did not see Jesus during his lifetime, but the universal significance of his death, proclaimed in the trilingual sign above the cross, was eventually made known to the Greeks by Jesus' disciples, and it seems likely that some of these Greeks were among the readers envisioned by the final form of the Gospel text.

If this scenario is correct, we cannot assume that all members of the Johannine community read the Gospel from the same perspective. A common Christian faith would have helped to foster a strong sense of solidarity within Johannine Christianity, but we cannot assume that it expunged all the variations in outlook that people of Jewish, Samaritan, and Greek background would have brought with them into the community of faith. The likelihood of such diversity increases when we recognize that there were almost certainly a number of Johannine congregations rather than a single community with all members residing in the same place. The Gospel itself is manifestly concerned about the children of God who were scattered abroad (11:52) and the Johannine Epistles reveal a situation in which Johannine congregations were geographically separated from each other and were comprised of Christians who did not necessarily know the members of their sister congregations.[11]

As the Johannine community came to include an increasingly diverse spectrum of readers, the Gospel could continue to be an important vehicle for its tradition because it conveyed a message that could be grasped at different levels. The text offered something for the maximally informed reader and

---

[11] Note especially the emphasis on welcoming fellow Christians who were strangers in 3 John 5-6. On the context generally, see Raymond E. Brown, *The Epistles of John* (AB 30; Garden City: Doubleday, 1982) 100-103.

something for the minimally informed reader. Readers did not need to comprehend the text fully in order to understand it in part. Some have argued, to be sure, that the meaning of the Gospel would be clear to insiders but opaque to the uninitiated and Martha sharp distinctions between truth and falsehood, light and darkness, what is "from above" and what is "from below," correspond to the distinction between the two types of readers.[12] Yet the Gospel also contains passages suggesting that truth is multidimensional and can be appropriated in stages.

Consider, for example, the story of the Samaritan woman. When she first encountered Jesus, she said, "How is it that you, a Jew, ask a drink of me, a woman of Samaria?" (4:9). Clearly the woman did not fully realize with whom she was speaking, but her perception of Jesus was true up to a point. Jesus was in fact a Jew, and in the course of their conversation he would speak as a Jew, by charging that the Samaritans worshipped what they did not know and by affirming that salvation would come from the Jews (4:22). Later, the woman rightly recognized that Jesus was more than an ordinary Jew, that he was a prophet, who knew her life story and prophesied the coming of worship in Spirit and in truth. Finally, the woman even wondered if Jesus might be the Messiah, and with that question she brought her townspeople to Jesus. They soon recognized that he was not only the deliverer of their nation but also the Savior of the World. At each stage, a new facet of Jesus' identity was recognized, without negating the aspects that had been previously identified: Jesus was simultaneously a Jew, a prophet, Messiah, and Savior of the world.

There is a similar progression in the Story of the blind beggar. Jesus placed mud on the man's eyes and commanded him to wash in the pool of Siloam. The man did so and regained his sight. Afterward, he returned to his usual haunts where the neighbors asked him what had happened. The beggar replied, "The man called Jesus made clay and anointed my eyes and said to me, 'Go to Siloam and wash'; so I went and washed and received my sight" (9:11). What the man said was accurate as far as it went, though it scarcely exhausted the meaning of his healing. Later, the depth of his perceptions increased, so that he told the Pharisees that Jesus must be a prophet (9:17) who had come from God (9:33)

---

[12] See, e.g., Wayne A. Meeks, "The Man from Heaven in Johannine Sectarianism," *JBL* 91 (1972) 4472, esp. 68.

and finally worshiped Jesus as the divine Son of man (9:35-38). Everything the beggar said was true and no single statement captured the full meaning of what had happened. Jesus was a man, but not only a man; Jesus was divine, but not only divine. Each of the beggar's statements revealed a new facet of meaning without negating what had been said before.

The story of the blind beggar also shows that the healing can be understood in ways that are not true. As the man born blind progressively unpacked the meaning of his healing and the identity of his healer, the Jewish authorities voiced their own erroneous understandings of the event. Jesus had healed the man on the sabbath by making clay and using it to anoint the man's eyes, actions that violated Jewish sabbath regulations. The Jewish law did make exceptions when an illness was life-threatening, but this was not the case with congenital blindness. Therefore, within this frame of reference, some of the authorities maintained that Jesus was not from God, since he did not keep the sabbath (9:16), and they concluded that the sign proved Jesus was a sinner (9:24). The literary context makes clear that these interpretations of the sign are patently false and stem from ignorance, not insight.

Reading the Good Shepherd Discourse

The way the man born blind "read" his own experience of healing is, in important ways, analogous to the way people read the text of the Gospel. At the level of the text, we find that a reader, like the beggar, has to reject certain false perceptions, while gradually moving toward a more complete understanding of the episode. The Gospel narrative contains much that is as ambiguous as the experience of healing, but it also guides readers toward a more complete understanding of its message by focusing attention on images that can be appreciated at various levels. Those who slowly wind their way through the Gospel's discourses may find themselves in a thick haze, engulfed by peculiar thought patterns, subtle allusions to the Old Testament and Jewish traditions, and apparent breaks in the logical sequence. Yet, through the bewildering mist certain key images recur, like flashes of a beacon helping readers to maintain their bearings as they make their way forward.[13]

---

[13] Meeks (ibid., 48), developing the insights of Edmund Leach, has noted how the Gospel communicates a basic message in different ways. On the dynamics of the Good Shepherd

An interesting example is the Good Shepherd discourse in John 10, which begins after the Jewish authorities cast out the blind beggar, when Jesus abruptly begins speaking about a sheepfold and sheep, a doorkeeper, shepherd, thieves, robbers, and strangers. Like the bystanders depicted in the narrative itself, modern interpreters have sometimes been confused about the identity of these figures, but Jesus if anything exacerbates the problem by adding a hireling, a wolf, and the mysterious "other sheep" to complicate the picture. Nevertheless, by repeating "I am the door"/"I am the door" (10:7, 9) and "I am the good shepherd"/"I am the good shepherd" (10:11, 14) Jesus establishes himself as the center of this swirling array of images and enables readers to begin making sense of the passage in terms of these leading ideas. Readers may not know the precise identity of the doorkeeper or the hireling, but they do know that Jesus is the door and the shepherd and that they must focus their attention on him. The text also helps readers by pointing to certain key functions of each image. The door is identified as the sole legitimate means of entry to the flock, and the shepherd as the one who enters the sheepfold by the door, calls the sheep by name, and leads them out to pasture. The text also adds that Jesus is the good shepherd, who knows the sheep intimately and lays down his life for them, so that the shepherd is sharply distinguished from the thieves, robbers, strangers, and hireling who do not care for the sheep.

The imagery remains evocative; there is much that is not defined and Johannine Christians may have understood the text somewhat differently depending on the kinds of associations they brought to the text. Therefore, we must now consider what sorts of associations people along the reading spectrum might have brought to the text. We begin by considering the minimal kinds of information early readers of the text would probably have had; then, we will turn to readers who were better informed.

At the broadest level, some of the associations would have come from the cultural milieu of the eastern Mediterranean. Those who knew Greek would have understood that the word *poimēn* referred to someone who tended sheep. A *poimēn* or shepherd was a common sight throughout the Greek-speaking

---

discourse, see also Robert Kysar, "Johannine Metaphor-Meaning and Function: A Literary Case Study of John 10:1-18," in *The Fourth Gospel from a Literary Perspective (Semeia 53;* ed. R. Alan Culpepper and Fernando F. Segovia; Atlanta: Scholars Press, 1991) 81-111.

world in the first century, and most readers probably would have connected the word with a fellow who had a weather-beaten face and was dressed in coarse homespun clothing, with a wooden staff in one hand, as he led a flock of sheep out to pasture.

Moving a step further, a *good* shepherd was regularly understood to be one who led and provided for the flock and who considered the welfare of the sheep instead of abusing them. Because of this role, images of shepherding were used throughout the ancient world for kings and other leaders. According to the Jewish Scriptures, some of the leading figures in Israel's history actually had been shepherds at some point in their lives. God appeared to Moses while he was tending sheep (Exod 3:1–6) and David learned the arts of war by defending his flock against predators (1 Sam 17:34–35). In other passages, the term "shepherd" was extended to Israel's leaders generally, and the prophets Ezekiel and Jeremiah castigated those who governed Israel, calling them shepherds who fed themselves instead of feeding their flocks (Ezek 34:1–10; Jer 23:1–4). A similar connection between good shepherding and good leadership was common among Greeks. The Greek classics, which were the mainstay of education throughout the Greco-Roman world, used the term "shepherd" for leaders like Agamemnon the king (*Iliad* 2.243ff.). In Plato's *Republic,* Socrates discussed ruling in terms of shepherding, insisting that the ruler or shepherd must seek out what is best for the people or the flock. Later, the philosopher Epictetus compared kings who mourned the misfortunes of their subjects to shepherds who wailed when a wolf carried away a sheep (*Discourses* 3.22.35).

The discourse could appropriate all these connotations of good leadership by describing how the good shepherd leads the sheep out of the sheepfold and goes before them (John 10:3–4). The discourse also redefines what it means to be a good shepherd or an ideal leader in light of the cross. Within the brief span of eight verses, Jesus speaks of laying down his life no less than five times (10:11–18). This self-giving sacrifice is the premier trait of Jesus the shepherd. Jews and Greeks alike would have expected gracious leaders, like good shepherds, to seek what is best for the sheep and perhaps even to risk their lives for the flock, but Jesus, *the* good shepherd, laid down his life for the sheep. By his crucifixion, Jesus showed that he was willing to give himself completely for the sake of the flock. Readers who had even minimal familiarity with eastern Mediterranean cultural patterns would be able to interpret the text in this way.

Now we can move a step further. Readers with more extensive knowledge of the Old Testament would discern other dimensions of meaning within the text without negating what has been said thus far.[14] In the Good Shepherd discourse, Jesus said, "I have other sheep that are not of this fold; I must bring them also, and they will heed my voice. So there shall be one flock, one shepherd" (10:16). The emphasis on "one flock, one shepherd" may well have prompted many readers to recall the extended discussion of shepherding in Ezekiel 34, where God castigated those who have failed to care for the flock of Israel and promised, "I will set up over them *one* shepherd, my servant David, and he shall feed them: he shall feed them and be their shepherd" (34:23). This text readily lends itself to messianic interpretation, and the connection between shepherding and messiahship is found implicitly or explicitly in other Jewish texts as well (cf. Jer 23:1–6; Ps. Sol. 17:40).

Readers who knew the Old Testament also may have detected divine overtones in Jesus' claim to be the good shepherd. The book of Ezekiel promised that David would shepherd Israel, but also said that the sheep would be gathered and tended by God himself. According to Ezekiel 34, God compared himself to a shepherd who gathers the sheep when they have been scattered, promising to provide good pasture for his flock, declaring, "I myself will be the shepherd of my sheep" (Ezek 34:11-15). The connotations of divinity would have been reinforced by other Old Testament references to God as the shepherd of Israel and to Israel as God's flock (e.g., Pss 23:1; 95:7; 100:3).

The way the evangelist portrays the reactions of listeners to Jesus' claims helps readers identify the range of meanings found in the image of the shepherd. In the scene immediately following the Good Shepherd discourse, people surrounded Jesus in the portico of Solomon and demanded to know if he was the Christ. He responded, "I told you, and you do not believe" (10:25). Jesus had not actually called himself the Christ, but he had repeatedly called himself "the

---

[14] On the Old Testament and other materials useful for comparison with John 10, see recently Johannes Beutler, "Der alttestamentlich-jüdische Hintergrund der Hirtenrede in Johannes 10," and J. D. Turner, "The history of religions background of John 10," in *The Shepherd Discourse of John 10 and its Context* (ed. Johannes Beutler and Robert T. Fortna; SNTSMS 67; Cambridge: Cambridge University Press, 1991).

good shepherd," which suggests that the shepherd imagery should be understood in messianic terms. But Jesus also went on to say, "I and the Father are one" (10:30), which suggests that the shepherd image should also be understood in terms of divinity.

The message of the text is multidimensional and can be approached at different levels by different types of readers. The more minimally informed readers would have been able to grasp that Jesus, as the good shepherd, realized, surpassed, and redefined the prevailing ideals of good shepherding and gracious leadership by giving himself up to death for the sake of the sheep. Readers who knew more could also see that he was claiming to be the messianic shepherd promised in the Scriptures, and finally that he was the one in whom God himself had come to gather and care for his people. What is significant is that all of these perceptions are true and no single dimension exhausts the meaning of the text.

The narrative also helps to rule out certain misreadings of the text. Returning to the broad level of cultural associations, we must ask how the text would speak to readers whose perceptions of shepherding varied in certain respects. For some people, the image of a shepherd may have evoked a sense of nostalgia for the idyllic life of those who "lie there at ease under the awning of a spreading beech and practise country songs on a light shepherd's pipe."[15] For others, a reference to shepherding may have aroused a sense of suspicion, since shepherds were often perceived as rough, unscrupulous characters, who pastured their animals on other people's land and pilfered wool, milk, and kids from the flock.[16] The text would mute the suspicion often leveled at shepherds by acknowledging that those who came before Jesus were indeed "thieves and robbers" (10:8), while stressing that Jesus was the *good* shepherd. The adjective "good" evokes the more positive attitudes toward shepherding, but the context tempers sentimentality by presenting a pastoral landscape that echoes with the

---

[15] Virgil, *Eclogues* 1.1-5. See also the works in J. M. Edmonds, *The Greek Bucolic Poets* (LCL; London and New York: Heinemann and Putnam's sons, 1923).

[16] Joachim Jeremias, *Jerusalem in the Time of Jesus: An Investigation into Economic and Social Conditions during the New Testament Period* (Philadelphia: Fortress Press, 1969) 305; idem, *"poimēn, ktl.,"* TDNT 6:488–489; Ramsay MacMullen, *Roman Social Relations 50 B. C. to A.D.284* (New Haven and London: Yale University Press, 1974) 1-27.

cry of a wolf, not the gentle airs of a shepherd's flute.

At another level, most Jewish listeners would have considered messianic claims and divine claims to be mutually exclusive. Jewish people generally expected the Messiah to be a human being, and many assumed that he would be a king, a leader of Israel on the order of David or perhaps Moses.[17] Within a Jewish frame of reference, however, the idea that a human being could be identified with God would have been considered blasphemous. This becomes clear in the crowds's attempt to stone Jesus after he declared, "I and the Father are one" (10:30–33). According to the Fourth Gospel, however, Jesus is both Messiah and God. Jesus was the Messiah, but he would not simply replicate the exploits of David or Moses. Jesus was also aid, but he was not a blasphemous usurper of divine prerogatives. By using the image of the good shepherd, which could refer to the Messiah and to God simultaneously, the evangelist helps create a new frame of reference, in which the human and divine facets of Jesus' identity are brought together in a new unity.

Modern readers will come to the text with their own frames of reference. Some may know something about shepherds from their own experience, but many will not; some may be familiar with an image of shepherding like that found in Psalm 23, but many may not. The Johannine Good Shepherd discourse assumes that readers will accept the brief sketch of shepherding presented in the text and will be able to apply the traits of the good shepherd to Jesus. The imagery in the text offers enough for even minimally informed readers to gain some sense of Jesus' identity, but it remains evocative enough to stimulate the kind of further reflection that can lead to recognition of other dimensions of meaning.

The identity of the other figures in the text is left unspecified. The thieves and robbers, the stranger, and the wolf are never named. Their common feature is the threat they present to the flock. The discourse is set in a literary context that suggests that these figures should be identified with the Pharisees who opposed the man born blind in chap. 9 and who presented a threat to all who would confess that Jesus was the Christ. Recent research has shown that it is quite likely that the Johannine community included Christians who had experienced such threats from the Jewish authorities of their own time. Yet the imagery is

---

[17] See, e.g., John 6:14-15; 12:13.

so supple that the adversaries mentioned could readily be identified with various figures who opposed Jesus and his followers or who could have been perceived as Jesus' competitors.[18] The ambiguity invites engagement with the text. The Good Shepherd discourse is clear enough to allow readers with only a little background information to appreciate its message at a basic level, but the imagery is evocative enough to prompt readers to continue exploring its significance. The literary and historical contexts provide clues to additional dimensions of meaning and help to exclude certain misreadings of the text without unduly restricting the meaning.

Conclusion

Some years ago, Robert Kysar introduced a survey of Johannine research by observing that the Fourth Gospel "is a book in which a child can wade and an elephant can swim."[19] What he meant was that those who first read the Gospel often find its meaning to be rather obvious and straightforward, while those who study it more carefully may wrestle with its nuances for a lifetime. Although scholars have sometimes suggested that the meaning of John's Gospel is clear to insiders but opaque to the uninitiated, the reverse is true in many cases: the Gospel's complexity and richness become increasingly apparent with rereading. A text that was accessible at a basic level to less-informed readers, yet sophisticated enough to engage better-informed readers, would have been an important means of communication within the Johannine community as its membership became increasingly diverse. Some aspects of the text probably would have been most meaningful to the Jewish Christians who formed the nucleus of the Johannine community, but many of the Gospel's images and characters also would have been engaging to other types of Christians, including Samaritans and Greeks.

The Fourth Gospel was written in order that "you" might believe. In Greek,

---

[18] Helpful on this is Rudolf Schnackenburg, *The Gospel According to John* (3 vols.; New York: Crossroad 1982) 2:287.

[19] R. Kysar, *The Fourth Evangelist and His Gospel: An Examination of Contemporary Scholarship* (Minneapolis: Augsburg, 1975) 6. He is quoting an anonymous source mentioned in Siegfried Schulz, *Die Stunde der vier Evangelisten* (Hamburg: Furche, 1967) 297.

the "you" is plural and we should keep this plurality in mind as we ask about the author's communicative strategy. Both literary and historical approaches suggest that the final form of the Gospel was shaped for a spectrum of readers, some of whom were better informed than others. By keeping this spectrum of readers in mind, we can better appreciate how the Gospel can continue to engage attention and shape the perspectives of the most difficult and diverse audience of all: those who read the Fourth Gospel today.

Chapter Two

The Making of Metaphor:
Another Reading of John 3:1-15

ROBERT KYSAR

Commentaries on John 3:1-15 have become nearly tiresome. The passage has been interpreted and reinterpreted until one would almost wish for a moratorium on the wearisome rehash of the Jesus-Nicodemus discussion with the standard repertoire of insights and observations. So, why still another reading of the passage? For one thing, the passage merits further discussion from the perspective of the author's strategies, that is, from a reader-response perspective. A number of recent publications have moved contemporary reading of the passage in that direction, especially those of Francis Moloney and Mark Stibbe.[1] More importantly, little attention has been paid to the way in which the metaphors in the passage are developed in the process of the dialogue-discourse. While it is commonplace to point out the use of puns and double entendre in the passage, less effort has been made to analyze how the surplus meanings of those words function metaphorically and what result they have in the reader's experience of the passage. How are they metaphorical and in what way does the author create their metaphorical quality?

Methodology: First-Time Reader

This reading of John 3:1-15 attempts a first try at such an examination. However, the method of my reading is not formal reader response. I am not primarily interested in using these formal methods, although I am indebted to them in ways that will be obvious. What I shall do employs a far less formal

---

[1] F. J. Moloney, *Belief in the Word. Reading the Fourth Gospel: John 1-4* (Minneapolis: Fortress Press, 1992). M. W. G. Stibbe, *John as Storyteller: Narrative Criticism and the Fourth Gospel* (SNTSMS 73; Cambridge: Cambridge University Press, 1992); *John* (Readings: A New Biblical Commentary; Sheffield: JSOT Press, 1993); and *John's Gospel* (New York: Routledge, 1994).

method. I want to imagine myself—as best I can—an innocent, virginal contemporary reader, encountering the passage for the first time and to explore it from that perspective. I shall ask what this hypothetical reader might experience in a journey through the passage and how that reader might perceive the work of the author. Naturally this effort is at best risky![2] Who of us can successfully put aside all we think we know about this passage and take on the role of a first-time reader? Risky as it may be, I should like to attempt it with the belief that some fresh understanding might be gained. So, for the most part I shall dispense with the standard categories of "implied" reader and "implied" author.[3]

However, for methodological clarity two descriptions are necessary at the beginning—one of the interpreter of the text and another of the imaginary reader the interpreter employs. A first reader methodology requires description of the one who attempts such an imaginative encounter with the text. As with any interpretative process, the social location of the interpreter is crucial. No reading is possible without a specific reader, and no reader's endeavor is without a peculiar perspective, shaped by her or his ethnic, social, and economic situation.[4] The location of the reader is, therefore, an indispensable methodological presupposition and all the more significant if some imaginative first reading of the text is undertaken. This particular interpreter is an affluent, empowered, white male who works as a full, tenured professor within an academic setting in the service of the church. My history provides little in the way of social or cultural oppression. I know social marginalization and disenfranchisement only indirectly, and hence am nearly blind to the possible meanings a passage might render for those who know first-hand oppression by virtue of gender, race, class, or economic condition. Furthermore, I assume that the passage functions within the context of the Christian community

---

[2] See S. D. Moore, *Literary Criticism and the Gospels: The Theoretical Challenge* (New Haven: Yale University Press, 1989) 78-81.

[3] See R. M. Fowler, "Reader-Response Criticism: Figuring Mark's Reader," *Mark and Method: New Approaches to Biblical Studies* (ed. J. C. Anderson and S. D. Moore; Minneapolis: Fortress Press, 1992) 54-55)

[4] See F. F. Segovia and M. A. Tolbert, ed., *Reading From This Place*. Volume 1: *Social Location and Biblical Interpretation in the United States* (Minneapolis: Fortress Press, 1994).

(specifically within the Lutheran tradition) as a source of authority and that academic inquiry is a servant of the faith community. Moreover, I have in the past served the scholarly and confessing communities primarily through the traditional historical critical methods of biblical study. My use of a synchronic, literary methodology reflects a new commitment and hermeneutical enterprise.

My imagined first reader will reflect my own social and ethnic experiences, as well as my religious convictions. Hence, the first reader I imagine will be predisposed to questions of faith. As a first reader motivated by concerns of a religious nature, I will read the text with a personal intensity, searching for resolutions to the issues surrounding the story's central character. But the fictitious reader is also astute and remembers what he has read earlier in the story, and he tries to use his earlier reading as a framework of comprehension for the present passage. I imagine a careful and sensitive reader, responsive to the nuances of the text. Moreover, my method requires a first-time reader who becomes vulnerable to the text. Immersed in the movement of the passage, this reader allows himself to be drawn into the text and to be subjected to its influence. Such an imaginative first reading experience is a productive enterprise only in terms of this sort of understanding of the invented participant in the procedure.

To accomplish the sort of reading I have in mind, I will first move through the passage, suggesting the possible experiences of the first-time reader. Then, the second part of the essay will reflect on what this reading experience offers in terms of our understanding of the author's enterprise in chap. 3. Finally, I will consider the way in which the author has fashioned the metaphors of the passage, what sort of metaphors they are, and what role they play. For the purposes of this paper, I have arbitrarily defined the perimeters of the text as vv. 1-15. No clear closures (however partial) are detectable before 3:21. Indeed, 3:1-21 functions, I think, as a literary whole.[5] I confess then that the division after v. 15 is irregular, made simply because vv. 1-15 offers a workable unit for the sake of this essay and includes the four major metaphors I wish to examine.

---

[5] Moloney's division *(Belief,* 106) is more commonly proposed. He suggests that vv. 1-10 and 11-21 constitute separate units. He is, of course, correct that in the latter Jesus speaks directly to the reader and Nicodemus is in the background.

I will conclude, however, that the reader experiences a climatic insight in v. 15, even though the literary unit continues through v. 21.

A First Reader Examination of John 3:1 -IS

Our imaginary first reader approaches the passage with a naive optimism. The prologue of the narrative rings in memory's ear, and the reader comprehends, however vaguely, the identity of the story's hero. Nothing in the succeeding passages has diminished the bright image of the Word now made flesh. I have heard the baptizer's witness, watched Jesus call disciples, marveled at his insight, wondered at the transformation of water into wine, and heard with awe his majestic—if puzzling—pronouncements. True, the promise of the early verses that the hero would suffer rejection still haunts me (1:10-11). But, that troubling promise remains abstract, with the one exception of a mention of the hero's death (2:22). Nearly everything has worked toward encouraging a simple optimism and excitement in our reader.

Everything, that is, except the immediately preceding verses (2:23-25). On the one hand, the excited anticipation is enhanced by the declaration that "many believed in his name." On the other hand, the narrator's insistence that Jesus would not trust himself to these believers begins to temper our reader's enthusiasm. I can only wonder what dreadful evil lurks in the human heart that would necessitate Jesus' reserve. Nonetheless, the first two verses of our passage rekindle my optimism.[6] Anticipation is piqued by the possibilities of a conversation between Jesus and a religious leader. Nicodemus takes the initiative to come to Jesus and acknowledges that Jesus must be a teacher from God because of the quality of his wondrous works. He immediately attracts me, for I share his view of Jesus. Now a prominent Pharisee will come to understand Jesus and believe in him, and the story will continue to unfold the pattern of Jesus' glorious success.

In that hopeful expectation, v. 3 shocks me! After the solemn, "Very truly, I tell you," Jesus speaks opaquely (again). This is his chance to win over a

---

[6] Moloney (ibid., 108) suggests that, unlike my imaginary reader, the implied reader (on the basis of 1:5) recognizes Nicodemus' coming out of the darkness into the light. Hence, in his view the reader is even more optimistic about this meeting of the two figures.

powerful leader. Why confuse the process with such a stern pronouncement? I am utterly puzzled me "born *anōthen."* What possible meaning could it have? The juxtaposition of *ginomai* and *anōthen* creates an ambiguity. It crosses two experiences with a shocking result: To be born and from above or again. I am forced to consider how one might be born but born either from above or born once again. I suddenly feel distanced from Jesus—alienated from this one with whose cause I have become identified. I cannot understand his words and feel threatened by that sense of confusion.

Moreover, Jesus redefines the issue of the conversation around entering "the kingdom of God." I hear that such an entrance depends on an *anōthen* birth. But the dominion of God itself has its own ambiguities. It conjures up a whole series of different references—among them God's power, the ideal human society, a political transformation. So, I am faced with one vague image (born *anōthen)* used along with another (the kingdom of God).[7] One metaphor refers the reader to another. I am forced me ask how it is that an *anōthen* birth empowers one to experience God's dominion. Does one illumine the other? If so, how?

Nicodemus' question in v. 4 triggers several different responses in me. First, his query somewhat calms my anxiety and puts me at ease. He, too, is puzzled by Jesus' words. Like Nicodemus, I wonder, "how is it possible?" I am, therefore, drawn to him, identify with him in his confusion, and become hopeful that with his help the obscurity of the saying will be clarified. In one sense, I now feel a comradeship with this character as a co-inquirer with me. But, second, Nicodemus' question ridiculously narrows the meaning of born *anōthen.* How is a second physical birth possible? At Nicodemus' expense, I recognize that born *anōthen* cannot refer to a second physical birth. The reference of the image is narrowed, and its literal meaning eliminated. Finally, now I feel superior to Nicodemus. Like him I am puzzled by Jesus' words, but I would not suppose that they refer me to a second physical birth. My sense of alienation from Jesus is eased just a bit by the failure of Jesus' dialogue partner.

---

[7] See the seminal and still provocative discussion of the metaphorical character of "kingdom of God" in N. Perrin, *Jesus and the Language of the Kingdom* (Philadelphia: Fortress Press, 1976) 29-32. What the reader senses at this point is the "tensive" quality of the symbol.

Hence, while I feel distanced from Jesus, I do not yet feel abandoned by the discussion.

The intent of Jesus' words in the next verses (vv. 5-8) at first seems to confirm my renewed sense of companionship with Jesus. That new affirmation is short-lived, however. Once again I read, "Very truly, I tell you," and ready myself for difficulty. Born *anōthen* is paralleled with birth out of water and spirit. The metaphor is now enriched, but the reader is confused and again pushed away from the speaker. Little more is accomplished than to replace the puzzle of *anōthen* with that of *hydatos kai pneumatos* ("water and spirit"). To be sure, I remember John the Baptist's distinction between his baptism with water and Jesus' baptism with the Spirit (1:33). But still, as I was first forced to ask what kind of *anōthen*, I am now compelled to ask what kind of water and what kind of *pneuma*.

V. 6 still further narrows the possible reference of the enigmatic *anōthen* birth. Confirming Nicodemus' erroneous impression that the birth is physical, Jesus distinguishes between being born of flesh and born of spirit. I feel still further encouraged. Read on, for the light of clarification may be visible amid the clouds of obscurity! But *sarx* further clouds the light and introduces yet another of the accumulating ambiguous terms. Is it pejorative in this context? Or, is it neutral? Is the contrast of birth by flesh and birth by spirit meant only to distinguish the first, physical birth from a second birth; or, is it intended to demean the physical? If we know what being born of the flesh is, what then can born of spirit mean? Jesus has led me to think of born *anōthen* as a spiritual birth. That conclusion is consistent with the distinction of the prologue between born of God and born of flesh (1:12-13). But the questions of what more precisely a spiritual or divine birth is and how such a birth is possible compel me on in my reading.

I have managed to squeeze some satisfaction out of Nicodemus' question and Jesus' distinction between spiritual and physical birth. But Jesus' words in v. 7 mock both Nicodemus and me in our lack of understanding. How can we not be astonished? Now I sense that I once again stand with the Pharisee in my struggle to understand. My alienation from Jesus is reestablished.

Yet Jesus goes on now, seeming to promise clarification. His words concerning the *pneuma* (in v. 8) encourage me to expect an elucidation of entering God's dominion through an *anōthen* birth by the Spirit. Spirit is the key to unlock the meaning imprisoned in Jesus' image. How disappointing and puzzling, then, is the fact that the key itself comes locked away in its own prison. The tiny metaphor of v. 8 stretches my mind between *pneuma* as spirit and *pneuma* as wind. Jesus speaks in the freedom of the *pneuma*, the perception of the sound in the wind, but the mystery of its origin and destination. An implied comparison of wind and spirit is supposed to illumine the *anōthen* birth by water and the spirit. But precisely how still evades me.

By v. 9 I feel that Nicodemus is inside my mind and speaks for me. My identification with him in his puzzlement and our mutual alienation from Jesus in complete. I, too, repeat Nicodemus' query, "How can this be?" ("this" referring to the entire discussion thus far). Consequently, Jesus' stern reprimand in Nicodemus in his reprimand of me as well: "Are you a teacher of Israel (or, have you read this far), and yet you do not understand this?"

The distance between Jesus and me increases with v. 11. It begins again with that signal that what follows in important and (in my experience) demanding: "Very truly, I tell you." I have heard the speeches and the witnesses, but now, by virtue of my failure to understand, Jesus says, I have rejected the witness. As a first-time reader, the first person plural of v. 11 in not troublesome, for I acknowledge the plurality into((speakers-witnesses thus far in the narrative, e.g., the narrator, John the Baptizer, and others. However, beginning with this verse, I experience the conversation opening into a community. Jesus speaks, but now from within a group that has "seen" and here "bear witness" to their experience.

The hole gets deeper. Jesus has spoken of "earthly things," and I did not believe? What are these earthly things, and what might the heavenly things be? My mind is driven back to the flesh-spirit distinction. But I am led to think that both of those are earthly, not heavenly things. Still clinging desperately to the hero's verbal coat tails, I suppose that Jesus speaks of heavenly things in v. 13. Yet I am ill-equipped to receive his words. Added to the quandaries already piled on me by the discussion thus far comes another distinction: ascending and descending. And with the distinction a title, Son of man. Yet I recall the promise to Nathaniel: "You will see heaven opened, and the angels of God ascending and descending upon the Son of man" (1:51). Again, here is an ascending and descending. But now it is the Son of man who descends and ascends. The connection between the two, plus the encouragement of the prologue to the narrative, nurtures my identification of Jesus with the Son of man. The descent, I suppose, speaks in a veiled way of the Word's becoming flesh. But what might the ascent be? Am I to assume that Jesus will ascend? What has all of this to do with *anōthen* birth?

I feel as if I am listening to a foreign speaker in a language of which I have only a few scraps of vocabulary. The sojourn thus far has left me with a sense of having been shoved rudely away from the story's hero. But I have been thrown enough scraps of meaning that I continue to trail along, still hoping to reach the banquet table.

Immediately on the heels of the hint that Jesus has descended and therefore must once again ascend comes the enigmatic v. 14. The promise now is that the Son of man will be "lifted up" in a way comparable to Moses' lifting up of the serpent in the wilderness. Sparks fly as this text rubs against another,[8] and I struggle to grab those tiny hints of light. I am now confident that Jesus speaks of himself with the title Son of man. "Ascending" and "lifting up" correspond with one another in their verbal image of spatial movement. I know I am working with spatial imagery for something else, but I have no other clue as to the meaning of the *hypsoō*.

Again, the reader is asked to wrestle with a puzzling, ambiguous expression. Along with *anōthen* and *pneuma, hypsoō* is another hurdle. From it I might conclude that Jesus anticipates enthronement, and my mind races back to God's dominion. Or, I might venture the dreadful possibility of crucifixion, only to be forced to recall the dire prediction of rejection in the prologue and the mention of death in 2:22. But I cannot choose between enthronement and crucifixion. I have no clues to help me.[9] Along with the other ambiguous terms of the passage, I am left to suspend judgment concerning the sense of *hypsoō* until further reading. But the puzzling word occasions another recollection from my reading experience: "Destroy this temple, and in three days I will raise it up" (2:19).

---

[8] J. Culler, "Presupposition and Intertextuality," *Modern Language Notes* 91 (1976) 1387.

[9] Moloney argues *(Belief,* 117*)* that the reader is expected to grasp the double meaning of *hypsoō* in vv. 14-15, even though what the event is may be a puzzle.

Raise up. Ascend. Lifted up. Could these enigmatic sayings illumine the earlier one? Or, the earlier one, these?'[10]

V. 15 jolts me with the seriousness of the matter at hand. The one who believes in the lifted up Son of man may have eternal life. I feel more threat than promise in those words, for, in my confusion, I have no basis for belief. I cannot believe, if I do not understand. My understanding, therefore, takes on ultimate significance. At this point, let us suppose that our imaginary reader puts the text down, exhausted by the strenuous demands of these fifteen verses. As that reader, my head is spinning with ambiguity, stretched by obscure references, exhausted by the pace of the discussion, and confused by its movement. Still feeling distance between myself and Jesus, I nonetheless have been intrigued by the puzzle in the passage. Moreover, I have taken seriously the claim that something vital is at stake. I shall in the future take up the text again to resume my pursuit.

Reflections on a First Reading Experience of John 3:1-IS

On the basis of our journey through the passage as an imaginary first reader, we are ready to make some observations regarding the text and the implicit strategies of the author encountered there.

PRESUPPOSITIONS IMPOSED ON THE READER

The first of these observations concerns what is presupposed of the reader in the passage.[11] Those presuppositions are of at least two basic kinds. First, the text presupposes a prior reading of other texts. This presupposed intertextuality involves at least the earlier parts of the narrative. Further, the passage seems to assume that the reader will complete the remainder of the story, that is, that the reader is reading the whole Gospel and the fullest meaning of the present passage is known only in the context of the whole document. Satisfaction with

---

[10] See the interesting work of A. Reinhartz (*The Word in the World: The Cosmological Tale in the Fourth Gospel* [SBLMS 45; Atlanta: Scholars Press, 1992] esp. 19, 33, and 43) who understands the language of vertical spatial movement in this and other discourses as evidence of the "cosmological tale" of the Gospel. Our reader is unknowingly immersed in a cosmic narrative.

[11] Culler, "Presupposition."

the present passage is possible, the reader is led to hope, with the remainder of the narrative. But beyond the text of the Gospel v. 14 presupposes the reader's knowledge of another passage in the canon, namely, Num 21:4-9.

The second kind of presupposition burdening the reader of this text has to do with values. It assumes from the very first the implicit worth of the kingdom of God and eternal life. "Seeing" or "entering" the kingdom and having "eternal life" are implicitly desirable. Without adherence to God's dominion and the quest for a higher quality of life as important values, the engine of the passage is rendered impotent. But the passage also takes for granted a certain willingness on the part of the reader to recognize and deal with polyvalence. The reading experience is moved along by the ambiguity of key words. Without the reader's desire to pursue the sense of this language for the sake of understanding what is required to enter or see the reign of God and have eternal life, the passage would have no motivating power.

The imagined reading experience I have sketched demonstrates that the passage makes enormous demands on the reader. There are discouragements, disappointments, confusion, and alienation from the story's hero. The text implicitly trusts its own intertextuality and the reader's values to sustain the reading. The reader survives the text only if and because, as a result of the previous two chapters, her or his imagination has been captured by the fascinating hero of the story.[12] The reader endures the abuse of the passage only if and because he or she senses that the kingdom of God/eternal life are of utmost importance. With the obscurity of the passage, its implied author risks the loss of the reader-endangers his or her patience. So stressful and bewildering is the passage that only its intertextuality and subject matter render it passable.[13]

---

[12] Stibbe's enterprise (*John*, 17) to demonstrate that the Johannine Jesus is "the elusive Christ" is clearly helpful and valid; see also "The Elusive Christ: A New Reading of the Fourth Gospel," *JSNT* 44 (1991) 20-39. Our reading of 3:1-15 is an experience of that very elusiveness. But for the reader the mystery of Christ's identity is also comprised of a certain fascination that compels her or him to pursue a resolution of Christ's hiddenness.

[13] Moloney (*Belief*, 199) cites 3:1-15 as one example of where the author tries to accomplish too much. Stibbe points out that here Jesus is guilty of a "discontinuous dialogue by transcending the level of discourse used by his questioners" (*John*, 55). These are others ways of saying that the text nearly demands too much of our imaginary first time reader.

On the positive side, what I have addressed as the author's risk might also be understood in terms of the enticement of the reader into participation. The arduous demands on the reader force her or his involvement, if the passage is to be other than pure nonsense. The "gaps" of meaning are bridged only if the reader ventures some preliminary sense that enables progress.[14] The striking thing about the first reader examination is how tenuous the reader's constructions of meaning are and what thorough and imaginative participation is required for a successful reading.

THE ROLE OF NICODEMUS

The second of my reflections focuses on the steadily decreasing role of Nicodemus in the discussion. On the one hand, he stands at the head of the section, taking initiative in the meeting and stirring the anticipation of the reader. On the other hand, he rapidly slips from prominence. He is assigned three speeches in the passage. The first of these in v. 2 is comprised of twenty-four words, the second in v. 4 of eighteen words, and the third at v. 9 of only four words. In the end, the reader's anticipation around Nicodemus is disappointed.

Without trying to engage the whole question of how the author employs characters, at the level of experience the reader is subtly encouraged to identify with Nicodemus as well as to draw excited anticipation from his entrance. Once the reader has identified with Nicodemus, she or he begins to be distanced from him, beginning with his first response to Jesus' words. But, finally, in his last speech Nicodemus articulates the reader's experience.[15] However, then the

---

[14] J. E. Botha, *Jesus and the Samaritan Woman: A Speech Act Reading of John 4:1-42* (NovTSup 65; Leiden: Brill, 1991) 190. Cf. C. H. Talbert who suggests that the gaps are "invitations for readers or hearers to fill in the narrative" *(Reading John* [New York: Crossroad, 1992] 103). On such literary gaps, see Fowler, "Reader-Response Criticism," 61-65.

[15] I cannot agree with Jeffrey Staley's suggestion that the implied reader joins the implied author in laughing together at Nicodemus and his obtuseness and thereby reestablishes a close relationship between them. The relationship between the reader and Nicodemus is, it seems to me, far more complicated and the reader's identification with either Jesus or the implied author made far more precarious than Staley seems to acknowledge (J. L. Staley, *The Print's First Kiss: A Rhetorical Investigation of the Implied Reader in the Fourth Gospel*

figure disappears. Nicodemus is a bridge character, that is, a means by which the reader begins to hear Jesus' words and to try to understand them. He is a scout who leads the reader into the midst of the skirmish. But once the reader has become involved in the process of the discussion—once the reader begins to struggle with the images of Jesus' words—Nicodemus' function has been accomplished, and he becomes an obsolete accessory to the reading process.[16]

But the reader's relationship with Nicodemus amounts to what Jeffrey Staley calls "reader victimization" and what Eugene Botha terms more simply "manipulation."[17] In particular, my reading experience led me to view the advent of Nicodemus as promising and as the beginning of a significant acknowledgment of Jesus' identity—a view that the passage utterly annihilates.[18] Consequently, I felt as though I had become a victim of the text.[19] Furthermore, my relationship with Nicodemus moved from identification to

---

[SBLDS 82; Atlanta: Scholars cress, 1988] 92).

[16] Moloney maintains *(Belief,* 116, 120) that Nicodemus represents one who is not able to move beyond his own categories. Unable to move him, Jesus shifts at v. 11 to a commentary on the whole discussion. Furthermore, for the reader he serves as an example of those described in 2:2325. Stibbe calls Nicodemus "the embodiment of misunderstanding" *John,* 54). My view of Nicodemus differs only in that I see him far more as an authorial construct to lead the reader into a one-on-one dialogue with Jesus. However, he remains, I think, a thoroughly ambiguous character in the whole of the Gospel. Cf. J. M. Bassler, "Mixed Signals: Nicodemus in the Fourth Gospel," *JBL* 108 (1989) 635-646, and M. Davies, *Rhetoric and Reference in the Fourth Gospel* (JSNTSup 69; Sheffield: JSOT Press, 1992) 336-38.

[17] Staley, *The Print's First Kiss,* 95-118; Botha, *Jesus and the Samaritan Woman,* 191192.

[18] However, Stibbe convinces me that Jesus' identity emerges as the readers see characters such as Nicodemus respond to Jesus. As "foils...they speak and behave in such a way that our understanding of who Jesus really is is enhanced" *(John as Storyteller,* 25). Therefore, even with the reader's disappointment in Nicodemus' failure, something of Jesus' identity may be clearer.

[19] Staley concludes his fascinating study with the suggestion that the Johannine text betrays the fact that it is intended for "insiders." The reader is brought "inside" by virtue of the prologue, if nothing else. But "the reader victimization strategies" push the reader "outside" *(Print's First Kiss,* 116). 3:1-15 functions primarily to evoke a sense of being an outsider and qualifying any sense the reader may have of being an insider.

superiority and back to identification. As a result there is a sense in which the text manipulated my attitude toward this character in what Botha calls "involuntary association and disassociation."[20] The reader's posture toward Nicodemus may, however, be only one of several ways in which the text subtly misdirects the reader.

THE LANGUAGE OF THE PASSAGE

The peculiar language of the discussion shapes the reader's experience in several different ways. Verbs of knowing *(oida* and *ginoskō)* are prominent in the whole of the discussion. Nicodemus knows (v. 2), and then does not know (vv. 8 and 10). In v. 11 Jesus and others know. Verbs of knowing dominate the discussion through v. 11 and then give way to belief *(pisteuō),* with which the passage climaxes (vv. 12 and 15). This shift skillfully leads the reader from a concern for knowing to one for believing and to the ultimate importance of knowing for belief. The reader's experience of struggling to understand (that is, to know) is vital in order that she or he might believe. On the basis of the reading experience of this passage, knowing and believing appear intertwined, if not synonymous.

Another feature of the language of the passage consists of the words referring to the use of the senses. The verb see *(horaō)* occurs twice (vv. 3 and 11). But words of sounds and hearing dominate the passage: In v. 8 the verb "to hear" *(akouō);* "said" and "say," seven times (vv. 2, 3, 4, 5, 7, 9, and 11); "answered," three times (vv. 3, 5, and 10). "Sound" (v. 8), "speak" (v. 11), "witness" (v. 11), and "told" (v. 12—twice) complete the repertoire of auditory expressions in the passage.

Of course, a dialogue-discussion passage is going to use many of these terms, so their prominence does not surprise us. Still, I propose that the reader has an auditory experience as a result of the passage. Not surprisingly, Jesus is made to refer to the sound *(phonē)* of the *pneuma,* so important is the experience of

---

[20] Botha *(Jesus and the Samaritan Woman,* 192) suggests that reader victimization functions in two ways:

> On the one hand, it maximizes reader participation and involvement, because they never know what to expect next, and on the other, it enhances the communication in such a way that the message is actually formulated by the readers themselves because they are forced to evaluate and reevaluate their opinions, beliefs and perceptions.

hearing. Combined with the use of the verbs of seeing, the reader's experience is essentially a sensory one. This suggestion is important, since the passage pivots around four metaphors, each of which has a sensory basis. "To be born," "to be born of water," "to hear and feel the wind," "to see the Son of man lifted up"—all of these appeal for their reference to an experience of the senses. The text sensitizes one to sensory experience and thereby opens the reader to the transformation effected by the metaphors. (Of course, the author of this Gospel consistently appeals to the senses, beginning the document with seeing the incarnation of the Word [1:14] and concluding it with a discussion of Thomas' seeing [20:24-29].[21])

But the language of the passage also subliminally bathes the reader in contrasts: knowing and not knowing (vv. 2, 8, 10, and 11); spirit and flesh (vv. 5, 6, 8); earthly and heavenly things (v. 12); ascend and descend (v. 13); born *anōthen* by spirit (vv. 3, 6, and 7) and natural birth (vv. 4 and 6); and the implicit contrast between lifted up for enthronement and for crucifixion. Still, another contrast is fundamental to the reading of the passage. It is the contrast of the possible and the impossible and is represented in the Greek text with the use of the word, *dynatai*. The contrast begins with Nicodemus' confession in v. 2, "no one can do these signs that you do, unless God is with him." Jesus claims that participation in God's dominion is possible only if one is born *anōthen* (v. 3) of the water and the spirit (v. 5). Three times Nicodemus asks how such a birth is possible (twice in v. 4 and again in v. 9). Jesus' interrogator begins with an affirmation of what is possible but disappears behind his last puzzling question, "How is it possible?" The contrast is between what is impossible from the human perspective and what is possible and necessary from the divine perspective.[22]

Meeting contrast after contrast, the reader gradually becomes aware of a fundamental opposition to which the passage propels her or him, namely, a contrast of belief and unbelief which becomes explicit only in v. 12: "If I have told you about earthly things and you do not believe, how can you believe if I tell you about heavenly things?" In general, the author frames the whole

---

[21] See R. Kysar, *John the Maverick Gospel* (rev. ed.; Louisville: Westminster/John Knox Press, 1993) 86-90.

[22] Stibbe points out (*John*, 57) that the author parodies Nicodemus' lack of knowledge.

narrative with polarities, which find their literary expression in the kind of contrasts we see in this passage. The deadly seriousness of v. 15 is gained in part by the polarities with which the reader must deal. The sense of seriousness is experienced because, in the environment of the contrasts of the passage, there is no alternative to the polarity of belief and unbelief.[23]

The unity, of the passage is attained on one level by its language. The author takes the reader by the hand to lead her or him on from one to another thought by means of something like catch-words. We have already observed this feature in the use of several words in the text: "see," leading from v. 3 to v. 11; "know," leading successively from v. 2 to v. 8 to v. 10 and finally to v. 11; "believe," directing the reader from v. 12 to v. 15. Two other bridge words are worth noting: "God" in v. 2 recurs in Jesus' words in v. 3; "born" is first used in v. 3 but then sequentially in vv. 4, 5, 6, 7, and 8. Establishing such a repertoire of words focuses the reader's attention and formulates a theme. Using them to lead the reader on provides transitional bridges, holding tightly to the reader's mind as the passage races on.

One more linguistic observation is necessary. In the passage as I have delimited it, Jesus is introduced with a saying about birth (v. 3). Jesus concludes the passage with a saying about life (v. 15). It is not accidental, I think, that my reading experience directed me from consideration of the origin of life to a claim about the authentic quality of life. The character of human existence is journey from physical birth to a search for the meaning and quality of genuine life. Therefore, the *anōthen* birth is implicitly about the authentic existence, i.e., eternal life.

READING STRUCTURE

The reader is carried through a threefold dialogue.[24] Each of the three parts is comprised of a statement or question by Nicodemus followed by Jesus' words. As Nicodemus' participation in the discussion is steadily shortened, Jesus' words become more lengthy. In each of the first two of the three

---

[23] Moloney *(Belief,* 119) expresses this point in terms of the necessity of decision and the impossibility of indifference. Such a view assumes the role of the reader's values, including those sketched above.

[24] See Stibbe, *John,* 53-54.

components, Jesus begins his speech with the solemn, *amēn, amēn.* In the third component v. 10 intrudes before "Very truly, I tell you." In the reading experience itself, the double *amēn* signals the reader that the forthcoming words are of vital importance but also that they will be puzzling.

In reading the passage, one begins only as an interested observer of a dialogue between Jesus and Nicodemus However, the dialogue soon evolves into a triangular discussion, including the reader's participation. Finally, it shifts abruptly to a dialogue between the reader and Jesus, who now stands within and speaks for a witnessing community. Hence, the tripartite structure entails three reading modes: observer; participant with Nicodemus and Jesus; and dialogue partner with Jesus and his community.

The Making of a Metaphor — The Metaphors of John 3:1-15

I have traced the experience of our imaginary first reader through the passage and drawn from that experience a number of observations about the text and the strategies of its author implicit therein. Only now are we ready to turn to the central topic of the reading: The making of the metaphors found there. The passage, I suggest, epitomizes the way in which this author creates a metaphor, fashions a metaphorical experience for the reader, and places the reader in the midst of a metaphorical ecosystem. In this case, the construction of the metaphor is through what I would like to call mini-images, that is, short uses of language (sometimes single words) to refer to something beyond the commonplace referent of the words. The process of that construction has a number of features, a few of which describe the way the text constructs metaphor.

EARTHLY PHENOMENA AND TRANSCENDENT REALITIES

Obviously the making of a metaphor in this case, as always, is begun by daring the reader to consider two phenomena placed side by side. In this passage the phenomena are four pairs: birth and *anōthen;* birth and *pneuma;* wind and spirit; lifted up for enthronement and lifted up for crucifixion. Additionally, the rule of God is compared with an earthly kingdom and authentic human existence is named "eternal." In each case, the metaphorical experience resides in the strangeness of the comparison, the shock of being asked to consider one by reference to the other, and the provocative and open-ended character of the comparison. Metaphor is created by aligning phenomena from this earthly existence with those of a transcendent realm. In particular, physical birth and birth from above (or by *pneuma),* physical wind and the divine spirit, and crucifixion and enthronement. In this way, the metaphors have an earthly quality about them, which in turn transforms the earthly into something more.

This leads us to a related feature of the making of the metaphors in the passage, "defamiliarization."[25] Obviously, the text requires the reader to deal with the familiar phenomenon of birth and wind in unfamiliar ways. In the process the power of the familiar is altered and a new potency infused. Birth becomes new creation in a novel sense. Wind is broken open to reveal the work of the Spirit. Two ordinary meanings of "lifted up" are challenged by the possibility that the two may become one. The text imposes on the reader the necessity to see the old and daily in new ways. Their entrance into the reader's consciousness is through their very familiarity. But once having gained entrance into the fortress of the reader's mind, they wreak havoc in his or her worldview.

But the category of defamiliarization is not quite appropriate to what we have witnessed in the experience of the reader. The familiar is not finally destroyed to make room for the new. Better, it is transformed by virtue of the metaphors, something more akin to **transfamiliarization.** The result is that the phenomena of birth and wind remain familiar and daily. But now the familiar threatens to carry within itself a transfamiliar reality—the reality of *anōthen* birth and the Spirit. The familiar meaning of the image is not cast aside, once it is defamiliarized. Rather, the familiar retains an essential role in the process of transfamiliarization and ever carries the peril of becoming unfamiliar.

METAPHOR OUT OF AMBIGUITY

Even more characteristic of the metaphors before us in the passage is the fact that they are constructed from the raw material of ambiguity (as all poetic

---

[25] B. B. Scott, *Hear Then the Parable: A Commentary on the Parables of Jesus* (Minneapolis: Fortress Press, 1989) 277. W. A. Beardslee speaks of the "deformation of language, a stretching of language to a new metaphorical meaning which shocked the hearer (the `dialogue partner') into new insight" *(Literary Criticism of the New Testament* [Guides to Biblical Scholarship. Philadelphia: Fortress Press, 1970] 11). See R. A. Culpepper, *Anatomy of the Fourth Gospel* (Philadelphia: Fortress Press, 1983) 199.

metaphors are). By ambiguity I mean the "verbal nuance ...which gives room for alternative reactions to the same piece of language."[26] The nuances of Jesus' language breed tension and constantly compel the reader on in the text. What is clarified leaves something else vague. One hand offers the reader some advancement in understanding, while the other hand rudely takes it away by providing still another ambiguity.

But in this passage it is precisely in ambiguity or surplus of meaning that the metaphorical quality of the words of the Johannine Jesus is to be found. That is, the comparison of the new origin from above with physical birth arises from the imprecision (or the overflow of meaning) of the word *anōthen*. Does it refer to another physical birth or another beginning occasioned by transcendent forces? Therein, as the reader, I am forced to ask how a spiritual rebirth is like a physical birth. The ambiguity of *pneuma* allows for an image of the Spirit as wind. The double meaning of *hypsoō* invites the reader to anticipate the meaning of the crucifixion by comparing it with a royal enthronement.

The surplus of meaning in the speeches of Jesus, in this case at least, gives the language its metaphorical quality. Metaphor is crafted out of ambiguity. That should not surprise us, since metaphor feeds on excess of meaning, often excess that is never conscious until the poet is brave enough to suggest it. Hence, the surplus meaning residing in a simple story of a shepherd who leaves ninety-nine sheep to search for a single stray lamb evades pedestrian thought and explodes our consciousness when it is offered. But the metaphorical use of ambiguity in this passage is linguistic rather than narrative. That is, it feeds on the ambiguity of single words or phrases, rather than on ambiguous plot line. There is no narrative of one who is born and then experiences a new beginning, or of a child

---

[26] W. Empson, *Seven Types of Ambiguity* (New York: Directions, 1966) 1. This classic study of ambiguity explores seven different types. Jesus' metaphorical language in this passage appears to me to be a blending of Empson's fourth and sixth types. He characterizes the fourth type as "two or more meanings of a statement [that] do not agree among themselves, but combine to make clear a more complicated state of mind in the author." The sixth type requires the reader "to invent statements of his [sic] own and they are liable to conflict with one another" (133, 176). Our passage shows that the Jesus' possible referents disagree and are complicated. But it also invites the reader's own imaginative constructs.

wondering about the sound and comings and goings of the wind. The metaphors of the passage are linguistic as opposed to narrative.

But that distinction may not be quite adequate, since each of the words or phrases miniaturizes a single basic story. The narrative quality of the metaphors in this passage then may be implicit. (How easy it would be, for instance, to create a story out of each of the ambiguous expressions of the passage.) However, such a thesis demands further and separate attention which we cannot afford on this occasion. Whether or not that thesis can be defended, it is still the case that metaphor in our passage is fabricated with the stuff of ambiguity.

STACKED AND PROGRESSIVE METAPHORS

Another feature of the making of metaphor in John 3 is the way in which the images are "stacked." The reader is systematically led to quest the resolution of the earlier metaphor in the next. Hence,

BORN *Anōthen* TO ENTER THE KINGDOM OF GOD

leads to

BORN OUT OF WATER AND SPIRIT

leads to

SPIRIT IS LIKE WIND

leads to

THE SON OF MAN BEING LIFTED UP.

The strategy of the author is to pile image upon image, letting each illumine and each conceal the others. Image is superimposed on image, creating a literary ecosystem of metaphor. Such a strategy is not limited to our passage, for one can witness just such a stacking of images in 10:1-8.[27] Furthermore, evidence of that strategy may be found elsewhere in the Fourth Gospel.

Yet there is an implicit progression discernible in the sequence of the images of our passage. The Spirit appears to be the key to the image of the *anōthen* birth. But Spirit is only understandable in the context of the event of the crucifixion-enthronement of the Son of man. There is no resolution of the metaphors, no explanation of the parable, no delimitation of the reference. But

---

[27] R. Kysar, "Johannine Metaphor-Meaning and Function: A Literary Case Study of John 10:1-8," in *The Fourth Gospel from A Literary Perspective (Semeia* 53; ed. R. A. Culpepper and F. F. Segovia; Atlanta: Scholars Press, 1991) 81-111.

there is direction for the reader's contemplation of these mysteries. Ultimately, the passage suggests that all the previous images must be considered in the light of the crucifixion-enthronement and witnessing the communion of heaven and earth in that event. From a theological perspective, the author has placed the cross at the apex of the images of the passage and of the discussion of entering the kingdom of God. From a literary perspective, the author has tantalized the reader at this point with the grand climax of the entire narrative (the crucifixion-resurrection). The reader's anticipation of Jesus' glorious triumph has been drastically qualified by the promise of a conclusion at the foot of the cross.

JOHANNINE METAPHOR AND SYNOPTIC PARABLES

A final, concluding observation about the making of metaphor in John 3:1-15 entails consideration of Johannine metaphorical language and the narrative parables attributed to Jesus in the synoptic gospels. My suggestion is simply that the two share a fundamental functional similarity. What we have come to think of as distinctive about the synoptic narrative parables is subtly evident in the metaphors of this passage.

Like the best of Jesus' synoptic parables, the metaphors of this passage are diaphorical as opposed to throw-away epiphors. They are both participatory in the sense that they clearly invite the reader to share in the discovery of meaning and surprising in that they both make startling comparisons. The narrative parables and the metaphors of 3:1-15 both explore another metaphor (the dominion of God) in relationship with very different earthly phenomena. Moreover, the Johannine metaphors share a paradoxical quality with the narrative parables, if only in the sense that meaning resides in the tension among the four images of our passage. The poetic quality of the Johannine mini-images and the parables is evident insofar as the metaphors of this text have power to initiate new experience, as do the narratives told by Jesus. The realism so well attested in Jesus' parables is retained in John 3:115 in the use of the familiar to invite consideration of the transcendent. The pairing of parables common in the synoptics (e.g., Mark 4:26-32) is witnessed here in the "stacking" of metaphors. The implicit narrative character of the Johannine images, hinted at above, might add still another possible common feature between them and the synoptic narrative parables.

I do not wish to venture d historical conclusion to a literary study. However, I propose only the possibility that the parabolic tradition associated with Jesus may be preserved in d very different way in the metaphors attributed to him in the Gospel of John.

Chapter Three

Toward a Psycho-literary Reading
of the Fourth Gospel*

MICHAEL WILLET NEWHEART

In recent years Johannine scholars have shown increasing interest in the literary study of the Gospel. This trend is perhaps best evidenced by the collection of essays in *Semeia* 53, entitled *the Fourth Gospel from a Literary Perspective*. In this volume, six scholars investigate the Gospel using a variety of literary methods, including narrative criticism, rhetorical criticism, and reader-response theory. In his rhetorical-critical study of the Lazarus story, Wilhelm Wuellner suggests one way to put life back into critical readings of the Gospel. Noting the bond between rhetoric and the emotive side of human nature, he calls for the rehabilitation of psychological exegesis to supplement the newer literary approaches.[1] This article is an attempt to take up Wuellner's challenge. It makes a case for a psycho-literary reading of the Fourth Gospel, that is, a psychological analysis of the reader's experience of the Gospel. First, it will be shown how recent literary studies in the Fourth Gospel seem to be paving the way for psychological analysis. Second, a psycho-literary model of reading will be presented. Finally, some initial soundings will be made in a psycho-literary reading of the Gospel.

Current Literary Studies in the Gospel

Current literary studies in the Gospel seem to be moving, albeit unconsciously, toward consideration of psychological issues. The *Semeia* 53 volume on literary approaches to the Gospel is perhaps the best place to begin,

* This research was made possible with support from the Faculty Research Program in the Social Sciences, Humanities, and Education at Howard University.

[1] W. Wuellner, "Putting Life Back into the Lazarus Story and Its Reading: The Narrative Rhetoric of John 11 as the Narration of Faith," in *The Fourth Gospel from a Literary Perspective (Semeia* 53; ed. R. A. Culpepper and F. F. Segovia; Atlanta: Scholars Press, 1991) 119.

for a number of essays, in addition to Wuellner's, make reference to the emotions of the reader, and others seem to carve out a place for consideration of the psychological, as well as social, location of the reader. I would like to deal first, then, with the essays by Robert Kysar, Fernando Segovia, and Jeffrey Staley, which discuss the reader's emotional response to the narrative, and then with Segovia's introduction to the volume and Tolbert's response, both of which address the reader's social location.

It is interesting to note how often the words "emotion" and "affective" appear in the *Semeia* volume, yet these words lie on the pages of the essays still-born and undeveloped. For example, in his essay on the Good Shepherd discourse, Kysar notes how the reader's experience of the metaphors in this passage is "affective" as well as cognitive, for they elicit "emotional instability" and "shock" on the part of the reader.[2] But what is the nature of this "affective response"? Why do the metaphors elicit "emotional instability"? Kysar has been a good shepherd in calling these insights by name, but now they must be led out.[3]

Segovia, in his essay on the plot of the Gospel, notes that one of the three axes of a plot is a content-emotion axis.[4] He contends that his own approach is midway on this axis, with an emphasis on the correspondence between patterns of the narrative and the patterns of emotional response.[5] Segovia then discusses the didactic, polemical, admonitory, consolatory, and exhortatory functions which the Gospel has for the implied reader.[6] But precisely how does the implied reader respond emotionally to the plot of the Gospel? If the Gospel has a polemical function, does it help the reader focus anger? If it has a consolatory function, does it help the reader deal with sadness? The question remains, therefore: How does the Word make the journey into the reader's psyche?

---

[2] R. Kysar, "Johannine Metaphor-Meaning and Function: A Literary Case Study of John 10:1-18," *The Fourth Gospel from a Literary Perspective*, 95-98.

[3] Unfortunately, in his paper on John 3 (see above), Kysar does not discuss the reader's affective experience, though he does note that the author entices the reader into participation.

[4] F. F. Segovia, "The Journey(s) of the Word of God: A Reading of the Plot of the Fourth Gospel," *The Fourth Gospel from a Literary Perspective*, 25-26.

[5] Ibid., 49.

[6] Ibid., 47-49.

Staley, in his essay on John 5 and 9, refers to Stephen Moore's criticism that New Testament reader-critics' readings are "overly cerebral and emotionally retarded."[7] Staley admits that he is still stumbling and reaching in this regard.[8] Yet the reader of the Gospel narrative–whether implied or real, critical or naive–responds emotionally as well as intellectually to the text. If critics are genuinely interested in "reader response," then they must plumb the affective as well as the cognitive.

But what is the critic's own response to the narrative? Is the implied reader's response so cerebral because that is the critic's own response to the narrative? Critical readers, then, must read themselves as well as the Gospel, a point which is made both by Segovia in his introduction and Tolbert in her response to the collection from a literary perspective. Both encourage readers to analyze their own social location, noting that a person's race, class, gender, religion, and politics will affect one's reading of the text.[9] Yet they must be critical of their psychological location as well. The psychological issues with which readers are wrestling will shape their readings as surely as social context. Indeed, social context shapes the psyche, so perhaps one should speak of the "psycho-social" location of the reader, which must be analyzed along with the text.

Reader-response criticism, then, seems to be knocking on the door of psychology. Reader-critics are beginning to talk about the emotions which the

---

[7] J. L. Staley, "Stumbling in the Dark, Reaching for the Light: Reading Character in John 5 and 9," *The Fourth Gospel from a Literary Perspective,* 70; see S. D. Moore, *Literary Criticism and the Gospels: The Theoretical Challenge* (New Haven: Yale University, 1989) 95-98, 107-08.

[8] Staley, however, seems to catch his breath and walk more confidently in a later essay, appropriately entitled "Reading with a Passion," in which he notes that his childhood values affect his interpretation ("Reading with a Passion: John 18:1-19:42 and the Erosion of the Reader," in SBLSP 1992 [ed. E. H. Lovering; Atlanta: Scholars Press, 19921 67).

9 F. F. Segovia, "Towards a New Direction in Johannine Scholarship: The Fourth Gospel from a Literary Perspective," The Fourth Gospel from a Literary Perspective, 16-17; Tolbert, "A Response from a Literary Perspective," ibid., 209. See also F. F. Segovia, "The Text as Other: Towards a Hispanic American Hermeneutic," a paper presented at the Casassa Conference on "Text and Experience: Toward a Cultural Exegesis of the Bible," Los Angeles, March 1992, 11, 23-24. The proceedings of this conference will be published by Sheffield University Press.

reader experiences, and they are calling for their colleagues to examine their own situation, which might include psychological as well as social location. The way seems clear for a psycho-literary model for reading the Fourth Gospel.

A Psycho-Literary Model of Reading the Fourth Gospel

Of what would such a model consist? In this section, I will sketch a psycho-literary model of reading the Fourth Gospel. It would consist of two elements: a literary component and a psychological component. The literary component is reader-response criticism, and the psychological component is analytical psychology.

First, reader-response criticism contends that the meaning of a text is determined by the interaction of text and reader. The reader is, therefore, instrumental in shaping meaning. Reader-response criticism, however, takes in a spectrum of approaches: from a text-dominant mode on the right, which discusses the text's strategies and constraints, to a reader-dominant mode on the left, which discusses the reader as an individual subject or member of an interpretative community.[10] The psycho-literary model that I am proposing here could function at either end of the spectrum. First, it could operate from the text-dominant mode, looking at the psychological situation of the "implied reader," the reader for whom the text is written.[11] What psychological moves does the implied author expect the implied reader to make? How does the rhetoric of the gospel effect these moves? But also it could function in the reader-dominant mode, focusing on the psychological situation of the real reader in experiencing the text. Such an application of the model emphasizes the reader as an individual subject, who brings to the text a unique set of psychological

---

[10] Segovia, "Towards a New Direction," 20-21; Tolbert, "Response," 204-05.

[11] This term has been popularized by Wolfgang Iser (*The Implied Reader: Patterns of Communication in Prose Fiction from Bunyan to Beckett* [Baltimore: The Johns Hopkins University Press, 1974]). For a discussion of it, as well as others such as "ideal reader" and "informed reader," see R. M. Fowler, *Let the Reader Understand: Reader-Response Criticism and the Gospel of Mark* (Minneapolis: Fortress Press, 1991) 26-40. Fowler concludes this discussion with his own "critical reader," which "has an individual persona (mine), a communal person (the abstracted total experience of my critical community), and a textual persona (the reader implied in the text itself)" (40).

issues, but it also recognizes that those issues have been shaped through the subject's membership in an interpretative community.[12] Questions to be asked include, What is the reader's psycho-social location? What psychological issues does the reader bring to the text?

One, however, needs a psychological method in order to plumb the reader's psyche. The method I will employ is the analytical psychology of the Swiss psychiatrist Carl Gustav Jung. I have found his psychology personally and professionally satisfying as I try to make sense of both my own psychological issues and the psychological issues which the text raises.[13] A growing number of biblical scholars in the last twenty years or so have attempted analyses of the biblical texts using Jungian categories.[14] Furthermore, Jungian literary criticism,

---

[12] Such a use of the psycho-literary model of reading, then, would go hand-in-hand with the intercultural model of reading outlined by Segovia ("Text as Other," 20-21; see also F. F. Segovia, "The Final Farewell of Jesus: A Reading of John 20:30-21:25," *The Fourth Gospel from a Literary Perspective,* 187-88). He emphasizes the subject's membership in an interpretative community, while I emphasize the individual subject.

[13] In saying this, however, I do not mean to imply that Jungian psychology is the only appropriate method to use in fashioning a psycho-literary model of reading. Some very provocative literary biblical interpretations have been produced by scholars using Sigmund Freud and Jacques Lacan. On the Gospels, see S. D. Moore, *Mark and Luke in Poststructuralist Perspectives* (New Haven: Yale University Press, 1992); "Deconstructive Criticism: The Gospel of the Mark," in *Mark & Method. New Approaches in Biblical Studies* (ed. J. C. Anderson and S. D. Moore; Minneapolis: Fortress Press, 1992) 84-102; and "Are There Impurities in the Living Water that the Johannine Jesus Dispenses? Deconstruction, Feminism and the Samaritan Woman," *Biblical Interpretation* 1 (1993) 207-27. On Genesis, see I. Rashkow, *The Phallacy of Genesis: A Feminist-Psychoanalytic Approach* (Literary Currents in Biblical Interpretation; Louisville: Westminster/John Knox, 1993).

[14] The pioneer in this regard is Walter Wink, whose early work in the psychological study of the New Testament *(The Bible in Human Transformation: Toward a New Paradigm for Biblical Study* [Philadelphia: Fortress Press, 1973]) is almost exclusively Jungian, while his more recent work on the concept of the powers in the New Testament *(Naming the Powers: The Language of Power in the New Testament* [Philadelphia: Fortress Press, 1984]; *Unmasking the Powers: The Invisible Forces that Determine Human Existence* [Philadelphia: Fortress Press, 1986]; and *Engaging the Powers: Discernment and Resistance in a World of Domination* [Minneapolis: Fortress Press, 1992]) supplements that emphasis with the work of social psychologists. Gerd Theissen uses Jung along with several other

which is nearly a century old, has enjoyed something of a boom in the last 15 years.[15] Jung's method is primarily a literary method, for Jung believed that the unconscious reveals itself in dreams, myths, folktales, art and literature.[16]

In reading a narrative, a reader responds emotionally to the characters, images, plot, and rhetoric of the narrative. The reader is afraid when the protagonist enters into a dangerous situation, angry when the antagonist threatens the protagonist, and glad when the protagonist emerges triumphant. In psychological terms, these emotional responses are a result of the flow of libido, or psychic energy, in the unconscious.[17] The narrative hooks an inner image, or

---

psychologists in his work on Paul *(Psychological Aspects of Pauline Theology* [Philadelphia: Fortress Press, 1987]). Wayne Rollins has written extensively on the relevance of Jungian psychology for the interpretation of the Bible *(Jung and the Bible* [Atlanta: John Knox, 1983]; "Jung, Psychological Hermeneutics and the Bible," in *Jung and the Interpretation of the Bible* [ed. D. L. Miller; New York: Continuum, forthcoming]). Schuyler Brown has produced Jungian analyses of aspects of the Gospels of Matthew ("Universalism and Particularism in Matthew's Gospel," in SBLSP 1989 [ed. D. J. Lull; Atlanta: Scholars Press, 1989] 388-99) and John ("The Beloved Disciple: A Jungian View," in *The Conversation Continues: Studies in Paul and John in Honor of J. Louis Martyn* [Nashville: Abingdon Press, 1990] 366-77). I myself have written on Jung and John ("Jung and John," *Explorations* 2 [Fall 1988] 77-92; "Word, Psyche, and Symbol: Johannine Symbols in Jungian Perspective," *Jung and the Interpretation of the Bible).*

[15] S R. P. Sugg, ed., *Jungian Literary Criticism* (Evanston: Northwestern University Press, 1992) ix

[16] James Hillman ("Healing Fiction," *Jungian Literary Criticism,* 129-38) is most responsible for bringing this aspect of Jung's work to the fore. From a psychoanalytic perspective, Stephen Moore ("Deconstructive Criticism," 98) makes a similar observation: "The unconscious is itself irreducibly literary in its workings. It is a realm of graphic images, startling associations, surrealistic spectacles, and multilingual puns." Moore notes that he is indebted at this point to Jacques Lacan, "Freud's foremost French disciple."

[17] Jung ("On the Relation of Analytical Psychology to Poetry," in *The Spirit in Man, Art, and Literature* [The Collected Works of C. G. Jung 15; Bollingen Series XX; Princeton: Princeton University Press, 1966] 82) makes this point about the author or artist of a work:

> The creative process ...consists in the unconscious activation of an archetypal image, and in elaborating and shaping this image into the finished work. By giving it shape, the artist translates it into the language of the present, and so makes it possible for us to find our way back to the deepest springs of life.

My approach here, however, is focused on the experience of the reader, for, as Jane Tompkins notes, "Reading and writing join hands, change places, and finally become

an archetype, in the reader's psyche, and the reader projects that image onto the narrative. The reader, then, is emotionally bound up with a character or situation in the narrative. Furthermore, the reader becomes caught up in conflict between characters because it expresses the conflict between the reader's own inner images. When a character with whom the reader identifies triumphs over conflict, the reader feels triumphant over the inner conflict. The narrative, then, has a compensatory function in the reader's psyche, in that it compensates or corrects some conscious attitude in the reader's psyche.[18] For example, a reader may feel frustrated because he or she feels alienated from society, but such a feeling is compensated by a narrative in which the protagonist is a loner who is vindicated in the end.[19]

A reader's emotional response to a narrative will depend not only on the rhetoric of the narrative and the way in which the author directs the reader, but

---

distinguishable only as two names for the same activity" ("An Introduction to Reader-Response Criticism," in *Reader-Response Criticism: From Formalism to Post-Structuralism* [Baltimore: Johns Hopkins University, 1980] x). Yet Jung ("Psychology and Literature," in *The Spirit in Man,* 104-05) seems to grasp this point intuitively when he writes,

> We let a work of art act upon us as it acted upon the artist. To grasp its meaning, we must allow it to shape us as it shaped him. Then we also understand the nature of his primordial experience. He has plunged into the healing and redeeming depths of the collective psyche, where man is not lost in the isolation of consciousness and its errors and sufferings, but where all men are caught in a common rhythm which allows the individual to communicate his feelings and strivings to mankind as a whole.

[18] Jung viewed this idea of compensation as a "law of psychic happening," and when he set out to interpret a dream, he always asked: What conscious attitude does this dream compensate? ("The Practical Use of Dream Analysis," in *The Practice of Psychotherapy: Essays on the Psychology of the Transference and Other Subjects* [The Collected Works of C. G. Jung 16; Bollingen Series XX; Princeton: Princeton University Press, 1966] 153). Jung also noted that art serves to compensate for a one-sidedness or imbalance in the conscious attitude of an age ("On the Relation of Analytical Psychology to Poetry," 82-83; "Psychology and Literature," 97-98).

[19] I use this example in light of Wayne Meeks' influential article, "The Man from Heaven in Johannine Sectarianism" (*JBL* 91 [1972] 44-72), in which he argues that the Johannine picture of Jesus as an alien in this world is a projection of the alienation which the Johannine community experience in the aftermath of expulsion from the synagogue. Might it also be said that such an interpretation of the Gospel and the history of the Johannine community is Meeks' own projection of his alienation from society as a scholar?

also on the psycho-social location of the reader. Readers from different psycho-social locations will have different experiences with the inner images, and they will project different things upon the text. A person's social context will shape how one responds to the images in a narrative, for the interpretive community of which one is a part will affect one's reception of the narrative. Such a community sets down rules as to how a narrative is to be read and what responses are appropriate. Readers' class, gender,' race, sexual orientation, educational status, and religion will influence their emotional response.

A reader, nevertheless, comes to a narrative individually, with all his or her uniquenesses, complexes, and struggles. Each person comes with a specific experience of the inner images and projects different things upon them according to his or her experience. A person's unconscious issues, then, will determine one's conscious reading of the text. A reader attempts to resolve his or her complexes through reading. A person reads in order to move toward wholeness.[20]

A critical reader, then, must be sensitive to his or her emotional response to the narrative. How does the narrative evoke such a response from the reader? What is it about the rhetoric of the narrative that evokes such a response? What images call forth such a response? Yet the reader must be critical of one's own response to the narrative. How has this response been shaped by the social context in which one is a part? What emotional issues are projected upon the narrative? How can these images in the narrative help one move toward wholeness?

Such is the psycho-literary model of reading a narrative which I have constructed. It consists of reader-response theory, which finds meaning in the interaction between text and reader, with emphasis on the reader's experience. Another major component is analytical psychology, which understands one's emotional response to a narrative as a result of psychic energy from the

---

[20] See Ralph Maud, who, under the influence of James Hillman, contends that a person brings "the sufferings of the soul" to the reading of a book. "We sit down with a serious book prepared to give the author something of ourselves to work on: we move toward the reading experience with our sorrows, all our woe" ("Archetypal Depth Criticism and Melville," *Jungian Literary Criticism*, 259).

unconscious occasioned by the projection of the reader's inner images on the text.

The Model Applied:
Toward a Psycho-Literary Reading of the Fourth Gospel

How, then, can this model be applied to the reader's experience of the Fourth Gospel? Time and space will permit only a sketch, but I will first give attention to the reader's experience of the characters of the Gospel, and then I will discuss how a reader's psycho-social location might affect the reading of the Gospel narrative. Characters to be considered will include first Jesus, then those who believe in him, and finally "the Jews." In my discussion of psycho-social location, I will first identify my own psycho-social location and then highlight how those from other psycho-social locations might read the Gospel differently.

Any discussion of characterization in the Gospel must begin with the character of Jesus, for he strides through the narrative like a colossus. He is the Messiah and the Son of God, but he is also the Word become flesh, the only Son from the Father; he comes down from above, works miraculous signs, speaks in long discourses, and returns to the world above through death, resurrection, and ascension. In other words, Jesus is presented in the narrative as a numinous, archetypal figure. In Jungian language, he is the symbol of the Self, which works toward wholeness in the psyche.[21] The reader projects this image onto the character of Jesus, and thus is established an emotional bond between this character and the reader. This bond is termed "faith" in the narrative. It has certain ideological components, such as believing that the Messiah, the Son of God is Jesus (20:31), but it also includes affective components such as love (13:1, 34-35; 14:15, 23-24; 15:9-10; 16:27), peace (14:27; 16:33; 20:19), and joy (15:11; 16:21-22; 17:13; 20:20). Believing in Jesus means having an emotional connection with him.

This connection between Jesus and the reader is formed primarily through Jesus' speech, which both interprets his actions and supports the narrator's

---

[21] For an extended discussion of the Self in Jung's thought, see Jung, "The Practical Use of Dream-Analysis." For Christ as a symbol of the Self, see "Psychology and Literature." In another place, Jung refers to the Self as "the God-image" within us ("On the Relation of Analytical Psychology to Poetry," 469).

speech. Jesus, however, does not use ordinary speech but rather archetypal images that stir the reader's emotions. I will highlight three aspects of Jesus' imagistic speech: sensory images such as bread, water, and light; relational images such as Father-Son; and spatial images such as the journey from above. Through the images he speaks, Jesus draws the reader into his bosom.

First, in his speech Jesus uses various sensory images, such as bread, water, light, and vine. These images have positive associations for the reader through experience in the world: Bread and water satisfy hunger and thirst (see 4:13-14; 6:35; 7:37-38), light gives guidance (see 8:12; 12:46), and vine emphasizes connectedness (see 15:1-11). Furthermore, the reader is aware that these images are associated in the Jewish tradition with God's relationship to the people of God (see e.g. Isa 42:6-7; 55:1-2; Ps 80:8-18). They, therefore, are already emotionally charged for the reader; they evoke warm feelings and help facilitate the reader's identification with God as symbol of the Self. In his speech Jesus applies these images to himself, often through "I am" sayings, and the emotion projected onto these images is now projected onto Jesus, with the result that the bond between him and the reader is cemented.

Jesus' images are not only drawn from the sensory world but also from the world of human relationships. He describes his relationship with God by naming God as Father, a name which scandalizes his opponents because it means that he is making himself equal to God (5:18). Yet the reader feels warmly toward Jesus and associates him with God. Jesus further defines his relationship with God by calling himself the Son and claiming an intimate relationship with the Father, characterized by knowledge, will, and love (see esp. 5:19-29).[22] The reader, then, is touched by this image of Father and Son; it evokes the reader's own longing for a deep sense of connection with his or her parent. Jesus carries a relationship with his parent for which the reader yearns, and thus the reader is further bonded to Jesus.

In addition to sensory and relational imagery, Jesus also uses spatial imagery to bring the reader into relationship with him: he says that he is on a journey from above. Jesus is not of this world, but he has come down from above (8:23; 17:14, 16; see also 3:31). Jesus, therefore, is the Mysterious Other, who is not

---

[22] See also M. E. Willett (Newheart), *Wisdom Christology in the Fourth Gospel* (San Francisco: Mellen, 1992) 68-74.

from this concrete world but from the imaginative world, not from this ego-consciousness but from the unconscious. As the Other, he evokes awe from the reader, so that the reader too is confronted with the unconscious and forced to come into relationship with it.

Although Jesus has come into this world, he does not become a permanent resident of it. Rather, he returns to the world above through death, resurrection, and ascension. Indeed, these events constitute the hour of Jesus' glorification, in which he returns to the Father (12:28; 13:31-32). Jesus, therefore, journeys into the world through incarnation, works signs and speaks in discourses while in the world, and then journeys out of the world through death, resurrection, and ascension. As Segovia has pointed out, this cosmic journey of the Word provides the overall framework for the plot of the Gospel.[23] Similarly, Adele Reinhartz calls this journey the "cosmological tale," which provides the interpretive key for the historical tale of the Gospel narrative.[24] Furthermore, she notes the "affective power" of the cosmological tale.[25] The tale derives its power because it touches upon an archetypal theme in the reader's unconscious, that of the journey.[26] Jesus' journey is not just a geographical journey from Galilee to Jerusalem, but a cosmic journey, from above to below and back to above. The reader is moved by the image of this cosmic journey, for it leads the reader to follow Jesus into the world above, the world of the imagination, the world of the unconscious.

Jesus' speech, then, functions to bring the reader into relationship with him, through his use of various images such as bread, water, and wine, through his statements about his intimate relationship with God, and through his references to his journey from above to below and back to above. The reader is thus emotionally bonded with Jesus.

This bond which the reader has with Jesus is lived out in the narrative by those characters who believe in him, such as the disciples, the man born blind

---

[23] Segovia, "Journey(s) of the Word of God," 33.

[24] A. Reinhartz, *The Word in the World: The Cosmological Tale in the Fourth Gospel* (SBLMS 45; Atlanta: Scholars Press, 1992) 30.

[25] Ibid., 29.

[26] See Segovia, "Journey(s) of the Word of God," 33 and the literature he cites there for the journey or travel account as a common literary form in ancient narrative.

and the Samaritan woman. The character who has an exemplary relationship with Jesus is not identified by name but is simply called "the disciple whom Jesus loved." He is first introduced as reclining in the bosom of Jesus (13:23); he is given the care of Jesus' mother at the cross (19:26); he recognizes that Jesus is risen (20:9; 21:7); when Peter is told by Jesus to follow, the beloved disciple is already following (21:20); and this disciple is the foundational witness for the Gospel (21:24). The reader is drawn to the beloved disciple, for he enjoys the kind of relationship with Jesus that the reader longs to have with the Self. With this Gospel, then, the beloved disciple takes the reader into the bosom of Jesus, which is a place of intimacy, of warmth, of care. The beloved disciple, then, facilitates the emotional bond between the reader and Jesus.[27]

The other disciples, however, do not seem to experience the kind of intimacy that the beloved disciple does. Indeed, they misunderstand, question, doubt, and even deny. Nevertheless, with the singular exception of Judas, whom Jesus (along with the reader) knows will betray him (6:64, 71; 12:4), the disciples persist in faith. Their failings do not alienate the reader, but rather the reader feels an even closer identification with them and with Jesus. The reader too desires union with the Ultimate but feels anxious about that relationship. These longings and anxieties are projected onto the disciples, and the successful resolution of their faith resolves the reader's faith too. The reader believes through the disciples.

The reader views other characters who come to faith in Jesus in much the same way. The reader identifies with the Samaritan woman, the man born blind, Mary and Martha, and Mary Magdalene, all of whom overcome various obstacles in order to come to faith. The reader experiences frustration with these characters for their momentary lack of faith or understanding but also experiences joy and relief when they come to believe. They carry for the reader his or her faith in Jesus.

While the reader identifies with characters who believe in Jesus, he or she is alienated from those who reject him. These include individual characters such as Judas and Pilate, but the primary opponent of Jesus in the narrative is a collective character: *hoi ioudaioi,* usually translated "the Jews" or "the Judeans."

---

[27] For an extended Jungian treatment of the beloved disciple, see Brown, "Beloved Disciple."

Also called "the Pharisees" (9:13, 16), they continually appear in the narrative debating with Jesus (2:18-20; 5:19-47; 6:25-59; et al). They seek to kill him (5:18; 7:1), and finally succeed by clamoring for Pilate to crucify him, saying that their King is not Jesus but Caesar (19:15). Jesus says that they are blind (9:40-41) and children of the devil (8:44). Characters who believe in Jesus do not express their faith openly because they are afraid of "the Jews" (7:13; 9:22; 12:42; 19:38; 20:19). "The Jews," then, evoke fear and anger from characters in the narrative, and the reader feels the same emotions toward them. They carry the reader's shadow, the sum total of what one refuses to acknowledge about himself or herself.[28] The reader, therefore, projects the archetype of the Self onto Jesus and the shadow onto "the Jews." The reader must read the narrative, then, with a divided consciousness: alienation toward "the Jews" through anger and fear, and identification with Jesus through love, peace and joy.

The reader, therefore, encounters various characters in the narrative such as Jesus, the disciples, and "the Jews." The reader experiences identification with or alienation from them, projecting onto them the inner images. The reader identifies with Jesus and feels warmly toward him because he is the symbol of the Self. The reader also identifies with the disciples and others who come to faith in Jesus, for they express the ego moving toward union with the Self. And finally, the reader is alienated from "the Jews" and is angry with them, because they carry the shadow.

I have been referring in this essay to the reader as the "implied reader." The "implied reader," however, is a construct—one might say, "projection"—of the real reader. A real reader projects his or her own responses, both intellectual and emotional, onto the "implied reader." When I speak in this paper, then, of "the reader," that is, the "implied reader," I am really speaking of myself as a reader of the Gospel narrative. As a reader, I come out of a particular psycho-social location. I am a white, middle-class, heterosexual, highly educated male Christian academic employed in providing theological education for those considered marginalized in society. I struggle with emotional issues surrounding Mother and Father complexes, and I have found analytical psychology of great

---

[28] For a brief discussion of the shadow, see Jung, "The Shadow," in *Aion: Researches into the Phenomenology of the Self* (2d ed.; The Collected Works of C. G. Jung 9/2; Bollingen Series XX; Princeton: Princeton University Press, 1969) 8-10.

assistance in dealing with those issues. My psycho-social location, then, shapes my reading experience of the Gospel. I identify with the character of Jesus in the Gospel because his professed sense of intimacy with God, whom he calls Father, meets my own sense of longing for parental connection. Furthermore, Jesus is depicted as an Other "not from this world," which gives expression to my own sense of alienation from the religious tradition in which I grew up and from society at large.

Readers from other psycho-social locations will respond differently to the Gospel than I do. For example, they will identify with different characters and situations in the narrative. They will also construct the implied reader in varying ways, projecting their own emotional responses onto that construct. Furthermore, they will come to a certain relationship with the implied reader, either accepting the claims of the implied author or rejecting them, thus becoming "resisting readers."[29] All such responses, however, are grounded in the psycho-social location out of which the reader approaches the narrative. A reader's psychological and social issues will shape how he or she responds to the narrative.

To take two examples, women and Jews will read the Gospel differently from the way I as a Christian man do. A woman who derives fulfillment through participation in the organized church will identify strongly with the female characters in the narrative, projecting her feelings toward the church onto the character of Jesus. Another woman, however, who feels estranged from the church because of its patriarchy will not accept Jesus as a symbol of the Self. She will feel angry toward him because of his exclusive use of male imagery for God, and he becomes for her the bearer of the church's oppressive patriarchy. Furthermore, Jewish readers will not identify with Jesus but rather with "the Jews"; they will feel angry toward Jesus and warmly toward "the Jews." For the Jewish reader, the Gospel narrative and the character of Jesus plant the seeds of Christian anti-Semitism.

---

[29] The term "resisting reader" is from Judith Fetterly, *The Resisting Reader: A Feminist Approach to American Fiction* (Bloomington: Indiana University, 1978). For a brief discussion of this idea and an application to the Gospel of Mark, see R. Fowler, "Reader-Response Criticism: Figuring Mark's Reader," *Mark and Method,* 73-81.

Other examples could be mentioned. African-Americans, homosexuals, homeless persons, and high school students will all have different reading strategies from one another and from me. But also those within particular social locations have various psychological locations. Everyone comes at the Gospel from a unique psycho-social location. For example, a reader struggling with depression might be drawn to the image of light in order to find relief from the enveloping psychological darkness. Another dealing with anger toward authority figures might see Jesus' polemic against "the Jews" as a vehicle for focusing anger. Someone else struggling with grief might be attracted to the narratives about the raising of Lazarus and Jesus' own resurrection. All readers read for psychological wholeness, for resolution of unconscious conflicts, for relationship with the Self.

A critical reader, then, will be critical not only of the Gospel narrative but also of oneself as reader. One will examine one's own psycho-social location and its effect on one's reading. What emotional issues does one bring to the reading of that narrative? What aspects of the narrative stand out, and how do those aspects meet one's emotional needs? How does one respond to Jesus as he interacts with the disciples and "the Jews," and how do those interactions express one's own unconscious issues? The implied author asks the reader, just as Jesus asks the first two disciples: "What are you looking for" (1:38)?

Conclusion

A psycho-literary reading, then, further extends the interest in literary studies in the Fourth Gospel. It takes seriously a reader's emotional response to the narrative. This psycho-literary model of reading takes as its literary component reader-response criticism and as its psychological component analytical psychology. When applied to the Gospel, this model considers the implied reader's dual response to the narrative: identification with Jesus as a symbol of the Self and alienation from "the Jews" as a collective shadow figure. A psycho-literary reading, however, realizes that real readers will have different responses to the narrative based on their psycho-social location. I will allow Carl Jung the last word:

> People will read the gospel again and again and I myself will read it again and again. But they will read it with much more profit if they have some insight into their own psyches. Blind are the eyes of anyone who does not know his

own heart, and I always recommend the application of a little psychology so that he can understand things like the gospel still better.[30]

---

[33] *Letters* (vol. 1; Bollingen Series XCV; Princeton: Princeton University Press, 1973) 463; quoted in Rollins, "Jung, Psychological Hermeneutics and the Bible," 1.

Chapter Four

Reading Myself, Reading the Text:
The Johannine Passion Narrative in Postmodern Perspective

JEFFREY LLOYD STALEY

> "[No] one has ever done exegesis of John's writings until the reader has received, as a vital reality, the message of the work and has felt its impact in his own life and existence."
>
> —Crossan

> "I am going to ...read the Gospel of St. John as an Indian. Secondly, this Indian is not a hypothetical being...whom I have imagined. This Indian is myself."
>
> —Amaladoss

> "[R]eading is a species of self-discovery, but it may also be a neurosis or hysteria."
>
> —Freund

Re-Reading Reader Criticism: Experiments in the New Testament

Reader-response criticism has survived as a vaguely defined subfield of literary criticism and literary theory for nearly twenty years now.[1] But its impact upon biblical criticism began to be felt only about ten years ago. Instead of being author-centered like so much of earlier literary and biblical criticism

---

[1] An earlier version of this essay appeared in the 1992 *SBL Seminar Papers* under the title, "Reading with a Passion: John 18:1-19:42 and the Erosion of the Reader," and was presented at the SBL Passion Narrative and Tradition in Early Christianity Group, where R. Alan Culpepper and Craig Koester responded to it. I wish to thank those scholars for their insightful remarks, and especially John Carroll, who initially invited me to present my work to that group. A still more developed version of this essay will be part of a book-length project, tentatively entitled, *Reading with a Passion: Formalist to Postmodern Reader-Response Criticism and the Fourth Gospel.*

had been—instead of answering questions such as, "What is the social/political/biographical context which best explains what this author is trying to do?"—reader-response criticism purports to be audience-centered. It has been interested in questions related to the effect of narrative upon audiences, theories of how texts effect particular responses, and illustrations of how a narrative can be transformed by the psychology of the individual reader or by particular interpretive communities.

When reader-response criticism burst onto the American literary scene in the 1970s, its popularity grew quickly. In contrast to most earlier approaches, reader criticism was keenly interested in describing and analyzing the persuasive side of literature.[2] The new breed of doctoral candidates in the late 1960s had had their mettle tested in protests against the military-industrial complex, the draft, the Vietnam war, racism, and sexism, and had seen how rhetoric could harm and heal. They had lived life with passion and zeal and had developed a distrust and distaste for ordered power structures. Now that they found themselves tenurously seated on the other side of the classroom desk, backs to the chalkboard, audience-oriented criticism was the natural, professional reaction to their mentors' clinical, white-gloved approach to literature. The old "New Critics" who thought they could analyze texts apart from their political, social, ethical, and personal effects were nearly extinct. A new species of reader was crawling out of the oozing slime.

Somewhat similarly to this development in English Departments across the United States, in the late 1970s many battle-tested New Testament professors

---

[2] In writing about literary critics' disenchantment with narratology, Christine Brooke-Rose ("Whatever Happened to Narratology?" *Poetics Today* 11 [1990] 284; my emphasis) argues:

> ...the chief problem came to be seen as arising not from inherent universal structures but from *reading*, as if analysers had a profound need to experience, not a text or even a story, but *their own mental processes* when faced with a poetic text or story that perhaps did not give them the immediate and unalloyed pleasures that its renown, its place in the canon or histories of literature had led them to expect.

If one were to take out her reference to *"universal* structures," leaving "structures" by itself, her observation would parallel the earlier reaction of reader-response criticism to New Criticism (see S. R. Suleiman, "Introduction: Varieties of Audience-Oriented Criticism," in *The Reader in the Text: Essays on Audience and Interpretation* [ed. S. R. Suleiman and I. Crosman; Princeton: Princeton University Press, 1980] 3-4).

and raw recruits just finishing their degrees were searching for an antidote to the hardline historical sourcery that had vivisected the biblical text and sucked out its readerly impulse. Having been inaugurated into literary criticism by the precision of structuralist thought, these scholars were soon opening up the rhetorically-oriented works of Wayne Booth, Wolfgang Iser, and the important collections of reader-response articles edited by Susan Suleiman and Inge Crosman, Jane Tompkins, and others.[3] The omens for change appeared to be good. Stephen Moore names this new breed of scholars and dissects their work up through 1988 in his chapter entitled "Stories of Reading: Doing Gospel Criticism as/with a Reader,"[4] and although new names might be added to his list, the reader-oriented critics' approaches to the Bible have not changed much in the intervening years.

In contrast to their English Department colleagues across the hall, who believed reader-oriented criticism was a much needed corrective to New Criticism's one-sided, constricting emphasis on "the poem itself," New Testament scholars initially saw the more synchronic, formalist, reader-oriented, narratological approaches as offering a way to hover closely over "the text

---

[3] W. Booth, *The Rhetoric of Fiction* (2d ed.; Chicago: The University of Chicago Press, 1983); W. Iser, *The Implied Reader: Patterns of Communication in Prose Fiction from Bunyan to Beckett* (Baltimore: The Johns Hopkins University Press, 1974) and *The Act of Reading: A Theory of Aesthetic Response* (Baltimore: The Johns Hopkins University Press, 1978); Suleiman and Crosman, *The Reader in the Text;* S. Tompkins, ed., *Reader-Response Criticism: From Formalism to Post-Structuralism* (Baltimore: The Johns Hopkins University Press, 1980). See also U. Eco, *The Role of the Reader: Explorations in the Semiotics of Texts* (Bloomington: Indiana University Press, 1979); S. Fish, *Is There a Text in This Class?* (Cambridge: Harvard University Press, 1980); S. Mailloux, *Interpretive Conventions: The Reader in the Study of American Fiction* (Ithaca: Cornell University Press, 1982); J. Culler, *On Deconstruction: Theory and Criticism after Structuralism* (Ithaca: Cornell University Press, 1982); R. Holub, *Reception Theory: A Critical Introduction* (New York: Methuen, 1984); and E. Freund, *The Return of the Reader: Reader-Response Criticism* (New York: Methuen, 1987).

[4] S. Moore, *Literary Criticism and the Gospels: The Theoretical Challenge* (New Haven: Yale University Press, 1989) 71-107.

itself" and breathe new life into it.[5] Thus, as New Testament scholars began to search for the "real, super, ideal, encoded, implied" reader in, with, and under the biblical text, they seemed to have had a threefold hope. First and foremost, they hoped that the analysis of biblical texts as narratives (complete with narrator, characters, and plot) could draw back together into one loaf the fragmentary crumbs of texts left over after historical-critical methodologies had departed. Texts would be interpreted as unified wholes.[6] Texts would be seen as mirrors and not only as windows to the past.[7] Secondly, these New Testament Scholars hoped that the analysis of the creatively affective and persuasive aspects of story worlds could add a third dimension to their mentors' two dimensional emphasis on historical events and community concerns. Text pragmatics would replace text semantics.[8] And thirdly, the scholars hoped that

---

[5] As Stephen Moore puts it so well: "The impression being fostered among biblical students and scholars ...is that secular literary criticism, as it pertains to literary narrative, is a discipline preoccupied with the unity of text and the autonomy of story-worlds..." (ibid., 11; see also 50-55). See R. Fowler, *"Let the Reader Understand": Reader-Response Criticism and the Gospel of Mark* (Minneapolis: Fortress Press, 1991) 9-12; M. A. Powell, *What Is Narrative Criticism?* (Minneapolis: Fortress Press, 1990) 6-21; R. Detweiler and V. K. Robbins, "From New Criticism to Poststructuralism: Twentieth Century Hermeneutics," in *Reading the Text: Biblical Criticism and Literary Theory* (ed. S. Prickett; Cambridge: Basil Blackwell, 1991) 248-252; and H. Boers, "Narrative Criticism, Historical Criticism, and the Gospel of John," *JSNT* 47 (1992) 37-38, 43-44.

[6] For example, note the unitarian emphasis in R. Fowler, *Loaves and Fishes: The Function of the Feeding Stories in the Gospel of Mark* (SBLDS 54; Chico: Scholars Press, 1981); R. C. Tannehill, *The Narrative Unity of Luke-Acts: A Literary Interpretation* (Philadelphia: Fortress Press, 1986); and R. A. Culpepper, *Anatomy of the Fourth Gospel: A Study in Literary Design* (Philadelphia: Fortress Press, 1983).

[7] N. R. Petersen, *Literary Criticism for New Testament Critics* (Philadelphia: Fortress Press, 1978) 19; S. Moore, "'Mirror, Mirror...': Lacanian Reflections on Malbon's Mark," in *Textual Determinacy (Part One) (Semeia* 62; ed. R. C. Culley and R. B. Robinson; Atlanta: Scholars Press, 1993) 168.

[8] J. L. Staley, *The Print's First Kiss: A Rhetorical Investigation of the Implied Reader in the Fourth Gospel* (SBLDS 82; Atlanta: Scholars Press, 1988); Fowler, *"Let the Reader Understand"*; W. Wuellner, "Putting Life Back into the Lazarus Story and its Reading: The Narrative Rhetoric of John 11 and the Narration of Faith," in *The Fourth Gospel from a Literary Perspective (Semeia* 53; ed. R. A. Culpepper and F. F. Segovia; Atlanta: Scholars

this new approach could bridge the growing gap between the academician studying the text as artifact and the layperson reading the text as article of faith.[9] The Bible would be a book motivating laity and scholars alike by its correctly interpreted persuasive power.

Without a doubt, early appropriations of reader-response criticism in the New Testament have been firmly rooted in formalist literary theory and rhetorical studies. They have typically argued that markers in the text itself guide and manipulate readers' responses. The role of the reader critic, then, has been to uncover and expose the New Testament narratives' rhetorical strategies and to make them obvious to the otherwise unsuspecting, twentieth century reader.[10] My own dissertation, written in 1985 and published in 1988, fell into this category of reader-response criticism but with some subtle twists. In it I explored the purpose of what I interpreted to be a "reader victimization" strategy in the Fourth Gospel: those places where the narrative forced the reader to the wrong conclusions (like false leads in a detective novel), only to correct the reader's mistakes later on.

But like its older sister in the secular realm, biblical reader-response criticism has watched many of its early adherents fly away from formalist, rhetorical constructions of readers to nest with feminist, deconstructive, and other poststructuralist understandings of readers. Along the way, more and more weight is being given to the "real reader"—either the elite, professionally trained, late twentieth-century Western (male) reader, or the feminist reader, or

---

Press, 1991) 40-54; J. E. Botha, *Jesus and the Samaritan Woman: A Speech Act Reading of John* 4:1-42 (NovTSup 65; New York: E. J. Brill, 1991).

[9] B. F. Meyer, "The Challenges of Text and Reader to the Historical-Critical Method," in *The Bible and Its Readers* (ed. W. Beuken, S. Freyne, and A. Weiler; Philadelphia: Trinity Press, 1991) 3-12; and L. White, "Historical and Literary Criticism: A Theological Response," *BTB* 13 (1983) 32-34.

[10] S. Porter, "Why Hasn't Reader-Response Criticism Caught on in New Testament Studies?" *Journal of Literature and Theology* 4 (1990) 278-283; more recently, see his "Reader-Response Criticism and New Testament Study: A Response to A. C. Thiselton's *New Horizons in Hermeneutics,*" *Literature and Theology* 8 (1994) 94-102. See Culpepper, *Anatomy of the Fourth Gospel,* 5-6; Staley, *The Print's First Kiss,* 27-49; F. J. Moloney, *Belief in the Word: Reading John 1-4* (Minneapolis: Fortress Press, 1993) 5-6, 9-13; and Botha, *Jesus and the Samaritan Woman,* 188200.

the third world, postcolonial reader. From these more recent perspectives those earlier appropriations of reader criticism in biblical studies have been criticized for the same reasons that they had been criticized in literary critical circles: for not really being reader-centered at all, but for being just as text-centered as was New Criticism.[11] Even in those places where the early biblical reader-response critics did talk of "readers" and the rhetorical responses that a narrative seeks to elicit from its "readers," what they were really talking about was merely their own idiosyncratic critical moves, lightly masked behind the neologisms and technical language of rhetoric and narratology.

To some scholars, the turn toward synchronic, reader-oriented analyses of New Testament narratives appears to be a radical reaction to problems left in the wake of historical-critical methodology. Yet biblical reader-response criticism has generated a number of challenging responses even from those scholars who, like themselves, are disenchanted with historical-critical methods.[12] One of the most pervasive criticisms leveled against biblical reader-response criticism comes from feminist and liberationist interpreters. These interpreters are quick to point out that the critic's social location has generally not been taken into

---

[11] As Mary Louise Pratt ("Interpretive Strategies/ Strategic Interpretations: On Anglo American Reader-Response Criticism," in *Postmodernism and Politics* [ed. J. Arac; Minneapolis: University of Minnesota Press, 1986] 26) notes,

> [although] reader-response criticism often presents itself as a corrective to formalist or intrinsic criticism[, t]his explanation... does not seem altogether adequate. On the one hand, formalism and New Criticism are already so discredited in theoretical circles that there seems little need for another round of abuse. On the other hand, much reader-response criticism turns out to be a notational variant of that very formalism so roundly rejected. An antiformalist theoretical stance invoked to uphold a neo- or covertly formalist practice is a contradiction not altogether unfamiliar these days, and one which suggests that in addition to the dead horses being flogged, there must be some live ones running around escaping notice. Gazes must turn outward, beyond the corral.

See also Gayatri C. Spivak, *The Post-Colonial Critic: Interviews, Strategies, Dialogues* (ed. S. Harasym; New York: Routledge, 1990) 50-52.

[12] D. Rensberger, *Johannine Faith and Liberating Community* (Philadelphia: Westminster Press, 1988) 115; Powell, *What Is Narrative Criticism?* 91-101; W. Wuellner, "Is There an Encoded Reader Fallacy?," in *Reader Perspectives on the New Testament* (*Semeia* 48; ed. E. V.. McKnight; Atlanta: Scholars Press, 1989) 41; Porter, "Why Hasn't Reader-Response Criticism," 283-290; and Moore, *Literary Criticism and the Gospels*, 98-107.

account by the largely white, elite males doing the readerly analysis.[13] In our quest to be part of the biblical critical guild, we reader critics have sacrificed one of the truly original insights of reader-response criticism (what real readers bring to the reading of texts)[14] for "scientific" (read "formalist"), exegetical objectivity.[15] From this critical perspective, the technical expressions of the reader as "in the text" as an "implied reader," or as an "encoded reader," are merely phrases which, once demythologized, betray the individual interpreter's unfocused ideological and political interests. These "readers" are not objective elements of texts at all. Instead, they are rhetorical devices naively used by the interpreter to convince an elite reading audience of the validity of the particular interpretation.[16]

So Temma Berg can write that, in general, biblical reader-response criticism needs:

> to keep looking at the words "reader" and "text" and "in" and re-examine what they mean ....The reader is in and not in the text. The reader can never be separated from the texts that surround him, partly because "reader" and "text" are interchangeable signs, but also because the reader is an active producer of what she reads. The text exists so that the reader may fill it. The

---

[13] J. C. Anderson, "Matthew: Gender and Reading," in *The Bible and Feminist Hermeneutics (Semeia 28;* ed. M. A. Tolbert; Chico: Scholars Press, 1983) 3-5, 21-24; Wuellner, "Is There an Encoded Reader Fallacy?" 49; T. Berg, "Reading in/to Mark," *Reader Perspectives on the New Testament,* 196; and Mary Ann Tolbert, "A Response from a Literary Perspective," *The Fourth Gospel from a Literary Perspective,* 208-209. In the secular realm, see especially P. Schweickart, "Toward a Feminist Theory of Reading," in *Gender and Reading: Essays on Readers, Texts, and Contents* (ed. E. A. Flynn and P. Schweickart; Baltimore: The Johns Hopkins University Press, 1986) 35-39; and Pratt, "Interpretive Strategies/Strategic Interpretations," 26-30.

[14] Berg, "Reading in/to Mark," 202-203; F. F. Segovia, "The Final Farewell of Jesus: A Reading of John 20:30-21:25," *The Fourth Gospel from a Literary Perspective,* 168-169; J. Beutler, "Response from a European Perspective," *The Fourth Gospel from a Literary Perspective,* 195-196; Tolbert, "Response from a Literary Perspective," 208-209.

[15] Moore, *Literary Criticism and the Gospels,* 106-107, 177-178.

[16] Wuellner, "Is There an Encoded Reader Fallacy?"; Daniel Boyarin, "The Politics of Biblical Narratology: Reading the Bible Like/As a Woman," *Diacritics* 20 (1990) 31-42; see Edgard V.. McKnight, *Post-Modern Use of the Bible: The Emergence of Reader-Oriented Criticism* (Nashville: Abingdon Press, 1988) 14-19, 161-162.

reader exists so that the text may fill her. Neither the reader nor the text has a single, stable center; both the reader and the text may be endlessly changed.[17]

Mary Ann Tolbert's criticism of my work sounds a similar refrain. She writes: "What Staley's generalized reader masks ...is the critic himself: Staley's reader reads the way Staley does. His analysis ...is not the reading experience of any reader, but the analysis of the modern biblical critic."[18] Here Tolbert is echoing an argument made by Stephen Moore, an argument which was first put forward by Stanley Fish in a critique of his own early "affective stylistics."[19] Moore's poststructuralist evaluation of reader-response criticism in New Testament studies concluded:

> [r]eader-response criticism of the Gospels, because it is an enterprise that tends to feel accountable to conventional gospel scholarship, has worked with reader constructs that are sensitively attuned to what may pass as permissible critical reading. That is why reader-oriented exegeses can often read disappointingly like the familiar critical renditions of the given biblical passage, lightly reclothed in a reader vocabulary. The reader of audience-oriented gospel criticism is a repressed reader. Its parents are mainstream gospel exegesis on the biblical side, and reader in the text formalism on the nonbiblical side?[20]

The signs are clear and unambiguous. Warning: Reading in Process. Wash your hands, disinfect your clothing, and check your personal effects at the door.

But on the other side of the critical debate, opposite Tolbert and Moore, stands the social world perspective of Bruce Malina. While he can agree with Tolbert that it is salutary to force reader-response critics and readers out from behind their individualistic and anachronistic reading masks, he has problems with the "increasingly diverse world of New Testament interpretation," which Tolbert and Moore laud. From Malina's point of view, the high value Tolbert

---

[17] Berg, "Reading in/to Mark," 202.

[18] Tolbert, "Response from a Literary Perspective," 206.

[19] Moore, *Literary Criticism and the Gospels*, 134-136; Fish, *Is There a Text in This Class?* 2167, 147-173. See Christopher Norris, *What's Wrong with Postmodernism: Critical Theory and the Ends of Philosophy* (Baltimore: The Johns Hopkins University Press, 1990) 79-83; and Porter, "Why Hasn't Reader-Response Criticism," 285-286.

[20] Moore, *Literary Criticism and the Gospels*, 107.

and Moore place on pluralistic and individualistic readings is just another sign of ethnocentric, elitist, middle-class American values being forced upon a radically different, ancient Mediterranean world.[21]

Malina's empirically defined, cultural-anthropological model of reading is one in which contemporary, considerate readers who value "U.S. fairness"[22] will "obviously make the effort to bring to their reading a set of scenarios proper to the time, place and culture of the biblical author." [23] Prom Malina's perspective, reading models that fail to make this effort are sinfully anachronistic, ethnocentric,[24] elitist, and grossly inconsiderate.[25] Strangely, the fairness doctrine to which he appeals seems to get lost in the agonistic rhetoric directed particularly at poststructural and postmodern readings.

In spite of the many important hermeneutical issues that separate social world critics like Malina from reader-response critics like myself, and from poststructuralist critics like Woke, we all nevertheless share a common rhetorical purpose: to radically undercut the churchly ordinariness of the text-that presumed connectedness of the biblical world with our own religious subculture-in order to confront the New Testament as other, as an alien thing.[26] The social world critics, for their part, do this by setting the biblical text in an ancient Mediterranean social context with a nearly unbridgeable chasm between

---

[21] B. J. Malina, "Reading Theory Perspective: Reading Luke-Acts," in *The Social World of Luke-Acts: Models for Interpretation* led. J. H. Neyrey; Peabody, MA: Hendrickson, 1991) 18-19, 21.

[22] Ibid., 22. See Stephen Moore's evaluation of North American capitalist economy and its influence upon biblical exegesis *(Mark and Luke in Poststructuralist Perspectives: Jesus Begins to Write* [New Haven: Yale University Press, 1992] 148-149).

[23] Malina, "Reading Theory Perspective," 16.

[24] Ibid., 23.

[25] Ibid., 17. Compare this with Edgar McKnight's comment: "A reader-oriented approach acknowledges that the contemporary reader's `intending' of the text is not the same as that of the ancient author and/or the ancient readers. This is not possible, necessary, or desirable" *(Post-Modern Use of the Bible,* 150, also 151-54). See Moore's discussion of intentionality in *Mark and Luke in Poststructuralist Perspectives,* 61-62, 74-75.

[26] C. Osiek, "The Social Sciences and the Second Testament: Problems and Challenges," *BTB* 22 (1992) 94.

it and our own world.[27] They may provide contemporary readers with a critical drop of water to cool their tongues, but that cultural chasm is one which only their own prophets can cross with ease. Conversely, some reader-response critics—and particularly poststructuralist critics—undercut the ordinariness to the biblical text to jarringly juxtaposing it to an ever-widening collection to contemporary literary theorists and intertextual reading frames.[28]

But let me give a different illustration of this rhetorical phenomenon from a related field: that to contemporary historical Jesus research. I find it not at all surprising that the Robert W. Funk-inspired Jesus Seminar has recently, in the final decade before the end of the second millenium, "discovered" that the historical Jesus was a profoundly prophetic, non-apocalyptic figure trying to transform and revitalize Judaism.[29] This peculiarly Lukan-sounding Jesus speaks out against the popular television-evangelist mode of Christianity which is saturated by a gross apocalypticism, a mode of Christianity which is largely uninterested in caring for or protecting the present world and its people.

But compare this latter-day reconstruction with Albert Schweitzer's turn-of-the-century work on the historical Jesus. Surrounded by a popular Christian culture that believed the twentieth century would herald the inbreaking of God's kingdom through the cooperative, humanizing agendas of church and state, Schweitzer's historical research uncovered a radically apocalyptic "Markan Jesus," a different Jesus, whose cataclysmic metaphors opposed the idealistic *Zeitgeist* of Schweitzer's day. Although Schweitzer's research and the Jesus Seminar's research reconstruct the teaching of the historical Jesus along totally different lines (the former accepts Jesus' apocalyptic words as authentic; the

---

[17] Among the social world critics there is a widespread emphasis upon the ancient Mediterranean "honor/shame culture" with its "dyadic view of person" and "limited good," which diverges widely from Euroamerican values (see, e.g., B. J. Malina, *The New Testament World: Insights from Cultural Anthropology* [Atlanta: John Knox, 1981] 25-93).

[28] Fowler, *"Let the Reader Understand"*, 228-266; Moore, *Mark and Luke in Poststructuralist Perspectives*, xv-xix; see D. Culbertson, *The Poetics of Revelation: Recognition and the Narrative Tradition* (Studies in American Biblical Hermeneutics 4; Macon, GA: Mercer University Press, 1989) 141-185.

[29] See, e.g., M. Borg's *Jesus: A New Vision: Spirit, Culture, and the Life of Discipleship* (San Francisco: Harper and Row, 1987) 14, 125-171, and his more recent article, "Portraits of Jesus in Contemporary North American Scholarship," *HTR* 84 (1992) 1-22.

latter rejects them as secondary), both share a common but unspoken rhetorical aim: to make Jesus different from their own culture so that "he" can critically speak to it.[30]

I believe that this same phenomenon can be found in the social world gospels as well as the reader-response and poststructuralist gospels. Although their methodologies differ radically, their goals (either conscious or unconscious) are similar: to defamiliarize the gospel narratives to such an extent that they can speak to contemporary culture in fresh ways.[31] Or perhaps their goals might be better described negatively: all three critical approaches, paralleling historical Jesus research, attempt to defamiliarize the gospel so that it is no longer able to speak in the traditional ways of the past.

Even the great contemporary Jesus scholar, John Crossan, is quick to point out (as did Schweitzer before him) that researchers' reconstructions of the historical Jesus have always had a strangely autobiographical element to them (that is, of course, all reconstructions except Crossan's own)." In other words, the interests and ideologies of the scholars doing the research are always replicated in their portraits of Jesus. I suspect that the same autobiographical point could also be made of biblical literary critics and their historical-critical counterparts. Indeed, it is precisely this autobiographical element that Tolbert's and Moore's criticisms attempt to uncover in us, the reader critics. Thankfully, however, they stop well short of disrobing their fellow scholars or themselves.

In summary, those who challenge reader-response criticism's appropriation by biblical scholars focus on two fundamental issues. The first criticism focuses on reader-response criticism's lack of critical apparatus for analyzing its own interpretive stance. Reader-response criticism often fails or refuses to investigate the social and rhetorical contexts of the interpreter and the implications of those contexts for interpretation. Thus, its interpretations lack a critically-reflected

---

[30] Not surprisingly, McKnight makes the same observation when speaking about scholars' reconstructions of "Paul" *(Post-Modern Use of the Bible,* 148-150).

[31] White, "Historical and Literary Criticism," 32-34.

[32] Crossan writes: "[H]istorical Jesus research is a very safe place to do theology and call it history, to do autobiography and call it biography" *(The Historical Jesus: The Life of a Mediterranean Peasant* [San Francisco: HarperSanFrancisco, 1991] xxviii; see xxxiv). However, his own methodologies and reconstructions are somehow free from these two viruses that inflict every other portrayal of Jesus (ibid.).

subjectivity—in spite of the fact that the interpretations are covertly rooted in the critic's experience as much as liberationist and feminist exegesis is explicitly rooted in the experience of oppression. Although the failure or refusal to address the social and rhetorical contexts of the interpreter may be due as much to academic or ecclesial politics as to any theoretical oversight, nevertheless more openness in this area will be necessary if reader-response criticism should ever solidify its place within the guild. The second criticism focuses on reader-response criticism's interest in appropriating the Bible for the contemporary reader. From this angle, reader-response criticism seems blatantly unconcerned about how canonical texts might have been understood and considered persuasive by first-century audiences.[33]

Thus, biblical reader-response critics fail at both ends of the reader spectrum. For historical and social world critics, reader-response criticism as it is applied to the Bible fails to understand the ancient Mediterranean world or its values—or worse yet, it has no interest in understanding them. Reader-response criticism is blatantly, pointedly anachronistic. And for feminist and liberationist critics, reader-response criticism fails to account for its own values and advocacy stance. Reader-response criticism is blithely elitist and anarchistic. In view of these pointed criticisms, I will begin my own leserly probing of the Johannine passion narrative at its most sensitive place—not somewhere in the text of the Fourth Gospel—but within a personal narrative that attempts to rip apart the seamless, scholarly tunic which protects my subjective nakedness. Or to use a more violent metaphor: I will begin with a personal narrative which intends to smash the bones of the dispassionate objective observer in me—the thing left writing long after the spirit has passed over.

Reading Myself: An Experimental Metaphor

Like many others in the academic discipline of New Testament studies, I have come to the guild of biblical scholarship through the roots of American Protestant fundamentalism. But the anti-intellectualism that I was raised with, in the fierce primitivism and sectarianism of the lay-led Plymouth Brethren, was tempered by a childhood spent exploring the eroded cliffs and canyons of the

---

[33] This point is often made in spite of many reader-response critics' expressed interest in orality (see particularly, Fowler, *"Let the Reader Understand"*, 48-52; Moore, *Literary Criticism and the Gospels*, 84-92).

Navajo Indian Reservation in northeastern Arizona. There, as the son of a missionary school teacher and a school cook, I encountered a culture radically different from that of my own family.

We lived our first fourteen months at Immanuel Mission in a two-room adobe and stone cellar, sharing the single bathroom with Yellowhair, an ancient Navajo who knew no English and was a survivor of the "Long Walk."[34] Yellowhair was more than a hundred years old when we first met him, and when he smiled his face would wrinkle and crease, making him look like the loose skin that covered the joint of my thumb. For twenty years he had been the only baptized Navajo in Morning Meeting.[35] Yellowhair's room adjoined the basement bathroom. And occasionally, on his way to empty his slop-bucket in the morning, he would stand and silently watch my mother getting dressed. With a sudden feeling of strange eyes upon her, she would turn and glimpse his shuffling shadow or hear his door scraping shut on the hard-packed dirt floor of his windowless room.

Within two years we had built our own four-bedroom, cinder-block house with all the conveniences of the modern world. Unlike the two-room cellar, it never flooded and it was much better at keeping out unwanted guests. Our new house had electricity, gas heat, running water, two indoor toilets, and we now owned a bright yellow, van-like "carry-all" (bought for fifty dollars at Army Surplus in Phoenix). But outside the mission compound no one had these comforts, and no one seemed to miss them. Most of the Diné[36] I saw rode horseback or in horse-drawn wagons. They lived in hogans—one-room mud huts with crude oil drum, wood burning stoves in the center. They traveled for miles to fill their barrels with drinking water, and their toilets were any bushes tall enough or ravines deep enough to hide them from the curious eyes of a roving white boy.

---

[34] This is what the Navajo people called their 1864 journey into exile at the Bosque Redondo in central New Mexico.

[35] We used the phrase "Morning Meeting," a term betraying its anti-sacramental, Quaker origins, to refer to our weekly communion service.

[36] This is what the Navajo people call themselves. It can best be translated as "the people."

Inside our house we read the Bible daily around the dining room table, and in Sunday School I memorized verses that spoke of a Holy Spirit poured out on Jews thousands of years ago. But outside our front door I was getting to know people who encountered spirits, witches, and holiness *(hózho', harmony)*—all within a quarter-mile walk of Immanuel Mission's fenced compound. Inside our house we kept a dog as a pet, and it usually slept at night curled up on our front doorstep. But beyond our front door the name for dog was *Xé chąą'i* (shit-eater), and I saw starving, cowering dogs kicked at every opportunity.[37] Occasionally, laughing Navajo children would throw live puppies into the mission's garbage dump fires. It was not unusual to find their small blackened bodies the next morning, mixed in among the empty cans and broken bottles.

My most vivid childhood memories are of dogs. They haunt my dreams. Their silvery shadows flit across the moonlit edges of my unconscious. I remember two dogs that we owned in Kansas, although the first, Chloe, lives in my memory only as a name. The second was named Bimbo, and from time to time my brother Greg and I would pretend that we were she. We would crawl around on all fours, bark ferociously, and eat her dry dog food from the bowl on our back porch.

In our first few years on the reservation, our family selected dogs for pets from among the many Navajo strays that made their home in the mission dump. Our first transformed stray was named Blackie. In our home she grew to be sleek, healthy, and alert. But to the Navajos, a well-fed, grinning dog meant only one thing: a cunning killer. She could only have gotten fat by killing and eating sheep. One day I found Blackie under the mission's old Studebaker, lying in a puddle of blood, turned inside out by a bullet through her side.[38] My eight-year-old eyes watched her life slowly pour out on the hard-packed adobe. She

---

[37] This translation of *Xé chąą'i* comes from somewhere in one of Tony Hillerman's popular Navajo mystery novels—the specific book and page I cannot recall. Although the Navajo word for dog was one of the first words I learned on the reservation, it never dawned on me to connect it with *chąą'* (excrement)—another word I learned very quickly—until I read it in the Hillerman story. Strangely, it was this particular translation, now lost to me, that rekindled my interest in my childhood years on the Navajo reservation.

[38] John 19:32-37.

had crawled home to her favorite hiding place, to nurse her four newborn pups one last time.

The second stray our family took in appeared to be part German shepherd. He was larger than Blackie and light-colored, and after a few weeks in our home he had changed from a cowering creature into a spirited and loyal friend. But one day his rightful owners came to our door accusing us of theft and the dog of killing sheep. They demanded the dog back. Then they took the dog and tied an old piece of briar-like barbed wire around his neck. With the husband pulling him, the wife kicked the dog the entire mile to their house. We children watched in horror as they made their way across the desert sand. The dog never got off his haunches. He cried like a newborn pup but never opened his mouth to bite them.[39] Two days later the dog returned to us. His tail was wagging and the wire was still wound tightly around his neck. We were overjoyed to see him, but our joy turned to anguish when our parents made us take him back to his original owners. He wouldn't leave us, so we threw stones at him to chase him away. I don't remember what happened to that dog. I can't recall its name.

Although we soon learned not to make family pets out of the stray dogs roaming the mission compound, it continued to be inundated by the troublesome pests. Invariably, the problem would be compounded early each spring when the females were in heat. Navajos would come to the mission for water, mail, or medicine, and after they left we would invariably find another four or five puppies foraging for food in the dump. Much to the annoyance of other mission staff, my mother had a habit of naming each stray and feeding them by tossing unwanted leftovers outside our yard, just beyond the mission fence. It wasn't long before she was stretching the boundaries of propriety even further by inviting Navajo women into her home for cookies, coffee, and conversation—a foolish and scandalous activity by most missionary standards.

Sometimes, in the white heat of a summer Sunday, the door of the two-room school where we had Morning Meeting would be propped open to circulate the cool Colorado Plateau breeze. Occasionally, a stray dog would wander in and slowly approach the communion table—perhaps drawn there by the smell of fresh baked bread and store-bought grape juice. But the alert eyes and quick hands of a senior missionary were always able to maintain the sanctity and order

---

[39] Isa 53:7.

of the hour. Much to the disappointment of us giggling children, no dog ever stayed around long. But after the service, if the dog had been patient and could follow its nose, it would find scraps of food under the outdoor picnic tables set up in the shade of tamarisk trees, where the Navajo faithful were fed hot dogs, beans, and Kool-Aid. In my more reflective moments, which sometimes jolt me with a sudden sharp pain, I have thought that perhaps the real communion on those Sundays took place outside, under the damask veil of those tamarisk trees.

When the stray dogs became too plentiful and threatened to run in wild packs, my father and other mission staff would gather the young ones together, along with the old and weak, stuff them into dusty potato sacks, and tie them to the exhaust pipe of our idling car. Before too long they would stop squirming and yelping. Then they would be buried in shallow pits at the far end of the mission garden. Afterward my brothers, sisters, and I could again run freely and play without fear in front of our home.

Because of the two different environments in which I was immersed as a child, I grew up with a natural curiosity about contrasting ways of perceiving the world. Existential questions regarding the inherent correctness of the order inside my home and the chaos outside it, and their corresponding claims of certitude, arose which otherwise might never have surfaced. Eventually, this same inquisitiveness led me to challenge the authoritarian, anti-intellectualism of my Plymouth Brethren upbringing, replacing it with a mindful curiosity and a natural pluralism.

Perhaps because of the doubleminded bind in which I grew up, this slow-forming New Testament scholar had no interest in studying John's gospel. The Fourth Gospel's message seemed too obvious, too transparent (3:7, 16-18). Everything divided up nicely into two camps: the seeing and the blind (9:39-40), the truth-holding believers and the unbelieving liars (8:44, 54-55). There seemed to be no room for openness, intellectual curiosity, or ambiguity in John's narrative world. Moreover, the Johannine Jesus was the type of character who pounded the truth into people's heads whether or not they wanted to hear his message—most, of course, did not. But then in graduate school, while I was taking seminars in literary theory, I began to use the text of John to teach beginning Greek. Suddenly, I began to read the Gospel with a new set of lenses. I began to see that although the Gospel had a clear message to impart (20:31), how the reader was transported to that end could be as important as the text's final words. And the *how* which I was beginning to find in John's Gospel was one which undermined, tricked, and played games with the reader's naive grasp of the story.

In my more objective moments of reflecting on my critical approach to the Fourth Gospel, I will argue that I have been drawn to reader-response criticism primarily because it has offered me a way to read the Bible closely and cohesively, yet critically and differently. And secondarily (a reflective perspective which I do not wish to make public), it has allowed me to do what I most like to do—read imaginatively and dramatically. Assuming that no text (or worldview) has the whole truth, reader-response criticism has given me a set of critical tools with which to ask questions about the Gospel's imaginative, dramatic story and how it intends to affect its audience. Narrative poetics and pragmatics are the operative words here.

As I noted earlier, reader-response criticism has always been concerned with analyzing the effects of literature. It is interested in the persuasive goals of texts: how texts work readers and how readers work texts. And in reader-response criticism's more formalist expressions, careful, "close readings" of texts are common practice. But in these two foci I also hear resonances from my past.

I grew up in a home where John Nelson Darby's torturous, literalistic readings of biblical texts (those that gave birth to dispensationalism and theories of a pre-tribulational rapture) were the ideal model of exegesis and translation. But in our house these were coupled to a devotionally focused ethos. "What does this verse mean to you? What is God trying to tell you today?" were the classic questions asked around our dinner table. We may have given lip service to Darbyite, "literal readings" of the Bible, but a self-taught, Spirit-centered devotion was what really mattered. So it is not coincidental that my family should emphasize the persuasive element of Scripture over everything else. And it is only natural that there should be little or no critical reflection on that element, and no sense of the differentness of Scripture. In our Plymouth Brethren home, scriptural meaning was always simple and crystal clear. Interpretive conflicts did not arise from honest intellectual questions but from willful acts of rebellion. In view of my family history, then, reader-response criticism functions as a chain linking my past to my present. Like a chromosome chain, it is wound tightly around the persuasive effects of narrative and my own personal history, yet it provides the critical tension (distance and attention) needed to assess those effects.

When I secured my first professional position in 1985 at a small university adjacent to the St. Johns district of Portland, Oregon, one of my goals as a teacher was to defamiliarize the Bible so that it could be reappropriated afresh by individuals and communities of faith. I firmly believed that in order for growth and learning to begin, one had to be able to see Scripture simply as different from one's own experience of the world—without necessarily being better or worse. Furthermore, I thought that difference, distance, and defamiliarization (sharpened and polished through my years of academic research) were crucial to the critical and hermeneutical task of the biblical scholar. Thus, for example, I sought to show my students how sensitivity to the Johannine manipulation of narrative order (a special emphasis in much of more formalist reader-response criticism) sometimes seemed to subvert the narrator's own explicit agenda. Among other things, this type of reading was intended to undermine students' naive assumptions that they were reading straightforward, historical accounts of events from the life of Jesus. My hope was that, as a consequence, students would more critically evaluate their own unexamined ideological, theological, and historical assumptions regarding canonical texts and the life of faith.

But again, the ability to "see things differently" is not something that came to me purely through reader-response criticism, nor was it necessarily something I "discovered" in the text of John. Contrary to my earlier assumptions, I do not believe that I developed this ability merely through appropriating the critical, distance-creating tools of scientific, objective research and the rhetorical techniques of academic discourse. As I have begun to think more recently in terms of how my own social context, geographic location, and personal experience interpret the biblical text, I have come to believe that difference, distance, and defamiliarization have been part of my psychological makeup from the age of seven, when my family moved to the Navajo Indian Reservation.

When I was a student at Shiprock High School on the banks of the San Juan River in northern New Mexico, the word *john* was pejorative reservation slang derisively used by Anglos and "town Navajos" for any Navajo who had not made the transition from traditional Indian culture to the dominant Caucasian culture and its values. Like a chapter from my childhood (like the red-letter text of John in my missionary parents' home), John seems to me to be a gospel that outwardly has a simple message, clearly stated and transparent. But underneath that message there is another which—like the john world outside my childhood front door—often seems to subvert and controvert the previously established norm. As I approach my fifth decade of life, I am beginning to think that I have long been the unsuspecting victim of two johns, two geographies, and two existential ironies.

Having long since left my fundamentalist roots and the Navajo Reservation, I am now discovering that that context with its values still remains with me, affecting the way I read and influencing my own persuasive, scholarly agenda.[40] But whether I am wrestling with geography or theology, Saint John or the San Juan Basin of northern New Mexico and Arizona, I will always treasure my initial probings into that Gospel. Like the red desert sand of my reservation childhood, the book is my blood. John's Gospel has been a place for me to abide. It has been my abode; an adobe-framed hiding place. In my childhood years on the Navajo reservation, St. John flowed with the muddied waters of the San Juan River of northern New Mexico and southern Utah. It lay deep beneath the snowcapped San Juan Mountains of southern Colorado. San Juan grit nourished me like Navajo fry bread. The air that scraped its peaks was a sweet-tasting, heady wine.

I know no St. John sans Juan—or, for that matter, sans Jean. For my wife and I both were carried in the wombs and suckled at the breasts of women named Jean.[41]

Reading the Text: An Exegetical Drama (John 18:1-19:42)

Now that the legs of the dispassionate, objective reader-critic in me have been smashed and my professional robes have been dispersed among the curious

---

[40] As the ancient Hebrew proverb puts it, "Like a dog that returns to its vomit is a fool who reverts to his folly" (Prov 26:11). Or to put it more positively, "Train children in the right way, and when old, they will not stray" (Prov 22:6).

[41] My mother's name was Mary Elizabeth Jean, and my mother-in-law's name is Marjorie Jean. Both of my sister's middle names are also derivations of the name John: Brenda Joan, and Beth Janette.

bystanders, be exegetical drama can begin. A Roman soldier begins to cut the leather thongs that hold the three bloodied bodies to their crosses. He rips the valuable iron nails from the still-warm flesh. They will be saved, straightened, and reused another day for another grim demonstration of Pax Romana. As he drops the first corpse on the ground, Death rattles their throats and the interpretive tale begins.

The first corpse falls in a heap, face in the dirt, and one of those left hanging addresses the other two. "You know, I must confess to you that I have never written about be Johannine passion narrative before, primarily because it has always struck me as a passionless passion. Ignace de la Potterie has recently said the same thing, only more in terms of character analysis. He says, 'The careful reader will be struck by two details: the complete self-awareness of Jesus, several times indicated, and also the majesty with which he goes forward to his Passion.'[42] But Raymond Brown describes it in a manner which I find to be more disturbing theologically, as a passion narrative where 'there is no victimizing of the Johannine Jesus, [who] is in such control that only when he affirms "It is finished," does he bow his head and hand over his Spirit' (19:30).[43] Suddenly, those strategies of subversion and victimization that so intrigued me in my earlier analysis of be Fourth Gospel's story world seem to have disappeared. If they're here at all, I'll have to work hard to find them."

The corpse lying free down in the dirt intones, "And I'm absolutely repulsed by this Johannine Jesus, a person sent from God who is so sure of himself, so hypersensitized and aware of be hour's significance that 'he passes through death without turmoil and with jubilation.[44] So how can I be anything less than a radically resistant reader to this 'take-two-aspirin-and-call-me-in-the-morning' story? I've got to know this passion narrative in a painful, passionate way, in a

---

[42] I. de la Potterie, *The Hour of Jesus: The Passion and Resurrection of Jesus According to John* (New York: Alba, 1989) 16.

[43] R. Brown, *The Community of the Beloved Disciple* (New York: Paulist Press, 1979) 118.

[44] E. Käsemann, *The Testament of Jesus According to John 17* (Philadelphia: Fortress Press, 1968) 20; M. M. Thompson, *The Humanity of Jesus in the Fourth Gospel* (Philadelphia: Fortress Press, 1988) 87-89.

carnal way. I will find a way to strip it and lay it bare, shuddering and convulsing, before the faithful mother and beloved disciple."

The third corpse, still hanging on its cross, enters the conversation: "Frankly, I'm repulsed by both of you. One of you has refused to talk about this text previously because it annoys your sophisticated literary and theological sensitivities, while the other of you dislikes the text's passionless characterization of Jesus, yet has decided to read it anyway—any way you want. You both seem to recognize intuitively that these crosses reflect the radical difference between two social worlds—the ancient Mediterranean and the contemporary Euroamerican—yet you can't let the difference stand by itself and try to understand that cultural difference for what it is.[45] So why don't we just let our crosses stand for difference, for the Other? Let's investigate, critically evaluate, question, and interpret the text, but then let's leave our crosses to turn to stone in the sun. Let them be discovered by chance as artifacts of a different time, culture, and place."

The second corpse, oblivious to the previous comments, plunges on in its soliloquy. Its voice deepens and grows more confident as it continues. "Listen to me for a minute, you two wind-filled bags of bones! From my vantage point up here I can see that the passion narratives are the most carefully, proleptically plotted parts of the Synoptic Gospels, and the Fourth Gospel is no exception to this. Straightforward predictions, foreshadowings, allusions, and reliable commentary all work together to announce significant elements of Jesus' final days, and purposely leave little room for passion, surprise, or imagination in the narrative. As many scholars have pointed out, from the opening scenes of the Gospel incidental characters, the narrator, and Jesus himself all make oblique or explicit references to his death and its significance. John's witness starts things off (1:29); Jesus alludes to it[45] and seems actually to contrive it (6:70-71;

---

[45] Part of that difference has to do with the contrasting experience of personhood in the ancient Mediterranean world and the contemporary Euroamerican world. Bruce Malina and Jerome Neyrey, following Mary Douglas, would argue that the Jesus of the Johannine passion narrative is a typical "strong group person" ("First Century Personality: Dyadic, Not Individual," *Social World of Luke-Acts*, 72; see also Mieke Bal, "The Point of Narratology," *Poetics Today* 11 [1990] 731-732).

[46] See, for example, John 2:4, 19; 3:14-16; 10:14-18; 12:7-8, 23-24, 31-32; 15:13; 18:11.

13:11-21; 17:12); the narrator expands upon it (2:21-22; 11:51-52; 12:33); and eventually even a minor character such as Caiaphas inadvertently prophesies it" (11:49-50).[47]

The other hanging corpse impatiently interrupts to interject a slightly different perspective. "I can play your literary game too, although I reject your anachronistic, ethnocentric notion of story worlds.[48] But, assuming for the sake of argument that I am reading the text as so-called closely as you are, I note that within the passion narrative itself the actions of political powers dominate the sequence of events as nowhere else in the story.

"For example, this is the only section of the narrative where Jesus is passively moved from one place to the other. Only in the passion narrative is Jesus bound *(deō:* 18:12, 24; 19:40),[49] brought *(syllambanō,* 18:12), or led to someone *(agō:* 18:13, 28; 19:4, 13). And it is precisely the actions and intentions of the soldiers and temple police that move your plot along—not Jesus' moment-by-moment decisions.

"As a matter of fact, earlier in the Gospel the chief priests had sent the temple police to arrest Jesus (7:32), but precisely because they were reluctant to do so, the action was not carried out (7:45-52). And at other times Jesus quite easily escaped or withdrew from people whenever he wished.[50] Finally, when Jesus was asked to intervene in situations of need, there was always an immediate sense that Jesus' own prerogatives governed the plot movement—not

---

[47] Culpepper correctly discusses many of these references within the context of "plot," (*Anatomy of the Fourth Gospel,* 86-98); see also D. Senior, *The Passion of Jesus in the Gospel of John* (Collegeville, MN: Liturgical Press, 1991) 31-44.

[48] The term "story world" expresses the biblical narrative critics' notion that stories can have their own natural laws, social codes, and symbolic connections which might be quite different from any "real world" outside the text. For example, science fiction and fantasy are two contemporary genres that construct story worlds which are often at odds with the world as we know it (see Powell, *What Is Narrative Criticism?* 6-8; Moore, *Literary Criticism and the Gospels,* 8-10).

[49] Note D. Sylva's discussion of the word ("Nicodemus and His Spices," *NTS* 34 [1988] 148-151).

[50] See, for example, John 4:3; 5:13, 18; 6:15; 7:1, 10, 19, 25, 30, 44; 8:20, 37, 40; 9:12; 10:39; 11:8, 54. See M. W. G. Stibbe, "The Elusive Christ: A New Reading of the Fourth Gospel," *JSNT* 44 (1991) 21-25.

the second party's interests.[51] So the intentions of both the protagonist and the antagonists do seem capable of affecting plot developments. Clearly, then, the Fourth Gospel's plot is not based upon a Greek idea of the Fates. Rather, Jesus is acting like a good and loyal son in a Mediterranean household. To paraphrase Malina and Neyrey, the Jesus of the Fourth Gospel is one who internalizes and makes his own what God, his 'father' says, does, and thinks about him because he believes it is necessary, if he is to be an honorable son, to live out the expectations of God, his 'father.'[52]

"Furthermore, although your implied reader has been given numerous clues early on that Jesus would willingly be 'lifted up,'[53] in the passion narrative there are only minimal references to Jesus' ultimate power over the events or the plot. These come equally from Jesus (18:5-8, 11; 19:28-29) and the narrator (18:4, 9; 19:30), but only at the beginning and end of the passion narrative. They seem to be clumsily tacked on by your timorous implied author. One would think that in such an important part of the story, your implied author could have given your implied reader consistently stronger clues regarding Jesus' self-awareness or commitment to God's purposes. But the closest we come to this is a remark by Jesus in his conversation with Pilate (19:11). By comparison, in the raising of Lazarus, your implied reader can find numerous references to Jesus' control and his near manipulation of events (11:4, 11-15, 23-27, 40-42).

"It seems to me, then, you could argue that in this juxtapositioning of power and powerlessness there is a subversive and doubly ironic undermining of the passion plotting. Jesus may indeed willfully step forward into his captors' arms at the beginning of the passion narrative (18:4-11),[54] but once he does that, he

---

[51] Note especially John 2:3-7; 4:46-49; 7:2-14; 11:1-6. In his study of these texts, Charles H. Giblin ("Suggestion, Negative Response and Positive Action in St. John's Portrayal of Jesus," *NTS* 26 [1979-80] 210) concludes that "there is [no] inconsistency or change of mind on Jesus' part." For Jesus is disassociated "from the predominantly human concerns of those who, by merely human standards, would seem to be rather close to him ....He never fails to attend to the situation presented to him, but in doing so he acts radically on his own terms."

[52] Malina and Neyrey, "First Century Personality," 73; see John 5:19-20, 22.

[53] See, e.g., John 3:14-16; 10:17-18; 12:32. See G. Nicholson, *Death as Departure: The Johannine Descent-Ascent Schema* (SBLDS 63; Chico: Scholars Press, 1983) 164-165.

[54] Stibbe ("The Elusive Christ," 23) wonders rhetorically whether Jesus' captors falling on the ground could not be understood as a response of amazement. Could it not be "[t]hat

becomes a mere pawn in the hands of Jewish and Roman authorities. And for a few moments, anyway, you can legitimately say that things move beyond Jesus' personal control. Why? Simply because the socio-political order *(kosmos)* hates and persecutes him (15:18-25; 18:36; cf. 11:50).[55] Even Jesus can't control that."

"Dogs! Dogs! There are dogs all around me!" The first corpse, face still in the dirt, suddenly screams out in its darkness. "Thin ones, with ribs protruding, ears down, and their tails between their legs. There are dogs in this story, *Xé chąą'i,* hungrily sniffing and licking my dried sweat, blood, and excrement—just like the dogs of Jezreel that gnawed Jezebel's bones,[56] First come the flies and dogs, then come the beady-eyed rats!"

The second corpse interrupts: "You're out of your mind! Lift your head out of the dirt and look about carefully, you babbling fool! If you just open your eyes you'll see that there are no dogs in this story world. Sheep, shepherds, and sheepfolds, yes. But nowhere in John will you find a dog mentioned. They're only the mad dreams of your disembodied mind."

"It may be true that there are no dogs in your Johannine story world," the third corpse breaks in, "but every Mediterranean crucifixion scene would have had them: the shameless dogs; watching, silently sitting on their haunches, waiting for the corpses to be dropped so they could finish the work left undone. The scavenging dogs surrounding crucified victims would have been one more element of the public shaming of criminals in that ancient social world."[57]

---

after so many great escapes Jesus is at last in a place where he will not and does not escape? Where he can be sought *and found"?*

[55] With regard to Pilate, who is a representative of the cosmos, Rensberger ("The Politics of John: The Trial of Jesus in the Fourth Gospel," *JBL* 103 [1984] 406) astutely observes that "he is callous and relentless, indifferent to Jesus and to truth, and contemptuous of the hope of Israel that Jesus fulfills and transcends ....Pilate is thus a hostile figure second only to `the Jews' themselves."

[56] 2 Kgs 9:30-37.

[57] In his study of honor in the ancient Mediterranean world ("Sanity and the Myth of Honor," *Journal of Psychological Anthropology* 5 [1977] 289), Paul Friedrich has shown how dogs are

...an illuminating key to the Illiadic idiom of honor. [They] emerge in the fourth line of the epic and reappear at least once in all but five of the remaining twenty-three books, thirty-five times in connection with the eating of corpses, mainly in metaphors, invectives, and similies. Dogs come

"So now you believe it too? A corpse with its nose stuck in our filth shrieks 'dogs,' and just like that you're off in the world of cultural-anthropology and honor/shame societies![58] That's precisely what I find so disconcerting about your kinds of interpretive moves," the second corpse says exasperatingly. "You have no sensitivity for how implied authors imaginatively create story worlds. You want to bring any and every detail of the ancient Mediterranean social world into the gospel — all from other first century *texts*, of course — and then you act as though they are part of this particular story world. But not every aspect of that ancient social world is in here!"

"Oh no, it *is* all here," replies the third corpse. "It's just that the ancient Mediterranean world is a 'high context society' which 'produce[s] sketchy and impressionistic texts, leaving much to the reader's or hearer's imagination ....Hence, much can be assumed.'[59] Western Europeans and Euroamericans, on the other hand, are 'low context societies,' which 'produce detailed texts, spelled out as much as possible, and leave little to the imagination.'"[60]

"Everyone here knows what a crucifixion is like. We don't have to spell out all the gory details."

"Your two-fold description may work for societies at large, but it won't work for storytelling," interjects the second corpse, trying to stretch out tall on its

---

in pairs, and packs, devouring the myriad corpses on the battelfield [sic] or even rushing in to gnaw the testicles of their dead master ....Numerous threats and entreaties involve being thrown to the dogs, the worst form of defilement.

See also J. D. Crossan, *Jesus: A Revolutionary Biography* (San Francisco: HarperSanFrancisco, 1994) 123-127, 153-154; J. H. Neyrey, "'Despising the Shame of the Cross': Honor and Shame and the Johannine Passion Narrative," *Semeia* [forthcoming]; P. Sloterdijk, *Critique of Cynical Reason* [Theory and History of Literature 40; Minneapolis: University of Minnesota Press, 1987] 167-169).

[58] For a comprehensive analysis of the ancient Mediterranean world as one whose values center around honor and shame, see B. J. Malina and J. H. Neyrey, "Honor and Shame in Luke-Acts: Pivotal Values of the Mediterranean World," *The Social World of Luke-Acts*, 25-65.

[59] Malina, "Reading Theory Perspective," 20.

[60] Ibid., 19.

cross. "It seems to me that narratives always reflect 'high contexts.,[61] No story can hold its hearers' attention if every detail of that narrative world must first be spelled out. Authors who had to do that would never get around to telling their stories! This is part of what is meant by beginning a story in media as, and it is as much a dictum of modern Euroamerican prose as it was of Greek literature when Aristotle first observed it. Enormously high context demands are placed upon readers of all narratives. It's not just a peculiar identifying mark of ancient stories from Mediterranean cultures.

"I will grant you the point that it is important to know how shaming and how shameful crucifixions were in your so-called honor/shame society. But I will still maintain, after all is said and done, that it is just as important to recognize how this implied author refuses to dwell on its most shameful details.[62] This implied author's narrowly constructed story world—no less socially constructed than any so-called real world, mind you—wishes to convince its implied reader of a different ideology: that in spite of outward appearances, the final event of Jesus' life is bringing honor to his 'father.' Thus, many shameful, real world elements have been purposely omitted from this particular 'fantastic' story world.[63] So don't go bringing into the story those elements which the author may have purposely left out."

"You don't think I understand how stories work? Well, you don't understand how different cultures work!" snaps the third corpse. "Don't you see that you can't understand what was 'left out' of a text without first understanding what

---

[61] Bruce Malina's concept of the socio-rhetorical "context" would be called the text's "repertoire" in Wolfgang Iser's theory of aesthetic response, which for him, "consists of all the familiar territory within the text. This may be in the form of references to earlier works, or to social and historical norms, or to the whole culture from which the text has emerged ...." (*The Act of Reading*, 69). Yet Iser (ibid., 83) can go on to make the important observation that,

> [l]iterary communication differs from other forms of communication in that those elements of the sender's repertoire which are familiar to the reader through their application in real-life situations, lose their validity when transplanted into the literary text. And it is precisely this loss of validity which leads to the communication of something new.

[62] The author of 4 Maccabees graphically depicts the torture of the Jewish faithful (4 Macc 5:28-6:30; 9:10-11:27).

[63] Käsemann (*Testament of Jesus*, 45) says: "Judged by the modern concept of reality, our [Fourth] Gospel is more fantastic than any other writing in the New Testament."

was socially implicit 'in' the text? Your ethnocentric dogmatism just appalls me!"[64]

The corpse crumpled on the ground tries to jerk out of its deathly slumber. "What is all the yapping I keep hearing? I've dreamed of those damned dogs, and I can still hear them sniffing and barking around me. Hidden inside every mad dog is a god, damned to suffer for our sins.[65] So I say let's keep them here beside us. They add a realistic note of passion to an otherwise passionless story. And besides, it's two against one. You're the odd corpse out."

"But you can't do that to the gospel!" The second corpse retorts. "You can't bring your personal, autobiographical *Xé chąą'i* into this story world so arbitrarily, so cynically, just because you've seen them in your dreams! Where's the logic in that? Where's the scholarly discourse; any semblance of plausible interaction with the text? At least the corpse hanging beside me has a reason for bringing in its scavenger dogs. Historical, social world reconstructions of first-century crucifixions would demand their presence. But you shamelessly add elements to the story based simply upon your own idiosyncratic desire to have them here."

"Oh, so you want a reason for the dogs' presence, do you? Some 'plausible interaction with the text?' If you require that for legitimizing interpretations, I can give it to you.[66] Everyone knows there are intertextual allusions to Psalm 22:14-18 in John 19:24 and 28. The narrator even adds, 'In order that the scripture might be fulfilled.' So what do you think is the subject of the third person plural verb *diemerisanto* and the antecedent of the reflexive pronoun

---

[64] See Mieke Bal's criticism of enthnocentrism in biblical literary criticism and ethnographers' need for narrative theory ("Point of Narratology," 730-737).

[65] David White writes, "There is much of man in his dogs, much of the dog in us, and behind this, much of the wolf in both the dog and man. And, there is some of the Dog-Man in god" (*Myths of the Dog-Man* [Chicago: The University of Chicago, 1991] 15). Or, I might add, there is some of the Dog-Man in Christ (see Sloterdijk *[Critique of Cynical Reason*, 161-162] and Crossan *[The Historical* Jesus, 72-88, 421-422] who both describe much of Jesus' behavior as dog-like, or Cynic-inspired).

[66] To paraphrase Mieke Bal, "the argument I am trying to make is to prove the presence of the absent, and it is up to the reader to evaluate to what extent they are there or not" *(Death and Dissymmetry: The Politics of Coherence in the Book of Judges* [Chicago: The University of Chicago Press, 1988] 239-240).

heautois in 'They divided my clothes among themselves' (19:24)? It's the 'dogs' of Psalm 22:16 and 20 *(kynes/kynos*, Ps 21:17/21 [LXX])![67] So you see, the dogs are here too. Some may watch us silently from their haunches, waiting to gnaw our bones. Others merely playfully tug and rip apart our discarded clothing."

But the second corpse continues to speak from its cross, dismissing its companions' voices with an attempted twitch of its head. "You can't have those dogs either. In Psalm 22:16 and 20 'dogs' is a pejorative epithet for 'evildoers.' Even there the dogs aren't real. They're just a metaphor. And besides, it's neither the third person plural verb nor the reflexive pronoun that is significant here in John, but rather the action of dividing the clothes. That's what 'fulfills Scripture.'"

"You bitches! You don't understand at all! What I want is precisely the metaphor: people as dogs, or dogs as people—either way, it doesn't make any difference to me. You say your implied author has historicized the Psalmist's metaphor, turning it into a prophetic reference to events at Jesus' crucifixion.[68] Well, I just want to retain the Psalm's original metaphoricity. What's wrong with that? Can't you hear my pain and my groaning? 'I have given a name to my pain and call it "dog." It is just as faithful, just as obtrusive and shameless, just as entertaining, just as clever as any other dog—and I can scold it and vent my bad mood on it as others do with their dogs ....'[69] So you can keep the sheepherders, the sheep, and the rock-enclosed corrals. I just want the dogs. And

---

[67] Robert Brawley recognizes this ("An Absent Complement and Intertextuality in John 19:28-29," *JBL* 112 [1993] 438).

[68] Ernst Haenchen argues: "The scene itself, the division of the clothes and the casting of lots for 'the tunic without seams,' is derived from Ps 22:18(19)" *(The Gospel of John* [Hermeneia; 2 vols.; Philadelphia: Fortress Press, 1984] 2:193). Raymond Brown, however, thinks that "the interpretation of the psalm is stretched to cover an incident that the evangelist found in his tradition rather than vice versa," since one would expect to find the psalmist's expression *ebalon klēron* for casting lots rather than the verb *lachōmen* (John 19:24) if the evangelist were simply inventing the scene *(The Gospel According to John* [AB 29-29a; 2 vols.; Garden City: Doubleday, 1966-1970] 2:920; see 2:903).

[69] F. Nietzsche, *The Gay Science: with a Prelude in Rhymes and an Appendix of Songs* (New York: Vintage, 1974) 249-250. Or as John Crossan writes, "if you seek the heart of darkness, follow the dogs" *(Jesus,* 127).

you can't take them away from me! They're here, they're mine, and they're eating me up inside!"

Attempting to get the scholarly discourse back on track, the second corpse decides to ignore the last outrageous outburst. "Irony. You had just brought up the issue of irony, if I remember correctly. Now there's an important topic in the Fourth Gospel and a Johannine strategy that we can all agree upon. Everyone says the Johannine passion narrative is highly ironic.[70] And, I believe, we were just talking about the contrasting views of power in the text, weren't we? Who is really in control? God, or the earthly, ruling authorities? Surely, as you said, the contrast between Jesus willfully stepping forward at his arrest and being led here and there is ironic.[71] And of course, Jesus' conversations with the 'powers that be' are ironic (18:19-24, 18:28-19:16).

"As everyone notes, those so-called powerful characters in the text think they are in control, but, in fact, the implied reader knows all along that they are not. Clearly, all Jesus' and the narrator's talk about *hōra/kairos* has been supplying the implied reader with that ironic, binocular perspective from the first scenes of the gospel.[72] So I don't see your focus on the contrasts in power and powerlessness as *subversively* undermining the theological theme of God's salvific power (10:17-18). As with the portrayal of the Jewish leaders' concern for pollution (18:28; 19:14, 31), these multifaceted ironies simply bind the implied author's and implied reader's ideological/theological points of view more closely together over against those of the ruling authorities: in spite of earthly appearances, God and Jesus are in control. Or to put it in your terms, the faithful, honorable son is acting out his socially prescribed role according to his father's wishes."

Another leather thong is cut and the third corpse drops to the ground beside the first. "I suppose it's time for me to jump back into your interpretive game.

---

[70] For example, see Culpepper, *Anatomy of the Fourth Gospel*, 173-174; P. Duke, *Irony in the Fourth Gospel* (Atlanta: John Knox, 1985) 129-137; Senior, *The Passion of Jesus, 68, 152;* C. H. Giblin, "John's Narration of the Hearing before Pilate (John 18,28-19,16)," *Biblica* 67 (1986) 238.

[71] Stibbe, "The Elusive Christ," 20-25, 29.

[72] See John 2:4; 4:21-23; 5:25-29; 7:6-8, 30; 8:20; 12:27; 13:1; 17:1. Paul Duke, following many before him, speaks of the "double-layered" quality of irony in the Fourth Gospel (*Irony in the Fourth Gospel*, 14).

So answer me this. Wouldn't you say that one of the most dramatic ironies is when Pilate asks the offhanded question 'What is truth?' (19:38) of the very one who had earlier told his disciples, 'I am the way, the truth and the life' (14:6)?[73] Yet curiously, neither Jesus, the narrator, nor Pilate respond to the question. In John 19:9-10 Jesus will again fail to answer Has, and there both the narrator and Pilate note Jesus' silence. But here, strangely, there is no narrative mark of the silence. Why not? Jesus responded to the high priest's earlier question, and he has responded to every other question of Pilate up to this point. Why is there no response, no uptake, not even a narrator's remark 'And he said nothing?'"

The second corpse quickly answers. "Well, obviously the implied author expects the implied reader to fill in the correct answer: 'Jesus is the Truth.'[74] And dilates question—is it asked in jest? pensiveness? or sarcasm?—proves only that he is an outsider.[75] So at Pilate's expense, Jesus, the implied author, and implied reader are all joined together. Ideologically they are one."

"But I'm not so sure," the third corpse interjects. "Did you know that this is the last time the noun *alētheia is* used in the book? Hats and your implied author both know that the answer to the question 'What is truth?' does not lie in some abstract quality of historical accuracy or confessional correctness (see 1:49-51; 7:27, 52; 11:27, 40). Irrespective of 'the truth,' Jesus only becomes a threat in this gospel when people rightly or wrongly 'believe in him' and 'follow him' (6:15; 7:3-9, 12, 45-49; 11:45-53; 12:12-19). So whether Jesus really is or is not a king is beside the point. Pilate's inscription on Jesus' cross and the chief

---

[73] Michel Foucault, *Power/Knowledge: Selected Interviews and Other Writings 1972-1977* (New York: Pantheon, 1980) 66.

[74] Paul Duke writes, "It is just as possible that the unanswered question concludes the scene because the Johannine ironist invites us to reflect upon what—and who—the Answer is" (*Irony in the Fourth Gospel*, 131). See M. Edwards, "The World Could not Contain the Books," in *The Bible as Rhetoric: Studies in Biblical Persuasion and Credibility* (ed. M. Warner; New York: Routledge, 1990) 192; Neyrey, "Despising the Shame of the Cross," 12).

[75] Following R. Schnackenburg (*The Gospel According to St. John* [3 vols.; New York: Seabury Press, 1980] 3:251) and R. Brown (*John*, 2:869), David Rensberger says that "Pilate's final 'What is truth?' (18:38) [is not] the question of a serious seeker; if it were, he would stay for an answer" ("The Politics of John," 403). See M. W. G. Stibbe, *John as Storyteller: Narrative Criticism and the Fourth Gospel* (SNTSMS 73; New York: Cambridge University Press, 1992) 107.

priests' objections to it will be the ultimate joke here (19:19-22).[76] Contrary to your opinion, here I think Pilate and Jesus are both aligned with your implied author."

"Yes! I think you've found the correct answer to this text's question, 'What is truth?' I would only want to add that whether Jesus fed 5,000 people with five loaves and two fish is also beside the point for your implied author (6:15, 21-65). Maybe even whether he is or is not a son of God is beside the point (5:18; 10:31-39). Neither who Jesus historically is, nor what people confess him to be—nor even who Jesus confesses himself to be—is the crucial question for your implied author or Pilate at this juncture. As the next dialogue between Jesus and Pilate will show (19:8-11), the important question underlying all others is whether Jesus is a threat to power (11:45-53; 12:12-19). The question of truth cannot be separated from the body that stretches out the hand" (18:22; 19:3; 20:27).[77]

"So as I was about to say, in 'handing over' Jesus (18:30), the chief priests have safeguarded their positions of power against the threat of their Roman overlords (11:48-50). In 'handing over' Jesus (19:16), Pilate is safeguarding his position of power (*exousia*, 19:10-11) against the possible threat of Caesar (19:12). And in 'handing over' his spirit (19:30), Jesus will safeguard his place of power (*exousia*, 17:1-5) before God (10:17-18). We all know that '[p]ower is cautious. It covers itself.'"[78]

"Thus, the power of the dialogue between Jesus and Pilate resides precisely in Jesus' possible threat to Roman power-not in the truth or falsity of his claim to kingship.[79] So Jesus doesn't answer Pilate's question and there is no uptake.

---

[76] Duke, *Irony in the Fourth Gospel*, 136-137; Senior, *The Passion of Jesus*, 153-154.

[77] In the ancient Mediterranean world, the hands of the human body represented power (Malina, *New Testament World*, 60, 66; see E. Scarry, *The Body in Pain: The Making and Unmaking of the World* [New York: Oxford University Press, 1985] 173, 252-253).

[78] Scarry, *The Body in Pain*, 59; see A. McKenna's discussion of "state agents" in *Violence and Difference: Girard, Derrida, and Deconstruction* (Chicago: University of Illinois Press, 1992) 160172.

[79] Charles Giblin instinctively recognizes this when he says, in regard to John 18:38b-40, that "[t]o Pilate's mind *thus far in the hearing* [my emphasis], the King of the Jews is no threat to Roman rule or to Pilate's own position" ("John's Narration of the Hearing Before Pilate," 227). Once he perceives Jesus to be a threat to his position, however, he immediately

Why? Because in the presence of power, the question of some independent truth source is ultimately irrelevant. Jesus, your implied author, and Pilate know that."[80] I guess what I'm trying to say is that '[t]ruth is a thing of this world [*kosmos*]: it is produced only by virtue of multiple forms of constraint.' It 'is linked in a circular relation with systems of power which produce and sustain it.'"[81]

"That's the most absurd, convoluted argument I've ever heard!" The second corpse shouts, its voice shaking with anger. "Why do you have to jump into this discussion too? First you tried to force your ridiculous Navajo dogs into the story, and now you're trying to turn one simple, off-handedly ironic question of Pilate into some radically deconstructive metaphor that shapes the entire narrative and empties its claim to truth. I wish you would just keep your mouth shut and your head buried down there in the dirt!

"From my vantage point up here, it is perfectly clear that right at the very start of the narrative the prologue revealed an implied author who would be vitally concerned with truth—who it is, where it comes from, what it does, and where it goes (1:14, 17).[82] I mean, *alētheia* and its cognates occur 48 times in the book! So let me tell you, your deconstructive agenda simply won't work here. I won't let it happen!

"But I do think the former observation, that there is no narrative uptake to Pilate's question, is an interesting one. Yet I can't see how it is significant—other than as a joke between the implied author and implied reader, both of whom, I will still maintain over your objections, are laughing at Pilate and his earthbound sensibilities.

"And if you really want to talk about power in the passion narrative, then talk about it in the resurrection account, where God's power is ultimately triumphant over human power.

---

moves to get rid of him (19:12).

[80] See M. Foucault, *Politics, Philosophy, Culture: Interviews and Other Writings, 1977-84* (New York: Routledge, 1988) 106-109, 118-119.

[81] Foucault, *Power/Knowledge*, 131, 133.

[82] M. Warner, "The Fourth Gospel's Art of Rational Persuasion," *The Bible as Rhetoric*, 176-77.

"Now, let's move on to talk about something more basic; something more objective, empirical, and countable. Let's look at the implied author's use of repetition in the story. This is an important topic, and the passion narrative is full of repetitions."

"Now wait just a minute! Who's talking about poststructuralist literary theory and a Johannine metaphor that deconstructs itself? I wasn't! I was thinking that perhaps what is operative in the Fourth Gospel is a commonly overlooked, ancient Mediterranean social-world code of patronage 'based on a strong element of inequality and difference in power.'[83] It does seem to fit. I mean, think of it this way: Jesus is the truth because he is the broker who has been 'sent' from the patron 'above,' the place of ultimate honor and power.[84] That's the language of patronage.

"Now, listen to what you were just saying. You were agreeing with me that in this narrative power (illustrated by your reference to the resurrection) is ultimately more important than some anachronistic, abstract quality of truth. The one with the power at the end, who has the right connections, is therefore the one who is 'the truth.' Power—either honorably acquired or ascribed—is truth, and in the Fourth Gospel truth does not exist apart from authority and power. That, my friend, is a description of the patronage system in an honor/shame society."

"All your talk of patronage sounds objective and scientific, but how far can you really press it in the Fourth Gospel? After all, Jesus never calls God his *prostatēs* in this story.[85] Instead, he always uses the relational language of *patēr/huios*. Isn't that difference in metaphors significant? Isn't fictive kinship finally more important than patronage?[86]

"You know me, I'd hate to have to give up any Johannine metaphor for some broader, ancient social-world scenario—regardless of its apparent usefulness—if it meant destroying the peculiar ideology and narrative world of the Fourth Gospel in the process."

---

[83] H. Moxnes, "Patron-Client Relations and the New Community in Luke-Acts," *The Social World of Luke-Acts*, 242.

[84] See John 3:31-36; 5:31-44; 7:16-18; 8:12-18; 10:36-39; 12:44-50; 17:25-26.

[85] See 1 *Clem* 36:1; 61:3; 64.

[86] See John 19:7, 26-27; 20:31.

"Well, don't forget that *patēr/huios* language is often used interchangeably with patron/client language in the Mediterranean world.[87] Fictive kinship and patronage are much more closely linked than you might think."[88]

"God! I'm confused. Am I awake or dreaming? Now that the two of you are on the ground, your voices are beginning to erode, intermingle, and coalesce. Perhaps if I could just lift my head from my chest to look at you ....But I can't. And I can't seem to connect voices with bodies anymore. Ancient Mediterranean social code of patronage or deconstructive metaphor—name it what you will, the effect still seems to be the same.

"For example, just look around us! No one is really listening to our conversation. Everyone who cared about us has left, convinced that we're dead. The only one still here is the cursing Roman, trying to cut me down from my cross before sunset. Needless to say, I'm worried that both of your strategies, no matter how necessary or novel for the modern world, will cut us off from the very communities we're seeking to nourish. This exercise is really beginning to bring me down."

"Oh come off it! You're the only corpse left up there with its head in the clouds, and you talk about us being cut off from community? As far as I'm concerned, the sooner you join us down here, the better off you'll be."

After a few moments of painful silence, the corpse remaining on its cross decides to ignore its own misgivings and the grunts and groans of the two on the ground below. Once more it picks up its commentary.

"Look, let's try this conversation one last time. As I noted earlier, the passion narrative is the most carefully plotted section of the story. Throughout it, repetitions of key words and phrases fill out and confirm the author's theological point of view. For example, the basic plot line is fourfold: (1) arrest (18:1-18); (2) legal charges (18:19-19:16); (3) crucifixion (19:17-37); (4) burial (19:38-42). But plot developments in each of the first three narrative sequences

---

[87] See, e.g., Matt 5:43-6:15.

[88] Halvor Moxnes ("Patron-Client Relations," 245) writes:

> In Roman models of society the relations between public, professional life and personal, family life were different from those of most modern societies. We make a clear distinction between the role of individuals as parents, spouses, or friends on the one hand and their role as public officials on the other. Within one set of relations we might expect them to show preferential treatment (parents, friends), but in others we expect strict impartiality (public officials). In Roman ideology, however, there were no such distinctions ....Even the emperor played a patronal[/paternal] role. He was looked upon more as a powerful father figure than as an imperial administrator.

are slowed down by the numerous repetitions, repetitions which primarily assess blame for the final events of Jesus' life. From the implied author's perspective, Jesus' arrest, trial, and death are the result of collusion within the *kosmos* of Jewish and Roman power.[89]

"The three most dominant repetitions are those which deal with 'the handing over' of Jesus to someone, the attempt to release Jesus, and his ultimate punishment by crucifixion. In the first case, *paradidōmi* is used twice as the narrator's epithet for Judas (18:2, 5). It is also used four times in reference tone Jewish leaders (by the Jewish leaders themselves, 18:30; by Pilate, 18:35; and by Jesus, 18:36, 19:11). Finally, the narrator uses it once in reference to Jesus' spirit (19:30). Interestingly, the six references of *paradidōmi* earlier in the gospel are all related to Judas. Moreover, the narrator never implicates 'the Jews' in Jesus' *paradidonai*. This is something `the Jews' themselves do, almost with a sense of pride (18:30), and it is echoed by Jesus and Pilate.

"The most common repetitions in the passion narrative are those that mention the crucifixion. There are fifteen references to it: 19:6 (twice), 10, 15 (twice), 16, 17, 18, 19, 20, 23, 25, 31, 32, and 41. The narrator uses the verb (*stauroō*) or noun (*stauros*) ten times, while 'the Jews' (chief priests and servants) only use the verb in the imperative mood (two times). Pilate, on the other hand, always uses the verb in questions (three times). Similarly, references of the kingship charge leveled against Jesus are repeated five times (18:33, 37, 39; 19:14, 15), four of which are couched in questions which Pilate asks. The remaining reference is the chief priests' climactic response to Pilate, 'We have no king but Caesar' (19:15). Finally, there are eight different references to Pilate's acquittal and intended release of Jesus (*aitian* in 18:38; 19:4, 6; *apolyō* in 18:39 [twice]; 19:10 and 12 [twice]). Six come from Pilate, one comes from the narrator, and one comes from 'the Jews.' Clearly, all these repetitions strongly reinforce the implied author's ideological point of view, one which cannot be misinterpreted by the implied reader."

The third corpse grins up at the second one still hanging above it. "Whenever I interrupt one of your dramatic soliloquies, you're forced to shut up for a while.

---

[89] John 15:18-19; 17:14-16; 18:36. David Rensberger correctly points out that "Pilate too becomes an agent of the `world'" in the Johannine trial scene" ("The Politics of John," 402; see further, 403-406).

So let me thrust another splinter in your tender, bloated side. Someone once said 'Sometimes the challenge posed by a text is not excessive obscurity but, rather, some form of excessive clarity.'[90]

"You talk of repetitions in the passion narrative, and how they seem to slow down the plot and emphasize your implied author's ideological point of view. But curiously, it is not until one gets to the crucifixion itself, which you argued earlier was the most emphasized element in the narrative's plot, that the action begins to speed up significantly. While it takes from 18:12-19:16 (five pages of Greek text) just to get a death verdict against Jesus, it only takes from 19:16b-42 (two and a half pages of text) to get Jesus crucified, dead, and buried. Thus, in the first half of the passion account, narrative time and story time more closely parallel each other. But in the second half, narrative time is greatly constricted, while story time remains roughly the same.[91]

"Furthermore, there are fewer repetitions in John 19:16b-37, more scene changes, and more characters on stage than in the first half of the passion narrative. Only the four unusual references to scripture being fulfilled (19:24, 28, 36, 37), the five references to Jesus' mother (19:25 [twice], 26 [twice], 27),[92] and the narrator's five necessary references to crucifixion (19:18, 20, 23, 31, 32) reflect those earlier, emphatic repetitions. Finally, and most importantly, at the crucial moment when Jesus is 'lifted up,' your implied reader's eyes are immediately averted from that central glorious event. Paradoxically, at this point, your implied reader is made to look anywhere but at Jesus" (19:19-25).

"If you ask me, you've still listed quite a number of repetitions for that section of text," snaps the hanging corpse. "And I must say that you've failed to mention one of the most fascinating redundancies in the entire passion

---

[90] B. Johnson, "Teaching Deconstructively," in *Writing and Reading Differently: Deconstruction and the Teaching of Composition and Literature* (ed. D. C. Atkins and M. L. Johnson; Lawrence: University of Kansas Press, 1985) 145.

[91] Alan Culpepper describes this narrative duration nicely, but in a general manner, without trying to point out the variations in duration on the last day of Jesus' life. He says: "The 'speed' of the narrative reduces steadily [throughout the gospel],...until it virtually grinds to a halt at the climactic day" (*Anatomy of the Fourth Gospel*, 72).

[92] Robert Brawley notes the fivefold repetition, calling it a "sentimental scene" ("An Absent Complement," 435), but surely this misses the rhetorical implications of the repetitions (see below).

narrative: the six additional references to writing which introduce the crucifixion scene (19:19 [twice], 20, 21) and conclude with Pilate's final words, *ho gegrapha, gegrapha* (19:22). It can hardly be inconsequential that Pilate's own writing, in a gross parody of Jewish Scripture, will not be modified (7:23; 10:35), and is an object of debate among 'the Jews' who read it (see 1:45-46; 7:51-52).[93] Nor can it be insignificant that it directly precedes the last three explicit citations of Jewish Scripture in the gospel."

"Yes, Pilate seems to be saying, 'I am one thing, [but] my writings are another matter,'"[94] the first corpse mumbles drowsily.

"What's that?"

"Oh nothing. It's just something else about intertextuality. An echo of another text, I suppose," responds the third corpse, trying to look at its companion.

"Well, I'm not interested in those sorts of intertextual echoes," the hanging corpse says. "That corpse beside you exasperates the hell out of me. Can't you get it to shut up? It has absolutely nothing to add to our conversation.

"Anyway, irrespective of your failure to note the important repetition I just pointed out, you would still need to account for the change in narrative point of view at the crucifixion scene. The focalization in 19:26-28 is from the perspective of Jesus. Jesus is the focalizer. This, I think, is really significant, for it means that the implied reader is indeed with Jesus at the moment of his glorification, gazing down at those around his cross." There are, therefore, other ways of emphasizing the implied author's ideological perspective besides

---

[93] Rudolf Bultmann correctly observes that Pilate's "inscription ...is undoubtedly to be understood as a prophecy" (*The Gospel of John: A Commentary* [Philadelphia: Westminster, 1971] 669), and Thomas Brodie calls it the "implication of a new scripture" (*The Gospel According to John* [New York: Oxford University Press, 1993] 546). But Brawley, strangely, fails to discuss any possible metaphorical or ironic connection between these references to writing and the subsequent fulfillment of Scripture ("An Absent Complement," 431-432).

[94] Nietzsche *(Ecce Homo,* 259), as quoted in J. Derrida, *The Ear of the Other: Otobiography, Transference, Translation* (ed. C. McDonald; Lincoln: University of Nebraska Press, 1988) 20.

[95] For, as Bultmann can say, in the crucifixion "everything has happened that had to happen; the work of Jesus is completed; he has carried out that which his Father had commanded him" (*John,* 674-675; see 632).

repetition. And in this case, the implied reader is uniquely made to share both Jesus' view of 'his mother and the disciple whom he loved standing alongside' (a person whom the narrator had left out of his earlier scenic description [19:25]), and Jesus' knowledge that 'all things were now finished' (19:28). So even if there isn't as much repetition here, the implied reader is clearly in a most privileged position."

The first corpse is aroused out of its restless dreams by this new turn. "Are the dogs gone yet? I'm sick of hearing them panting and sniffing around my head. Where the hell did they go?

"It's true that your implied reader is where Jesus is, seeing what Jesus sees, and knowing what Jesus knows, but I wouldn't say your implied reader is in a privileged position because of that. Your implied reader is actually offered only the most literal, rudimentary interpretation of Jesus' words. Jesus' statements to his mother and the beloved disciple (19:26) are interpreted by the narrator simply as Jesus' interest in her welfare ('the disciple took her to his own home' [19:27]), something which is a rather mundane concern for oldest sons in ancient Mediterranean kinship structure.[96] And Jesus' next statement initially seems to be a straightforward fulfillment of Scripture (19:28). Yet almost everyone sees Jesus' 'mother/son' language as reflecting more than a mundane concern for his mother and Jesus' thirst as more than a request for a drink. People say these must be symbolic, related somehow to the foundation of the new community and Jesus' mission.[97] But why do people say that? Where are the explicit textual clues?

"Damn it! The dogs are back. Now I think they're beginning to dig a hole to bury my bones.

"You know, I once heard how in ancient Mesopotamia (which is not too far to the east of here, I need hardly add) dogs were often severed in two, split longitudinally, so that the offerer could then 'pass between...[the] two parts

---

[96] Neyrey, "Despising the Shame of the Cross," 15; see Stibbe, *John as Storyteller*, 161-166.

[97] See, e.g., Brown, *John*, 2:922-927, 929-930; Senior, *The Passion of Jesus*, 113-120; D. Foster, "John Come Lately: The Belated Evangelist," in *The Bible and the Narrative Tradition* (ed. F. McConnell; New York: Oxford University Press, 1986) 127-128; Brawley, "An Absent Complement."

which, like a magnet, attracted ...impurit[ies].'[98] Rituals such as this are good illustrations of how 'the body tends to be brought forward in its most extreme form only on behalf of a cultural artifact or symbolic fragment or made thing (a sentence) that is without any other basis in material reality: that is, it is only brought forward when there is a crisis of substantiation.'[99] Well, as far as I'm concerned, our own little 'crisis of substantiation' here makes this the perfect time to cut up those cowering canines. Now, if I could just find something sharp ...."

"Well you can forget about chopping up your phantasmic dogs. There are actually substantive, intratextual clues that Jesus' mother, the beloved disciple, and thirst have symbolic significance here. Just look up John 2:1-11; 4:1-30; 6:52-56; 7:37-39; and 13:2125."

"Yes, you're probably right," adds the third corpse. "Those probably are intratextual cues. But I think what really interests my companion is how real readers get sidetracked, entangled, and mesmerized by the narrator's seemingly mundane observations, wanting to turn them all into deeply symbolic codes. I mean, here, at what appears to be the moment of greatest clarity, when the 'hour' comes, when all things converge at the cross—that place of Jesus' 'lifting up'— your implied reader is suddenly overwhelmed by the narrator's excruciatingly attentive descriptions of seemingly peripheral and extraneous details."[100]

"For example," chimes in the first corpse, "why should anyone care that Jesus' robe is seamless, woven in one piece from the top (19:23-25)? Simply because your implied reader knows Psalm 22:18? Or is it because your implied reader also knows the high priest's vestments were seamless (Ex 39:27-31)?[101] Perhaps your implied reader is expected to recall Mark 15:38 and the ripping of the temple veil. Who knows?"

---

[98] P. Wapnish and B. Hesse, "Pampered Pooches or Plain Pariahs? The Ashkelon Dog Burials," *BA* 56:2 (1993) 72; see L. E. Stager, "Why Were Hundreds of Dogs Buried at Ashkelon?" *BA* 17:3 (1991) 30-42.

[99] Scarry, *The Body in Pain*, 127, see 14; Gen 15:7-11.

[100] Robert Brawley writes, "Petty detail repeatedly takes on notable importance," and "[t]he insignificance of details can be the other side of their importance as symbols" ("An Absent Complement," *434;* see Moore, *Literary Criticism and the Gospels*, 161-163, 166).

[101] See Senior, *The Passion of Jesus*, 105-107; de la Potterie, *The Hour of Jesus*, 98-104.

"And just to continue that line of questioning," the third corpse adds, staring up into the sky, "how much ink has been spilled over the symbolic significance of the hour of crucifixion (19:14); the mother and the beloved disciple near the cross (19:25-27); the jar and the hyssop stalk which cannot support a sponge dripping with wine (19:29); the thirst that completes Scripture; the lance thrust, the unbroken bones, and the wound that pours forth water and blood (19:3435)? As the extensive repetitions we talked about earlier diminish, readers have a need to find more and more intertextual and intratextual allusions in order to give themselves some interpretive direction and a sense of control over the text. But instead, overt opacity and a strange, metaphoric murkiness abound."[102]

"So it's not the referentiality of all the scenic minutiae which I find so intriguing," says the first corpse, trying one last time to lift its face out of the dirt. "Rather, it's the fact that the inconsequential details are so concentrated here and tied so tenuously to the fulfillment/completion of Scripture—or to anything else, for that matter. What clues is your implied reader given in order to understand these concrete statements as allusions and metaphors? Why don't these kinds of illusive allusions appear earlier or elsewhere in the passion narrative?

"Most think that a seismic semeion is on the verge of erupting. If so, it would appear to be one which calls into question the apparent clarity and translucence of those carefully constructed semeia preceding this climax.[103] Ironically, when Jesus whispers 'It is finished/completed' (*tetelestai*), your implied reader's task is just beginning."

"Well, at least we've established from the preceding narrative that the implied reader knows this is the key scene in the gospel," sniffs the hanging corpse. "And if that is the case, the implied reader has been primed in every way to overread the death scene."

---

[102] Marianne Thompson has a nice summary of the text's various symbolic possibilities and intertextual connections (*The Humanity of Jesus*, 109-110; see Senior, *The Passion of Jesus*, 99). For a deconstructive analysis of the Johannine crucifixion and signs, see Moore, *Literary Criticism and the Gospels*, 161-163.

[103] For example, at this point in his interpretation of the crucifixion scene, Moore says that he is "as interested in what might be out of the control of the Johannine writers ...as in anything that has traditionally been said to be within their control" (*Literary Criticism and the Gospels*, 162).

"Yes, I can agree with that. Like Jesus, we have been led to cry 'I thirst!' We want to wring the text dry; to squeeze from it every last bit of wet, slippery symbolism that we can, in order to satisfy our craving for unity and meaning."

"Wait, you can't do this to me!" screams the last hanging corpse as it is finally cut loose from its cross and dropped down on the ground next to the other two. "I'm not finished! I still want to talk about the use of emphatic pronouns in the passion narrative. *egō*! *su*! *hymeis*! They're all over the place, and no one has ever made a detailed study of their usage here. I think I can squeeze them in, if you'll let me—but you're not going to! Now I can't even find them! Someone help me! Tie me back up where I belong!

"Oh no, it's dogs! My God! It's the dogs! I can hear them sniffing around my face. They're here and the bitches are gnawing[104] my eyes! My eyes! They've eaten my eyes!"

"Don't get so upset," laughs one of the dogs, its mouth full of dirt, sinew, and bone. "Just think of it as part of erosion."

"Yes, that's it," whispers the second corpse. "It must be erosion, and it's going to destroy the text in the same way that it's eating away every trace of us.

"Once upon a time there was an implied or encoded reader, who, with penetrating force, was erected upon this hallowed, hollow hill. But now there is only an eroded reader.[105] Our titular should have read, 'Here hung the eroded reader. Broken and pierced, stripped bare of its outer and inner tunics, it was finally devoured by the dream dogs of a croaking corpse.' Put that in Latin, Hebrew, and Greek, hang it over our heads, and see what real readers do with it."

"At least the image of erosion fits you," chuckles the third corpse. "And when rosy-fingered Eos appears you'll be completely gone. But perhaps the dog was inventing some narratological neologism, and yelped 'errorscission.' Maybe the cut of that Roman blade is beginning to bring you to your senses."

---

[104] The Greek verb here would be *trōgō* (John 6:56).

[105] "Listen to this. 'The top of the hill is round and smooth, worn down by centuries of eroticism.' Is she pulling my leg...?"

"I suppose she means 'erosion.'"

"I suppose she does. But yearning speaks betweeen the lines" (W. Stegner, *Crossing to Safety* [New York: Penguin Books, 1987] 49).

"No, no, you two still haven't gotten it!" hisses the first corpse. "The dog said 'erosion.' 'Eros-eon.' It's all about eros, can't you see? 'The cravings for unity, for essence, for the total picture, for the real and the true, are primitive,"[106] and eros will live on in readers for eons, regardless of what happens to us or the text. No wine-sopped hyssop can quench the tanha-like thirst for completion, nor will a tightly wrapped linen cloth ever silence its voice."

Post Mortem Reflections

"Socialization is training in allegorical interpretation," Barbara Johnson says,[107] and the strong temptation for me at the end of this drama is simply to defer any conclusion, allowing my readers to infer their own allegorical preferences from their own particular ideological perspectives and social locations. However, if confessions and original intentions count for anything in allegory (and I suppose that they do not), I should also add that I did not intend to write this exegetical exercise as a drama. I did not begin with a plan to fictionalize scholarly discourse.

The exegesis began like any other academic project: with sniffing out a text, developing a bareboned thesis, digging into the secondary literature, and carefully covering the various perspectives. But as I began to reflect on some of the objections raised against reader-response criticism and how I might "own my own views,"[108] I realized that I could not simply begin with autobiographical reflections and then let that stand apart from the critical discourse on the Johannine passion narrative. To do that would be to perpetuate uncritically the very problem that critics have been raising against biblical reader-response criticism. So I decided that I would somehow have to find a Way to integrate my autobiographical self into my professional reading of the Johannine passion narrative in such a Way that Whatever came out Would express the polyvalence and intersubjectivity of interpretation.

---

[106] B. Szabados, "Autobiography after Wittgenstein," *Journal of Aesthetics and Art Criticism* 50 (1992) 10.

[107] Johnson, "Teaching Deconstructively," 148. See N. Frye, *Anatomy of Criticism* (Princeton: Princeton University Press, 1957) 89.

[108] Tolbert, "Response from a Literary Perspective," 206; Moore, *Literary Criticism and the Gospels*, 105106; Porter, "Why Hasn't Reader-Response-Criticism," 283-290.

As Stephen Were states, "you must be several in order to write, and you must write with several hands."[109] So, at the risk of error or self-deception, the double-edged polyvalency of text and reader has been represented bra trinity of voices in my exegetical play. No doubt there are more voices in me,[110] but three is a fine number. It has held a position of honor in the Christian tradition, and sounds surprisingly contemporary when placed alongside postmodernism's rejection of the modernist fascination with binary oppositions. And besides all that, the three subjects were right there in the text from the very beginning.

But, "Whatever happened to narratology?" asks Christine Brooke-Rose plaintively.[111] Is there still a place in biblical exegesis for the more formalist type of reader-response criticism with which you began your literary-critical analysis of the New Testament?

I stammer for an answer. After all, my professional career began with narratology—with Genette, Bal, Brooke-Rose, Chatman, and others as my guides. Indeed, what *has* happened to narratology? But Christine replies before I can collect my thoughts, "It got swallowed up into story seems to be the obvious answer," she responds to her own question. "It slid off the slippery methods of a million structures and became the story of its own

---

[109] Moore, *Mark and Luke in Poststructuralist Perspectives,* 154-155. In biblical criticism, I might add, we have more often had to pretend we were writing with "severed hands" than with "several hands" (see Scarry, *The Body in Pain,* 176; J. P. Tompkins, "Me and My Shadow," in *The Intimate Critique: Autobiographical Literary Criticism* [ad. D. P. Freedman, O. Frey, and F. M. Zahaur; Durham: Duke University Press, 1993] 31-36).

[110] To paraphrase Szabados, "I have a feeling that many people speak through my mouth. Yet my aim has been to create myself out of this chaos of voices" ("Autobiography after Wittgenstein," 5). Or as Mikail Bakhtin *(Discourse on the Novel,* as quoted in H. L. Gates, "Editor's Introduction: Writing, 'Race' and the Difference it Makes," *Critical Inquiry* 12 [1985] 1) puts it:

Language ...lies on the borderline between oneself and the other. The word in language is half someone else's ....[T]he word does not exist in a neutral and impersonal language ...but rather it exists in other people's mouths, in other people's contexts, serving other people's intentions: it is from there that one must take the word and make it one's own.

See also W. C. Booth, *The Company We Keep: An Ethics of Fiction* [Berkeley: University of California Press, 1988] 238-239).

[111] Brooke-Rose, "Whatever Happened to Narratology?" 283.

functioning ...."[112] And then comes her final challenging query. "[So] was it a good story?"[113] Again I'm silent. I don't know, and I'm not sure I care. Let others be the judge of that, if it is important. But, like a pup happily chasing its own tail, I can't resist telling one more story; the true story of how the dogs made their way onto the paper, or how they were housebroken.

The dogs were not a part of the first draft of this article, which was originally read at the Pacific Northwest Regional Meeting of the Society of Biblical Literature, in May, 1992. The dogs made their way into this article, first in the autobiographical section, in order to illustrate dramatically the difference between Navajo values and the dominant values of my Euroamerican home. Only after some thought did I decide to add the dogs to the developing exegetical drama of the passion narrative. In this latter part of the article they were simply intended to stand as a metaphor for how we read our own interests and proclivities into canonical texts—or better yet, they would become a sinister allegory for the intermingling of text and reader—the erosion of the one into the other.

The more I thought about the dogs, the more they seemed the perfect metaphor for this intermingling phenomenon. First, dogs were despicable creatures in some ancient Mediterranean cultures, and thus could symbolize the "social world" perspective of many New Testament scholars. Secondly, dogs were despised animals in Navajo culture, and thus reflected my own cross-cultural childhood experiences and memories. Thirdly, and most importantly, I knew that there were no dogs in the Gospel of John, and so any imposition of them on the Johannine text would appear incongruous and artificial.

But now I had a real problem: how could I make dogs "appear" in a text where they were so obviously absent? The narratologist in me wanted some quirky evidence of their presence in the Fourth Gospel—and the more fantastic the argument for their presence, the better. An illusory sighting of dogs in John would point out the arbitrariness and subjectivity of some types of reader-responses and the masked illogic of some of our guild's interpretive moves.

---

[112] Ibid. Perhaps Brooke-Rose has exaggerated slightly in saying. "It slid off the slippery methods of a *million* structures..." (my emphasis). In my story, for example, only three methods have slid off their slippery structures.

[113] Ibid.

Knowing the word *kuōn* did not appear in the Fourth Gospel, I began by looking for a backwards *kuōn*. The genitive form of night *(nuktos)* seemed to offer possibilities, as did several participial constructions. But nothing fit "perfectly." I couldn't find a dog in John to save my soul, no matter how cynically I toyed with the text. It made no difference whether I was reading the text forward or backward, up or down.[114]

Then, totally by chance, and to my complete surprise, the dogs reared up in the passion narrative itself, in the quotation from Psalm 22. I just hadn't seen them there before—or had I? If I had seen them before, they had long since been reburied, like an old bone, deep in the dirt of my subconscious. But they were obvious to me now. Why hadn't I seen them there before? Suddenly, arguments about the arbitrariness of signifiers and signifieds took on new meaning. For what had begun as a conscious attempt to read something purely arbitrary into a text had ended up cohering nicely, intertextually stuck in the muck of a Johannine narrative world.[115]

As I sit typing these lines, I remember a phone call I received from my family just last night. It began with my seven-year-old son getting on the line and barking like a Chinese dog. Once, twice.[116] Then a long, pregnant pause.

"Daddy, two big dogs chased Allie tonight and knocked her down."

My wife picks up the phone in the bedroom. "Yes, that's right. And she has cuts and bruises all over her face to prove it. She was flat on her back, in the middle of the street, screaming, and these two dogs were pawing her and drooling in her face. She was petrified, but the dogs just thought it was a game.

---

[114] I guess I am not the first to read the Fourth Gospel in peculiar ways. Ernst Käsemann *(Testament of Jesus,* 75, n. 1) writes:

> Eighteen hundred years of exegesis have investigated each line and each syllable from all possible perspectives, reading it backwards and forwards, turning it upside down ....It is [therefore] easy for outsiders to ridicule us, that we think we can hear the grass grow and the bedbugs cough.

For the relationship of the apostle John to bedbugs, see The Acts of John, 60-61.

[115] Not long after I had made the intertextual connection between dogs and the Johannine passion narrative, John Crossan established a similar connection on historical-critical grounds (see his chapter entitled "The Dogs Beneath the Cross," in *Jesus,* 123-158).

[116] There is an ancient Zen koan that goes something like this: "When asked by a monk, 'Is there a Buddha-nature in a dog?' Chao-chu barked, 'Wu.'" (Wu is the negative symbol in Chinese, meaning "No thing" or "No.")

One of the neighbors kept yelling at the dogs' owner, 'God damn it, that's why cities have leash laws! To keep dogs like yours under control! '"

"Keep your dogs under control!" I can hear my fellow biblical scholars echoing that response. "You can't do critical, responsible exegesis with a bunch of half-wild dogs cavorting about your neighborhood, living room, or study, continually disrupting your work and pissing all over it."[117]

Yet if my readers (both the formalist ones inside the text and the real ones outside the text) have proven to be fictions, fossilized remnants on the verge of eroding away into nothing, then who—or what—is left to control the free-roaming, boundary-breaking, barking dogs that remain behind? For as surely as the sun rises, there will be caninical constraints and controls. I suppose the answer to that question, dishearteningly, is to be found among the same whos and whats that have always been in control: those cosmos-creating, sociopolitical structures which stand together as a human wall against the ever present chaos outside. Paradoxically, however, those structures are nourished by the "life-giving power" of the monstrous chaos they seek to exclude.

---

[117] Using words that, today, still describe many New Testament scholars' dogged resistance to new developments in biblical studies and hermeneutics, Robert Roberts admiringly wrote fifteen years ago of Rudolf Bultmann: he "has not ambled through his career sniffing every pole and fire hydrant of modernity [or postmodernity, we might now add] for an object upon which to bestow his theological blessings" *(Rudolf Bultmann's Theology: A Critical Interpretation* [Grand Rapids: Wm. B. Eerdmans, 1976] 9; see also L. E. Vaage, "Like Dogs Barking: Cynic parresia and Shameless Asceticism," in *Discursive Formations, Ascetic Piety, and the Interpretation of Early Christian Literature, Part 1 (Semeia* 57; ed. Vincent Wimbush; Atlanta, Scholars Press, 1992) 38.

THEOLOGICAL APPROACHES

Chapter Five

The Gospel of John as a Document of Faith in a Pluralistic Culture

R. ALAN CULPEPPER

Globalization, pluralism, and multicultural experience have become buzzwords in higher education today. As the world shrinks and American society becomes increasingly pluralistic, colleges and churches are facing old issues in a new way. We are also discovering that interpretation is both a distinctly personal, subjective enterprise and a communal one. Interpretation requires the interaction of a person in a particular context with a particular text, but the interpreter is never isolated from his or her tradition of interpretation, and interpretations of biblical texts exert powerful influences on communities of faith. My concern for the implications of using the Gospel of John as a document of faith in our increasingly pluralistic culture is grounded in my own pilgrimage as a reader of the Gospel.

The Gospel of John has always been for me a document of faith. I was raised in the home of Southern Baptist foreign missionaries in Chile and Argentina. I cannot remember a time when the Bible was not read and discussed in our home. I have always accepted the Protestant principle of the centrality of Scripture, and in my early years it never occurred to me to question the adequacy or suitability of the Gospel of John as a document of faith. Here As a Gospel that has spoken to people of different cultures and different ages, transcending cultural barriers as it communicates the essence of the Christian gospel. The increasing pluralization of our culture, changes in our understanding of the nature of biblical interpretation, and heightened ethical sensitivies force us to examine a question seldom discussed in either the academy or the church: *Can the Gospel of John continue to function for Christians as a document of faith in the increasing pluralism of American culture?* What problems or resources does it present to believers who live in a pluralistic culture?

The question is framed deliberately. I am concerned with the function of the Gospel of John for Christians. By "a document of faith" I mean a text that shapes the character and content of one's religious beliefs. Traditionally,

Christians (and Protestants in particular) have confessed that the scriptures were the sole sufficient guide in matters of faith and practice. In other words, we say that the scriptures are our authority when it comes to defining what we believe and how we are going to live. My question, therefore, juxtaposes the authority of the Gospel of John with the increasing pluralism of American culture. As the culture in which we live becomes increasingly pluralistic, religious communities are beginning to confront issues posed by the beliefs, experiences, values, and religious traditions of individuals from widely different social, ethnic, racial, and religious backgrounds. To put it in other words, *does using the Gospel of John as a document of faith lead to a faith stance that is adequate to the challenges a pluralistic culture poses for believers?*

Before attempting to fashion a response to the question, let us briefly remind ourselves of two challenges to the use of the Gospel of John as a document of faith in earlier eras.

Challenges to Gospel as Document of Faith

ANCIENT CHALLENGES: VALENTINIANS AND MONTANISTS

In the second century, questions were raised about the *theological orthodoxy* of the Gospel. The Gospel of John first appeared as a document of faith among the second-century Gnostics. One Gnostic school in Rome took the name of Valentinus, who lived between 100 and 175 and founded a school with the purpose of raising Christian theology "to the level of pagan philosophical studies."[1] We cannot be sure that Valentinus knew the Gospel of John, but it is clear that his followers used it. Ptolemy, one of Valentinus's early students, wrote a commentary on the prologue of John, and Heracleon, another Valentinian, wrote the first commentary on the Gospel about A.D. 170. Sketchy as the evidence is, it shows that while the Johannine writings were used only tentatively by the Church Fathers before Irenaeus (about 180), the Gospel was treated as an authoritative writing by the Valentinian school in Rome.[2]

Between 150 and 180 several sources confirm that John was widely known,

---

[1] B. Layton, *The Gnostic Scriptures* (Garden City, NY: Doubleday, 1987) 267.

[2] See my *John, the Son of Zebedee: The Life of a Legend* (Columbia, SC: University of South Carolina Press, 1994) esp. 114-119.

but the status of the fourfold gospel was still fluid: Marcion accepted only an edited version of Luke; the Valentinians added the Gospel of Truth; and Tatian wove the four gospels into one continuous account.

When others began to use the Gospel of John, Gaius, a presbyter and noted orthodox scholar at Rome, rejected the Gospel and denied that it was written by an apostle. Gaius was an opponent of the Montanists an enthusiastic group in Asia Minor who based their claims regarding the Spirit on John. While his basic concerns seem be have been theological, Gaius sought to discredit John by carefully noting its historical discrepancies and the places where it contradicted the synoptic Gospels. Gaius is significant because he shows that the authority of John was not so firmly established that it could not be challenged by one of be leaders of the church. The form of his argument is also telling: he sought to discredit be Gospel of John by showing that it contradicted be synoptic Gospels, which by implication served as the standard by which a gospel could be judged.[3]

Moreover, if the Muratorian Canon is to be traced to Rome during this same period (A.D. 180200), it can be seen as a defense of the authority of the Gospel of John in a social context in which it had been called into question. Specifically, it reports that the other disciples urged John to write his Gospel. Together they fasted for three days, and it was revealed to Andrew that all of be disciples were to go over the Gospel, but John should write everything down in his own name.[4]

Irenaeus, more than any other figure, mounted a defense of the Gospel of John as an orthodox gospel and fashioned a powerful anti-gnostic theological synthesis. He was also be first writer to offer a defense of the apostolic authorship of the Gospel of John, the first to claim that it was written in Ephesus, and be first to report that the apostle John lived to an old age in Ephesus. A major element in Irenaeus's defense of be Gospel was his appeal to a chain of tradition reaching back to be apostle John. Irenaeus reports that he had heard Polycarp, the bishop of Smyrna, who was martyred about A.D. 156.

---

[3] Ibid., 120-122. The place of Gaius in this history has been significantly clarified by J. D. Smith, "Gaits and the Controversy over the Johannine Literature," diss., Yale University, 1979.

[4] Culpepper, John, *the* Son *of Zebedee,* 128-129.

Irenaeus claims that Polycarp was "instructed by the apostles" and that Irenaeus himself, in his youth, had heard Polycarp. Even so, the credibility of Irenaeus's testimony has been sharply debated.[5]

Given the uncertainty of the evidence, exaggerated claims—either that John was used only by the Valentinians and Montanists before Irenaeus or that the authority of the Gospel was clearly established before Irenaeus—are out of place. Nevertheless, with Irenaeus the battle for the fourfold Gospel was won. The authority of the Gospel of John as scripture was never again in question.

MODERN CHALLENGES: K.G. BRETSCHNEIDER AND D.F. STRAUSS

The second challenge to the use of the Gospel of John as a document of faith was signaled by the publication in 1820 of a work by Karl Gottlieb Bretschneider and its influence on David Friedrich Strauss's *The Life of Jesus Critically Examined* (first published in 1835). This time the issue concerned primarily the Johannine discourses and their implications for the messianic consciousness of Jesus. In the Johannine discourses Jesus speaks not about the kingdom of God but about his own identity as the Son of God and his role as the revealer of the Father. More broadly, the question was to what extent the Gospel of John gives us a reliable portrait of Jesus. Is it the historical memory of the apostle John or the theological construction of a later writer? The theological issue was again tied to comparisons between the Synoptics and John. Bretschneider argued:

> It is accordingly quite impossible that both the Jesus of the [first] three Gospels and that of the Fourth can at the same time be historically true, since there is the greatest difference between them, not only in the manner of discourse but also in the argumentation and the behavior of the two; it is also quite incredible that the first evangelists invented Jesus' practices, teachings, and method of interpretation; but it is quite believable that the author of the Fourth Gospel could have created his Jesus.[6]

Prior to Strauss, the Gospel of John had been the favorite of post-Enlightenment German theologians, including Friedrich Schleiermacher, who

---

[5] Ibid., 123-128.

[6] Quoted by W. G. Kümmel, *The New Testament: The History of the Investigation of Its Problems* (trans. S. M. Gilmour and H. C. Kee; Nashville: Abingdon Press, 1972) 85-86.

constructed his argument that Jesus is the ideal archetype from the Gospel of John. For Schleiermacher,, Jesus was the model of human consciousness in his awareness of being dependent on God. Although Strauss waffled on his judgments regarding the Gospel of John in the third edition of his work, he mounted arguments against the credibility of the Fourth Gospel that profoundly shaped subsequent scholarship. Repeatedly, Strauss subjects the Johannine materials to detailed comparisons with the synoptic accounts. Whereas in the Synoptics Jesus speaks in aphorisms and parables, in John he offers extended discourses which employ an entirely different style and vocabulary. The discourses of Jesus in John resemble the idiom of the evangelist (or the elder of the Johannine epistles), not the style of the parabler of the synoptic gospels.[7] The synoptic sayings are brief, pithy, and memorable, but it is inconceivable that anyone should have remembered the long and repetitious Johannine discourses word for word.[8] Strauss concludes, "We therefore hold it to be established, that the discourses of Jesus in John's gospel are mainly free compositions of the Evangelist."[9]

The challenges of Bretschneider and Strauss did not lead to a reconsideration of the Gospel's canonical status, but they set the stage for a century and a half of debate over whether John should be read as history or theology. Although the debate is by no means settled, today most interpreters recognize that John is both history and theology: the fourth evangelist used historical traditions while composing the Gospel with considerable freedom and creativity.

CONTEMPORARY CONCERNS AND CHALLENGES

For many contemporary believers, however, the battles of the past no longer seem relevant. Generations of theologians have shown that whatever the circumstances of the composition or early use of the Gospel of John, its thought complements and extends the theology and christology of the rest of the New Testament. Indeed, many would say that it forms the pinnacle of theological

---

[7] D. F. Strauss, *The Life of Jesus Critically Examined* (ed. P. C. Hodgson; trans. G. Eliot; Lives of Jesus Series; Philadelphia: Fortress Press, 1972) 384.

[8] Ibid., 381-382. On p. 647, Strauss adds, "it is scarcely conceivable how John could accurately remember these long discourses."

[9] Ibid., 386. Strauss adds, "but we have admitted that he has culled several sayings of Jesus from an authentic tradition."

reflection in the New Testament. Neither do the challenges to the Gospel's historical reliability form the center of concern for many today. In place of the theological and historical challenges of earlier eras, a series of new concerns has arisen. These concerns are not primarily theological or historical but ethical: (1) Is the Gospel of John anti-Jewish? (2) Does the Gospel have anything to say to the marginalized and the oppressed? and (3) How should we interpret the theological exclusivism of the Gospel in a pluralistic culture? I will treat each of these questions individually.

The Gospel and the Jews

My own early responses to the charges that John is anti-Jewish or anti-Semitic were probably not unlike those of many others for whom the Gospel is a treasured book of scripture. I readily turned to counter-arguments that John does not teach hatred of Jews: (1) it reflects a historical period in which there was tension within the synagogue and Jews and Christians were not clearly distinct; (2) Jesus and the disciples were all Jews, and the first Christians were Jews; and (3) the Gospel of John opposes not Jewishness but the response of unbelief. In John, therefore, the Jews are simply representatives of unbelief. I still believe these points are correct, but they no longer constitute an adequate response.

Jewish friends and scholars have persuaded me that such responses to the issue do not take sufficiently seriously the Gospel's role in fostering anti-Jewish sentiment in Christian communities. We may be able to demonstrate historically or exegetically that the Gospel of John does not condemn Jews as a people, but what are we to do with the statements that vilify the Jews or, to be precise, the *Ioudaioi* in John?

The Gospel of John contains some of the most hostile, anti-Jewish statements in the Christian scriptures. So sharp is the contrast between Jesus' exhortations to his followers to love one another and the hostile references to "the Jews," that Kaufmann Kohler, an eminent Jewish scholar at the turn of the century, commented that John is "a gospel of Christian love and Jew hatred."[10]

The following passages give only a sample of the statements in John which

---

[10] K. Kohler, "New Testament," *Jewish Encyclopedia* (1905), 9:251.

refer to the *Ioudaioi* in a hostile manner:[11]

> -"But I know that you [Jews] have not the love of God in you" (5:42).
>
> -Then Jesus said to the Jews who had believed in him[!] ...."you look for an opportunity to kill me, because there is no place in you for my word. I declare what I have seen in the Father's presence; as for you, you do what you have heard from your father ....You are from your father the devil, and you choose to do your father's desires. He was a murderer from the beginning and does not stand in the truth, because there is no truth in him. When he lies, he speaks according to his own nature, for he is a liar and the father of lies ....Whoever is from God hears the words of God. The reason you do not hear them is that you are not from God" (8:31, 37-38, 44, 47).
>
> -"They [the Jews] will put you out of the synagogues. Indeed, an hour is coming when those who kill you will think that by doing so they are offering worship to God. And they will do this because they have not known the Father or me" (16:2-3).

The effect of these and other passages, when read as part of the scriptures of the church, has often been to incite anti-Jewish feelings in Christian communities. In eastern Europe in particular, Jews feared the celebration of Easter because they knew that it frequently led to pogroms or organized massacres of Jews.

It is now widely accepted that the Gospel of John reflects a period of sharp controversy with the synagogue about the time the Gospel was written. John has

---

[11] See M. J. Cook, "The Gospel of John and the Jews," *RevExp* 84 (1987) 260-261. In light of our earlier discussion of Strauss's arguments and their influence, it is interesting to note that later in this article Cook observes that the Johannine dialogues "convey no impression of verisimilitude" (266). One may compare Strauss's comment: "Hence, I confess, I understand not what is the meaning of verisimilitude in the mind of those who ascribe it to the discourses of Jesus in the Gospel of John" *(The Life of Jesus,* 381). Cook also poses the question whether John should be considered primarily as a historian, a polemicist, or a theologian. Discrepancies between John and the Synoptics are again marshaled against the view that John was primarily a historian. While maintaining that John is "assuredly anti-Jewish," Cook recognizes that "anti-Judaism is hardly foremost on John's agenda" (267). He therefore contends that John should be understood primarily as a theologian. Long established issues have therefore been given a new focus by the increased sensitivity of both Jewish and Christian scholars to the need to find effective ways of blunting the effects of John's anti-Jewish pronouncements.

therefore interpreted Jesus' debates with the religious authorities in the light of the experience of his own community. In this process, references to scribes, chief priests, and in places even the Pharisees have given way to a polemic against "the Jews."[12] Even if the Greek term *hoi Ioudaioi* once denoted Judeans or the Jewish authorities, the Gospel of John generalized and stereotyped those who rejected Jesus by its use of this term and elevated the bitterness and hostility of the polemic to a new level.[13] Perhaps even more importantly, the Gospel is the first document to draw a connection between the authorities who condemned Jesus and the Jews known to the Christian community at a later time. By means of this transfer of hostility, effected by merging events in the ministry of Jesus with the conflict with the synagogue in the time of the evangelist, the Gospel allowed and perhaps even encouraged Christians to read the Gospel in an anti-Semitic fashion.

Christians after the Holocaust—and indeed in a time of resurgence of "ethnic cleansing"—can no longer ignore the role of anti-Jewish statements in John and elsewhere in the New Testament in inciting or justifying prejudice and violence against Jews. We may argue that in its historical context the Gospel of John cannot have been anti-Semitic. Nevertheless, since the influential work of Rosemary Radford Ruether,[14] Christian scholars have begun to recognize that the Gospel rejects Judaism, contends that its festivals and observances have been replaced, and uses the generalizing tern *hoi Ioudaioi* to identify those who rejected God's revelation and persecuted Jesus and his followers. We must therefore reckon with the legacy of the Gospel and its effects on those of us who read it as Scripture. Is it possible for Christians who are sensitive to these issues to interpret the Gospel in such a way that does not foster antipathy and violence toward Jews, or should the Gospel be set aside as a document of faith?

Constructive proposals have taken various forms. Christian interpreters may begin to sensitize others to the dangers of John's anti-Jewish references and the

---

[12] R. T. Fortna, "Theological Use of Locale in the Fourth Gospel," *Gospel Studies in Honor of Sherman E. Johnson* (ed. M. H. Shepherd, Jr., and E. C. Hobbs; *Anglican Theological Review,* Supplementary Series 3 [1974]) 90.

[13] R. Fuller, "The 'Jews' in the Fourth Gospel," *Dialog* 16 (1977) 35.

[14] R. Radford Ruether, "Theological Anti-Semitism in the New Testament," *Christian Century* 85 (1968) 191-196.

difficulties of translating the term *hoi Ioudaioi* in John. Some have called for limiting the use of certain passages in John by excluding them from the common lectionary used by many churches. Others have proposed altering the translations of the Gospel on the logic that if it did not originally condemn Jews as Jews, then modern translations should not support or even allow for such an interpretation of the Gospel.[15] Most would agree, however, that if translations are altered, it should be because the text demands it, not because translators are seeking to change or diminish the anti-Jewish tone of the Gospel.

The Greek term *hoi Ioudaioi* can mean "the Jews," as it is usually translated, but it can also mean "the Judeans." In the Gospel of John the group designated by this term appears to be variously "Judeans" as opposed to Galileans or Samaritans, the "Judean leaders" (where it is used interchangeably with "the Pharisees"), or—less frequently—"Jews" as opposed to Gentiles. The meaning of the term *hoi Ioudaioi,* which is used seventy-one times in the Gospel, must therefore be determined by the context of each occurrence. There are places in John where the term can hardly mean "the Jews." A different translation would actually convey the sense of the text more accurately. For example, although the crowd in Jerusalem at the festival of Booths must have been predominantly Jewish, they still fear the *Ioudaioi* By translating *hoi Ioudaioi* as "the Jews" in this context, the NRSV and other translations produce a reading that makes little sense.

> The Jews [*hoi Ioudaioi*] were looking for him at the festival and saying, "Where is he?" And there was considerable complaining about him among the crowds. While some were saying, "He is a good man," others were saying, "No, he is deceiving the crowd." Yet no one would speak openly about him for fear of the Jews [*hoi Ioudaioi*] (John 7:11-13, NRSV).

Here it is clear the *hoi Ioudaioi* refers to a more limited group opposed to Jesus, either certain Judean Jews or the religious authorities. The same difficulties appear elsewhere in the Gospel.

Improving translations by translating each reference to *hoi Ioudaioi* contextually may contribute to eradicating anti-Jewish readings of John. However, if the Gospel is to continue to have a viable place in shaping Christian

---

[15] See *The American Family Bible* (Philadelphia: The American Institute for the Study of Racial and Religious Cooperation, 1986).

faith and practice, biblical scholars and Christian theologians are going to have to continue aggressively promoting awareness of John's anti-Judaism. John's circumscribed love command—that you love one another, that is, fellow Christians—is no longer adequate. To paraphrase Matthew rather ironically, "Do not even the Gentiles do the same?" (Matt 5:47). The anti-Judaism of the Gospel of John must be repudiated, and hard questions must be addressed regarding its theological exclusivism, but more on this shortly.[16]

THE GOSPEL AND THE MARGINALIZED AND OPPRESSED

The second major challenge to the Gospel of John is whether it has anything to say to the marginalized and the oppressed. Various groups have raised this question. What does the Gospel say to women who are striving for a place in the church as well as a voice in society at large? What does it offer the African-American who is searching for a story and a heritage for those whose ancestors were violently displaced and forced into slavery, and who themselves have been oppressed by racism? What does the Gospel offer to Hispanics, to Asian Americans, and—lest we forget—to the Native Americans we displaced from their lands?

Unfortunately, biblical scholarship at least until recently has been dominated almost exclusively by white, male, Europeans and Euro-Americans. The voices of those who have been culturally marginalized have scarcely been heard. The methods of critical biblical scholarship were developed and defined by European scholars, and the concerns they brought to the text were defined by their own academic, ecclesiastical, and cultural context. Women, African-Americans, and third world readers rightly point out that the authority of the Bible has been wielded in the interests of the status quo, the powerful, and the educated. As a result, even our Bible dictionaries, encyclopedias, and

---

[16] See further N. A. Beck, *Mature Christianity in the 21st Century: The Recognition and Repudiation of the Anti-Jewish Polemic of the New Testament* (rev. ed.; New York: Crossroad, 1994), esp. 321-328; and my essay, "The Gospel of John and the Jews," *RevExp* 84 (1987) 273-288, subsequently revised and published under the title, "The Gospel of John as a Threat to Jewish-Christian Relations," *Overcoming Fear Between Jews and Christians* (ed. J. H. Charlesworth with F. X. Blisard and J. L. Gorham [New York: Crossroad, 1992]) 21-43.

commentaries are not free from hermeneutical bias.

The interpreter must exercise a "hermeneutics of suspicion": whose interests are being served by this or that interpretation, and whose voice is being suppressed? What do we communicate when we treat the blind man in John 9 and scarcely note that he was a beggar, or when we interpret John 4 and pay little attention to the social location of a Samaritan woman? On the other hand, the patriarchal bias of the biblical stories is often taken as normative for society today.

Along the margins, however, we are beginning to hear the call for a reading of the Bible that grows out of the struggle of various groups for freedom, economic equality, and the integrity of their own voice:

> Thus, for example, *Itumeleng J. Mosala,* a black South African, writes:
>> The particularity of the black struggle in its different forms and phases must provide the epistemological lenses with which the Bible is read. Only such a position seems to us to represent a theoretical break with dominant biblical hermeneutics. Anything less is a tinkering with what in fact must be destroyed.[17]

Likewise, *Elsa Tamez,* reading the Bible from a Latin American woman's perspective, says:

> It is precisely the Gospel's spirit of justice and freedom that neutralizes antifemale texts. A reading of the Bible that attempts to be faithful to the word of the Lord will achieve that goal best when it is done in a way that reflects the liberating meaning of the Gospel, even when sometimes fidelity to the Gospel forces the reader to distance herself or himself from the text. Therefore, a time has come to acknowledge that those biblical texts that reflect patriarchal culture and proclaim women's inferiority and their submission to men are not normative ....The rationale behind this statement is essentially the same as that offered by the Scriptures: the proclamation of the gospel of Jesus calls us to life and announces the coming of the kingdom of justice.[18]

---

[17] I. Mosala, "The Use of the Bible in Black Theology," *Voices from the Margin: Interpreting the Bible in the Third World* (ed. R. S. Sugirtharajah; Maryknoll, NY: Orbis Books, 1991) 59.

[18] E. Tamez, "Women's Rereading of the Bible," *Voices from the Margin,* 65.

In a similar vein, *Gustavo Gutiérrez* calls for identification with the struggles of the poor:

> Prophetic language makes it possible to draw near to a God who has a predilection for the poor precisely because divine love refuses to be confined by the categories of human justice. God has a preferential love for the poor not because they are necessarily better than others, morally or religiously, but simply because they are poor and living in an inhuman situation that is contrary to God's will.[19]

The examples could be multiplied, but these eloquent voices suffice. The influence of the perspective, the culture, and the social location of the interpreter is being recognized. No text, and no interpretation, is ever completely unbiased or neutral. Some interests are advocated, privileged, or defended, while others are denied or subjugated. The implications of this shift in critical theory are just beginning to be considered. If no interpretation can claim to be neutral, and if the quest for scholarly objectivity and detachment has often functioned as an excuse for failure to recognize the ethical, political, or social implications of our work, then *the challenge of increased pluralism for interpreters of the Gospel is to be deliberate about the ethics of our interpretations.* The quest for objectivity and detachment should now be replaced by a quest for an ethics of interpretation that arises out of the highest ideals of the Bible and the Christian tradition, an ethic that is adequate to guide the interpretive community as it seeks to live out these ideals in a pluralistic culture.

As a step in this direction, interpreters are beginning to take seriously what may be called the "p" codes within the text: power, privilege, property, poverty, and persecution. Who is privileged and who is oppressed, and how are each treated in the text? The issues of power and social stratification—land, education, social class, religious obligation, and work—often guide us to readings of the text that respond to its ethical implications. In what ways does the text undermine prevailing power relationships: male—female, master—servant, rich—poor, patron—client, citizen—alien? Whose interests are protected or advanced by our reading of the text? Does it protect the status quo or empower the dispossessed?

---

[19] G. Gutiérrez, "Song and Deliverance," *Voices from the Margin,* 131.

This challenge calls us to examine our interpretations as well as the texts we seek to interpret. What do they have to say to the poor and the marginalized? Do they perpetuate the interests of the privileged or liberate the oppressed? And where must they be read with a hermeneutics of suspicion, looking in the gaps and silences for what is not said?

Various interpreters are already leading the way. Three recent, small books illustrate that John need not be read from the perspective of the empowered. Richard J. Cassidy states his thesis clearly at the outset: "In depicting Jesus' identity and mission within his Gospel, the evangelist John was concerned to present elements and themes that were especially significant for Christian readers facing Roman imperial claims and for any who faced Roman persecution."[20] Such a perspective allows Cassidy to read the Gospel's claims for the sovereignty of Jesus, the Roman trial, the farewell discourses, and John 20-21 in light of how they would have been understood by persecuted communities under Roman rule.

David Rensberger notes that John seems to be the least likely of the gospels to support a theology of liberation because of its overriding focus on christology. Nevertheless, Rensberger cautiously notes that although John does not offer a political program, and the situation of its first readers was different in significant respects from that of oppressed communities today, the Gospel of John is "the product of an oppressed community."[21] John 15:18, 15:20b, and 16:2b show that the Johannine Christians at least saw themselves as oppressed: "If the world hates you, be aware that it hated me before it hated you ....If they persecuted me, they will persecute you ....Indeed, an hour is coming when those who kill you will think that by doing so they are offering worship to God."[22]

Rensberger then interprets Nicodemus as one faced with the decision whether to identify publicly with the oppressed, marginal Christian community:

> The choice that faced Nicodemus was whether or not to side, no longer in private but openly, with a specific oppressed group in his society-indeed,

---

[20] R. J. Cassidy, *John's Gospel in New Perspective: Christology and the Realities of Roman Power* (Maryknoll, NY: Orbis Books, 1992) 1.

[22] D. Rensberger, *Johannine Faith and Liberating Community* (Philadelphia: Westminster Press, 1988) 110.

[22] Ibid., 111.

with those whom the members of his own rank and class, the people whose
company he truly preferred, were oppressing ....In essence, Nicodemus is to
be found wherever one whose life is secure must face those whose life is
insecure, or who struggle in the cause of God, and decide to say, "I am one
of them." [23]

When read in this light, John's passion narrative and ethic of love also speak
prophetically to contemporary readers who are sensitive to the situation of the
oppressed.[24]

In a little book entitled *Jesus and the Marginalized in John's Gospel,* Robert
J. Karris calls attention to the neglect of this subject in Johannine studies.'
Successive chapters deal with the poor, those who are ignorant of the raw, the
physically afflicted, geographically marginalized people, and women in John's
Gospel. "Those who do not know the law" in John 7:49 are interpreted on the
basis of rabbinic materials as "people of the land" who may not necessarily have
been poor but who were marginalized by the religious authorities because they
did not know the Law. The lame man in John 5:1-15 and the blind beggar in John
9 are treated as representatives of the "people of the land" who were also
physically afflicted. The Galilean *basilikos* in John 4:46-54 and the Samaritans
represent those who were geographically marginalized. In a helpful excursus,
Karris argues that the military context is absent in John 4:46-54, leading to the
conclusion that in this context *basilikos* designates a "Jewish royal official,
directly subject to 'King' Herod Antipas."26 As a Galilean, he was held in low
regard by the Judean rabbis. Because of their marginalized status in antiquity,
women often exerted influence through religious communities and activities.
Gathering up these threads in the concluding chapter, Karris contends—building
on the widely held thesis that the Johannine community was experiencing
conflict with the Jewish authorities—that the Jewish authorities opposed the
community because it gathered in the poor, Galileans and Samaritans, the
physically afflicted, those ignorant of the Law, and women. The result of such

---

[23] Ibid., 115, 116.

[24] Ibid., see esp. 116-132.

[25] R. J. Karris, *Jesus and the Marginalized in John's Gospel* (Zacchaeus Studies: New
Testament; Collegeville, MN: Liturgical Press, 1990).

[26] Ibid., 61.

compromising of the traditional standards of election was that the Johannine Christians were drummed out of the synagogue. The Gospel consequently encourages believers to remember that the Messiah to the marginalized was himself marginalized.[27]

In sum, Cassidy, Rensberger, and Karris have each contributed to sensitizing readers of the Gospel to its concern for the persecuted and those marginalized in various ways by society and religion. When read in this light, the Gospel challenges contemporary believers to oppose prevailing structures and social patterns that oppress the marginalized.

THE GOSPEL AND EXCLUSIVISM

The third sign of the emerging challenge to the use of John as a document of faith is expressed in the question: How should *we interpret the theological exclusivism of the Gospel in a pluralistic culture?*

The Gospel of John is not alone in the New Testament in asserting that salvation is attained only through confession of Jesus as Lord, but the Gospel's pronouncements are at the center of dialogues between Christians and persons of other religious faiths. While the following passages articulate the core of their faith for some, they pose an insurmountable obstacle to faith for others:

-"I am the way, and the truth, and the life. No one comes to the Father except through me" (John 14:6).

-"No one can come to me unless drawn by the Father who sent me ....Everyone who has heard and learned from the Father comes to me ....unless you eat the flesh of the Son of Man and drink his blood, you have no life in you" (John 6:44, 45, 53).

-"Whoever does not abide in me is thrown away like a branch and withers; such branches are gathered, thrown into the fire, and burned" (John 15:6).

These verses raise the problematic issues of exclusivism. Does the Gospel of John offer the Christian reader any basis for dialogue with persons from other religious traditions, or does it demand that there is no hope of salvation apart from confession of the Lordship of Jesus?

Global questions are sometimes best approached through the struggles of a

---

[27] This summary of Karris, *Jesus and the Marginalized in John's Gospel,* has been adapted from my review, published in *CR* (1992) 224–225.

particular individual. I have learned a great deal about the issues of exclusivism and pluralism from a Japanese Christian. Dickson Kazuo Yagi has written of his struggle to shape what he terms "a yellow theology."[28] Yagi is a third-generation, Japanese-American convert from a Shingon Buddhist home. For over twenty years he has taught Christian theology and world religions at Seinan Gakuin University in Japan. His grandfather prayed daily for the family before his Buddha altar. On his deathbed, the grandfather asked Yagi if he would pray for the family. At first, the grandfather wanted to pass on his altar, but he realized that his grandchildren would know little of the Japanese language and nothing of Buddhism, so he asked Yagi to pray for the family, saying "Of course, you are not a Buddhist, but a Christian minister. Yet surely the Buddhas would understand the cultural problem and accept your Christian prayers."[29] And so Yagi asks, "Will the God of Abraham, Isaac, Jacob, and Jesus Christ also understand ...the collision of the absoluteness of the Christian Cross and the cultural relativity of our multi-religious modern world"?[30]

The difficulty, he observes, is that Christianity is a gospel with two centers: faith (epitomized by Paul) and love (epitomized by John). A gospel with two centers results in two questions that cannot be answered:

> The first is what can we say about those who believe in Jesus Christ but do not love? The second is what can we say about those who do not believe in Jesus Christ and yet love their neighbor? Because there are two centers to the gospel, not one, these two questions are unanswerable. Just as Christians who do not love are solidly rejected by one center, non-Christians who do love are affirmed by the other center .[31]

Yellow theology rejects a gospel with only one center.

The most serious problem faced by Christianity in Asia is ancestor worship. As a response to the abuse of indulgences, the Reformation cut all ties to the dead, committing them to the hands of God. But because the dead are honored daily in Asian homes, the Asian Christian can hardly abandon hope for those

---

[28] D. Kazui Yagi, "Christ for Asia: Yellow Theology for the East," *RevExp* 88 (1991) 357-378.

[29] Ibid., 358.

[30] Ibid.

[31] Ibid., 364-365.

who die without confessing Christ. After all, only .08 percent of the population is Christian.[32] Questioned about his hope of seeing his grandfather after death, the Japanese Christian responded, "If I got to heaven, though, and could not find him, I would immediately go to be with him wherever he was—be it hell or purgatory. Why should I go to heaven to be with white folks while my people are burning in hell?"[33] Yagi therefore calls on whites and blacks in the West to recognize the "gravitational pull" of this issue on Asian Christians as they fashion a yellow theology that expresses an authentic biblical faith. One of the avenues to such a theology that Yagi considers is that of the Cosmic Christ in John 1:9. According to John 1:9, Christ is the true light that enlightens every man.

The Gospel's opening gambit is to describe the work of the Logos by drawing from the Wisdom tradition.[34] As Wisdom, the Logos was the creative agent. Wisdom manifests God's design and power in all the creation. As John N. Jonsson observes,

> The universal phenomenon of wisdom, impregnated within the human consciousness across the world, highlights how pathetically inappropriate all our exclusivist religious belief systems are in the light of the stern realities and anomalies of our contemporary pluralistic world.[35]

The exclusivist claims of the Fourth Gospel, such as those cited above, must therefore be understood in the context of the opening claim that the revelation that came through Jesus Christ is the same as that which is universally present in the Logos. To cite Jonsson once more:

> Wisdom belongs to the diversity of human pluralism, necessitating a pluralism in theological expression in the prolongation of the mystery of the incarnation, i.e., God becoming a human being absorbed into the cultures of all people of the world. Here there is a paradox in faith between the

---

[32] Ibid., 369.

[33] Ibid.

[34] See the recent monographs by M. E. Willett, *Wisdom Christology in the Fourth Gospel* (San Francisco: Mellen Research University Press, 1992) and M. Scott, *Sophia and the Johannine Jesus* (JSNTSup 71; Sheffield: Sheffield Academic Press, 1992).

[35] J. N. Jonsson, "Wisdom: The Threshold of God in Human Existence" (unpublished ms. to be published in a collection edited by John A. L. Saunders), 3.

particularity of the Jesus of Nazareth and the universality of the cosmic
Christ, the "logos" of God.[36]

Because the Gospel presents Jesus as the incarnation who made known the
work of the Logos from the creation and through all time, it undercuts the
triumphalism of claims that Christendom has a monopoly on the revelation of
God. The further implication is that what one says about the nature of revelation
has direct implications for salvation through the work of the Logos. Just as the
Logos brought a saving knowledge of God to Abraham, Moses, and Isaiah, so the
Logos continues to speak to persons through other religious traditions as part of
God's effort to draw all people to a knowledge of God. The cosmic
understanding of wisdom personalized in Yahweh, the one God, is the antecedent
on which John's Logos Christology rests. One of the cruxes in the interpretation
of the prologue of John is whether vv. 9-13 refer to the work of the pre-existent
Logos or to the period of the incarnation. Obviously, if this section describes the
former, it further clarifies that the work of the preexistent Logos was not only
creative but redemptive. Accordingly, John's Logos Christology allows
Christians to affirm that adherents of other religious traditions may come to know
God through the work of the Cosmic Christ.

If Christian theologians have hesitated to draw the implications of these
biblical perspectives on revelation, it is due in part to understandings of salvation
that are too narrow, inflexible, and legalistic. Permit me a personal reference.
After a full career as a missionary and later professor of missions and world
religions, my father's last published statement may be a brief expository article
in which he deals with the problem of exclusivism by interpreting Acts 4:12. He
translated the verse quite literally, as follows: "and there is not in any other one
salvation. For neither is there another (kind) of name under heaven given among
men in whom it is necessary for us to be saved."[37] His comment calls for a
reconsideration of the meaning of language about "being saved":

> The understanding of this last word, "saved," is crucial to the exposition of
> this verse. If we follow the popular understanding of salvation as being
> something objective which we can "have" or "not have," i.e. as being an

---

[36] Ibid., 9. Here Jonsson cites Frederick Cawley, *The Transcendence of Jesus Christ*
(Edinburgh: T. & T. Clark, 1936) 10-101.

[37] H. H. Culpepper, "Acts 4:12," *RevExp* 89 (1992) 85.

objective status, we miss the mark. It becomes legalistic, juridical, judicial. It has nothing of the personal, of what we are in ourselves, or of the relational, of how we relate to God and other human beings. If God is the ultimate reality, our vocation is to be such as is in harmony with him.[38]

His concluding affirmation is a reflection of his own understanding of the work of Christ as the Logos:

If there is a God beyond all gods, surely he uses every culture, all the differing religious traditions, even all history in seeking to get through to as many people as possible and bring them voluntarily into relationship with himself![39]

Yagi's quest for a yellow theology, John Jonsson's reflections on the significance of Wisdom, and my father's reflections on persons of faith from other religious traditions have sensitized me to both the difficulties and the values of taking the Gospel of John as a document of faith—both for Asian Christians and for American Christians in our increasingly pluralistic society.

Concluding Comments

The question we began with was: *Can the Gospel of John continue to function for Christians as a document of faith in the increasing pluralism of American culture?* In large measure the answer to that question depends on how we interpret the Gospel. Whereas previous challenges to the use of the Gospel as a document of faith were based on theological and historical concerns, we are witnessing the emergence of a third challenge based on what we might characterize as ethical concerns. I would readily admit that there were social and ethical differences between interpreters in both the second century and the nineteenth century. The questions that face us now, however, are clearly more ethically defined than previous challenges: How should those of us who derive our religious teachings from the Gospel of John respond to Jews who are concerned that the Gospel is anti-Jewish, those who have been marginalized and oppressed by the church and by Christians in society, and persons of other religious traditions? These questions concern the very character of religious faith.

---

[38] Ibid., 85.
[39] Ibid., 86-87.

They also raise new sensitivities and concerns for those who interpret the Gospel. The position toward which I have been moving assumes that the role of the Gospel of John as a document of faith will depend on the hermeneutics of the ecclesiastical and scholarly reading communities: it depends on how we interpret the Gospel. One could argue that the two challenges we have discussed from earlier eras contributed to the definition of new methods of interpretation—the first to the allegorical method and the second to historical criticism. Our quest then is for critical methods—now much more self consciously hermeneutical— that will be adequate to the challenge of reading the Gospel in an increasingly pluralistic culture.

I have no program to offer, only some principles that may be useful in our common search:

1. For the sake of clarity, it is important to question interpretations that claim to be objective, neutral, or non-partisan and to seek to be clear about the assumptions, commitments, and interests that guide our own work as interpreters.

2. One of the issues to be discussed is whether the biblical texts are themselves inherently liberationist or oppressive and how to treat those texts that are oppressive.[40] Interpretation always calls for the interpreter to identify the elements of the text that shape his or her interpretation and show how those facets of the text undermine antithetical or incongruous elements of the text. Part of the solution, therefore, may be for the interpreter to allow the voices of the oppressed and excluded to raise new sensitivities and concerns for those of us who interpret the Gospel of John.

3. Because the challenge, we face is in many respects an ethical one, our reading of the Gospel must be informed not only by theological tradition and historical criticism but also by concern for the effects and ethical implications of our interpretation. Only by asking whether our interpretation of the Gospel serves to put an end to violence against Jews and other ethnic minorities, to give voice and power to the marginalized and oppressed, and to bring understanding and acceptance between persons of different religious traditions can we expect that our interpretation will be relevant to the challenges of our culture.

---

[40] Consider the challenges of I. J. Mosala and E. Tamez in the works cited above.

Sensitized to the challenges of our pluralistic culture—indeed, of our world—the interpreter may find that another part of the solution comes from the Gospel itself. That is, he or she may be able to identify facets of the text that resonate with our quest for what we may call *a hermeneutics of ethical accountability*. For example, the Fourth Gospel's declaration of God's boundless love for the world undermines its polemic against "the Jews." Its concern that the community of faith may be one undermines social and ethnic barriers between believers, and its affirmation that the work of the Logos cannot be confined to the period of the incarnation opens the way for affirming the experience and heritage of persons of faith in other religious traditions.

Christian interpreters still have much to do. Accountability requires us to seek interpretations that are both faithful to the text and ethically responsible. Only by asking whether our interpretation of the Gospel serves to put an end to violence against Jews and other ethnic minorities, to empower the marginalized and oppressed, and to bring understanding between persons of different religious traditions can we expect that our interpretations will stand the test of accountability when they themselves are read with a "hermeneutics of suspicion."

Chapter Six

Metaphysics and Marginality in John

WERNER H. KELBER

We must face squarely the violence of language in our traditions, and squarely ask, What is the theological stance that we must take toward texts of such terror?

—Michael Fishbane

But what if the text in question were ethically flawed? What if it were misogynistic, say, or anti-Jewish?

—Stephen D. Shore

In Christian teaching and preaching, the Jew was too often presented as the quintessential "other," the mythical enemy of Christianity, less than human.

—Irvin J. Borowsky

But if there were a lesson to be drawn, a unique lesson among the always singular lessons of murder, from even single murder, from all the collective exterminations of history...the lesson that we can draw today—and if we can do so then we must—is that we must think, know, represent for ourselves, formalize, judge the possible complicity between all these discourses and the worst (here the final solution).

—Jacques Derrida

Spirituality and Anti-Judaism

When Clement of Alexandria espoused the thesis that the author of the Fourth Gospel, "urged on by his close friends (*protrapenta hypo tōn gnōrimōn*), and divinely moved by the Spirit (*pneumati theoporethenta*), composed a spiritual gospel" (*pneumatikon poiēsai euaggelion*), he (Clement) intended to draw a distinction between the Johannine narrative and the other three canonical gospels. Whereas the Synoptics had grasped the "corporeal things" (*ta sōmatika*), John had come into existence under the special guidance of the

Spirit.[1] To be sure, Clement's invocation of the metaphysical dualism of body versus Spirit fails to capture the relation among the canonical gospels. But the issue of John versus the Synoptics aside, there is no denying that the Fourth Gospel entertains a high estimation of the Spirit. Descending from above, the Johannine Logos is endowed with the Spirit (John 1:3233), proclaims a birth from above and from the Spirit (3:3-6), anticipates true worship in Spirit and truth (4:23), promises the "living water" of the Spirit to the believers (7:39), announces the sending of the "Spirit of Truth" in the form of "another Paraclete" (14:16), and dispenses the Spirit among the disciples following his own glorification (7:39; 20:22) while he is reunited above with the Father (14:28-29). In John, the Spirit embodies the world above, provides illumination in the world of the flesh, and comes to rest in the Paraclete, Jesus' alter ego, while Jesus himself prepares for his return to the world above. Clement and the ancient tradition he relied upon rightly sensed the spiritual, indeed metaphysical, underpinnings of the Fourth Gospel.

There is, however, a growing awareness of a feature seemingly at odds with the Gospel's spirituality: its profound anti-Judaism. Alarmed no doubt by the holocaust, which brought to calamitous heights centuries of Christian anti-Jewishness, theologians and biblical scholars find themselves under obligation to reexamine the foundational documents of Christianity.[2] It is tempting to claim that the animosity John exhibits toward the Jews and most things Jewish is antithetical to its spirituality and irreconcilable with its theological profundity. Would it not make theological sense to suggest that the Gospel carries unspiritual elements which run counter to its metaphysical loftiness? Should it not be possible to isolate and excise John's unspiritual elements in the interest of highlighting its spiritual grandeur? But this is not the argument we will pursue in this essay. The thesis presented here is that John's spirituality and his anti-Jewish animus are tragically intertwined features. Hatred of the Jews and

---

[1] Eusebius, *The Ecclesiastical History* (LCL; London: Heinemann; New York: Putnam's, 1932) 6.14.5-10.

[2] A model of critical examination of anti-Judaism in the New Testament documents is N. A. Beck, *Mature Christianity in the 21st Century. The Recognition and Repudiation of the Anti-Jewish Polemic of the New Testament* (expanded and rev. ed.; New York: Crossroad, 1994).

philosophical ambitions are concurrent phenomena in this Gospel. Our quest will be for the metaphysical roots of Johannine anti-Judaism.

Facing Johannine Anti-Jewishness

Efforts to face the issue of John's anti-Judaism are numerous ranging from the patently apologetic to the intellectually astute.

1. It is sometimes suggested that language lies at the heart of the problem. We must strive for accurate translation and allow the original to speak for itself, as it were. It is said, for example, that in the Johannine text the tern *Ioudaioi* does not always connote the Jewish people as a whole. Attention to literary context and social milieu provides evidence that the term can refer to "those leaders who hold some influence over their Jewish constituency in the region known to the Fourth Evangelist."[3] A return to the semantic origin, it is felt, will tell the truth and make us free.

John's use of words surely deserves scrutiny because it is through the medium of language that the implied author casts Jews and Judaism in an unfavorable light. But it is facile to assume that translation lies at the heart of the problem and linguistic correctness would redeem the violence in the text. To imply that the polemic against the Jews is correctible by application of greater translational precision is to belittle the magnitude of the problem. We need to probe and penetrate Johannine language and narrative more strenuously to uncover the depth of its involvement in the hostilities.

2. Another thesis posits that to stay with Jews and Judaism as the principal opponents of the Johannine Jesus is to settle merely for the literal meaning. On the surface level the controversy is acted out between the earthly Jesus and the Judaism of John's time. Those who fail to understand Jesus and go after his life and those who are provoked by Jesus and subjected to his riddling and egocentric language represent the Judaism of the first century. But what typifies the Fourth Gospel is its inability to remain for long on the literal level. In a sense transcending literalism, the controversy is with "the Jews as the representatives of the world," and it is on that level that it takes on "an

---

[3] R. Kysar, "The Gospel of John and Anti-Jewish Polemic," *Explorations* 6 (1992) 3.

exemplary significance for a larger, more extensive religious realm."[4]

It is arguable that John's narrative "describes the progressive alienation of Jesus from the Jews."[5] As heavenly savior of the world, Jesus comes "into the world" (1:9) and "to His own" who "did not receive him" (1:11). While those who gravitate toward the light are selected from the world (15:19), the unbelieving world is left in darkness. As the conflict with the Jews intensifies, they are progressively identified with the world. The world that rejects Jesus and hates his followers is represented by the Jews. One cannot join the Johannine community "without making the decisive break with the 'world,' particularly the world of Judaism,[6] Dramatically, it is thus plausible to argue that Judaism gradually modulates into the notion of the world, and vice versa. But we must press the issue and emphasize the heinousness that underlies the notion of the Jews as representatives of an unbelieving world which "is in essence existence in bondage."[7] Far from moderating Johannine anti-Judaism, it magnifies it to cosmic proportions.

3. If one approaches Johannine language from the perspective of ancient rhetoric, the prevailing polemics of the Gospel invite a reassessment in a new light, for the ancient rhetorical culture was adverse to dispassionate thought abstracted from the human lifeworld. Reasoning evolved out of argumentation with others. Thought and conviction were born out of assertion against opposition. In like manner, it is argued, John's narrative, as any effective narrative in antiquity, "needs an antagonist as much as it needs a hero figure."[8] Hatred of the other was a rhetorical fact of life in the ancient Gentile, Jewish, and Christian world. Rhetorical considerations would thus enable us to locate John's language of invective more broadly in the context of other, harshly polemical passages in the Hebrew Bible, the Dead Sea Scrolls, and the Church Fathers.

Undoubtedly, the adversarial style grows directly out of the rhetorical culture

---

[4] E. Käsemann, *The Testament of Jesus. A Study of the Gospel of John in the Light of Chapter 17* (Philadelphia: Fortress Press, 1968) 24.

[5] W. A. Meeks, "The Man from Heaven in Johannine Sectarianism," *JBL* 91 (1972) 69.

[6] Ibid.

[7] R. Bultmann, *Theology of the New Testament* (vol. 2; trans. K. Grobel; New York: Charles Scribner's Sons, 1955) 16.

[8] Kysar, "The Gospel of John," 4.

of antiquity. Polemics is an intrinsic feature of rhetoric, although by no means an exclusive or even predominant one. The art of producing conviction in others was already a world removed from the brute force exerted in warfare. Apart from the fact that rhetoric is synonymous with persuasion more than with hostility, we must face up to the animosities as they exist in our sacred texts "because they have been appropriated for further hatred."[9] Rather than accepting violence as part and parcel of ancient culture, we need to analyze the texts for their ideological allegiances and for the way in which they construct positions of dominance and submission. We further need to acknowledge that we, the readers, also operate out of social locations.[10] And ours is a post-holocaust world.

4. In recent years evidence has been accumulating that in addition to its anti-Jewish polemic, the Fourth Gospel was also marked by intra-Christian tensions. Focusing on the sayings traditions, D. Bruce Woll postulated a charismatic community which was faced with "*too much* 'salvation,'" that is to say, too many claimants to saving powers, too many successor figures, resulting in rivalry and 'charismatic competition'."[11] In this context, no sharp line was drawn between the earthly Jesus and the ascended and/or risen Christ.[12] Reacting to the charismatic collapsing of the hierarchical distance between Jesus and his followers, the farewell discourse makes a concerted effort at subordinating the disciples to Jesus. James Robinson, approaching the Gospel from a somewhat different but related perspective, focused on the chronological divide between open and concealed language, a hermeneutical device which was intrinsic to the

---

[9] M. Fishbane, "Saving Scripture and Our Mortal Souls," *Explorations* 7 (1993) 6.

[10] M. A. Tolbert, "A Response from a Literary Perspective," *The Fourth Gospel from a Literary Perspective* (ed. R. A. Culpepper and F. F. Segovia; *Semeia* 53; Atlanta: Scholars Press, 1991) 203-12.

[11] D. B. Woll, *Johannine Christianity in Conflict: Authority, Rank, and Succession in the Farewell Discourse* (SBLDS 60; Chico, CA: Scholars Pres, 1981) 32; D. E. Aune, *The Cultic Setting of Realized Eschatology in Early Christianity* (NovTSup 28; Leiden: E. J. Brill, 1972); D. M. Smith, *Johannine Christianity: Essays on its Setting, Sources, and Theology* (Columbia, SC: University of South Carolina Press, 1984) 1-36.

[12] M. E. Boring, *Sayings of the Risen Jesus: Christian Prophecy in the Synoptic Tradition* (SNTSMS 46; Cambridge: Cambridge University Press, 1982) 49.

sayings/discourse genre.[13] There the risen or living Christ speaks openly, casting a shadow of concealment over his earthly career. Robinson finds this technical terminology of concealed versus revealed language recurring in John 16:25 and 16:29.[14] Whereas Jesus anticipates a time when he will no longer speak figuratively *(en paroimiais),* the disciples assume—probably mistakenly—that he is already speaking openly *(en parrēsia).* In other words, they mistake the earthly Jesus for the risen Christ in charismatic, gnostic fashion. According to the rationale of John's narrative, however, it is, and was, only with Jesus' resurrection/glorification that the time of remembrance was ushered in (2:22; 12:16; 20:9), and what had to be remembered was the story of Jesus' life and death, and not exclusively the words of the risen Christ.

The notion that conflictual relations with a prophetic, charismatic, gnosticizing type of Christianity are inscribed in the Gospel constitutes a stunning reversal of the classic assumptions that John has "spiritualized old apocalyptic traditions"[15] and "eliminated apocalyptic parousia expectations,[16] because he felt that "the traditional, futuristic eschatology is no longer meaningful."[17] But even if John was seeking to curtail an oral, mystical, gnosticizing emphasis on the *praesentia Christi,* rather than reacting against the futuristic scenario of apocalypticism, the polemics against Judaism are equally strongly inscribed into his narrative. While much work still needs to be done to grasp the historical and narratological logic of the coexistence of these dual polemics, it will not alter, let alone justify, the anti-Jewish posture of the Gospel. After all, the Gospel narrates a rationale for the break with Judaism while it holds out hope for believers in post-resurrectional times.

5. Historical criticism, more than any other single approach, has uncovered the source of John's anti-Judaism. We are indebted to historical research, which

---

[13] J. M. Robinson, "On the *Gattung* of Mark (and John)," in *Jesus and Man's Hope* (2 vols.; Pittsburgh: Pittsburgh Theological Seminary, 1970) 1:99-129; rpt. in *The Problem of History in Mark and Other Marcan Studies* (Philadelphia: Fortress Press, 1982) 11-39. See also his "Jesus: From Easter to Valentinus (or to the Apostles' Creed)," *JBL* 101 (1982) 5-37.

[14] At this point our reading of John differs from Robinson's interpretation.

[15] Käsemann, *Testament,* 72.

[16] H. Conzelmann, *Grundriss der Theologie des Neuen Testaments* (Munich: Chr. Kaiser Verlag, 1968) 388.

[17] R. Kysar, *John: The Maverick Gospel* (Atlanta: John Knox, 1976) 92.

has assembled plausible evidence with regard to the schismatic experience that lay at the root of Johannine self-consciousness. Few have made a more persuasive case for the trauma of separation as a determining factor in the composition of the Fourth Gospel Inn J. Louis Martyn.[18] In his classic study on the ancient setting of John's Gospel, he reconstructed the drama of the building of the wall of separation which came to divide an ancient synagogue from the self-consciously Christian community of John. What precipitated the crisis, according to Martyr, was neither the issue of the Torah, nor that of the Gentile mission, but rather Jesus' messiahship, or more precisely, allegiance to his Mosaic-Prophetic messiahship. At some point in time, "not far removed from the end of the first century,"[19] the authorities of a synagogue perhaps located in Alexandria,[20] reached a formal agreement to expel members who had pledged allegiance to Jesus, the Mosaic, messianic miracle worker, whom they may also have worshipped as god alongside of God. Invoking the 12th benediction, these synagogal authorities proceeded to take formal action against the Messianic heretics by excluding them from their community. Those displaced from their cultural home fashioned a socio-cultural identity of their own, which was both grounded in their Jewish matrix and distanced from it.

In illuminating the Gospel's cultural environment and in bringing to light the synagogal conflict, Martyr has taught us a model lesson in historical criticism. After Martyn we cannot help but read the Gospel as a dramatization of deeply conflictual relations. But historical criticism, if used as the sole and solely privileged access to the text, is not without its problems. By locating the source of crisis in external causation, one has to some degree prejudged the internal problematics of the text. If we allow external causality to become the defining hermeneutical criterion, we fail to grasp sufficiently the intrinsic narrative rationale, including the full force of its anti-Jewishness. And in placing the crisis at the heart of the synagogue, we have subtly allocated responsibility.

---

[18] J. L. Martyr, *History & Theology in the Fourth Gospel* (2nd ed. rev. and enlarged; Nashville: Abingdon Press, 1979). See also Klaus Wengst, *Bedrängte Gemeinde and verherrlichter Christus: Der historische Ort des .lohannesevangeliums als Schlüssel zu seiner Interpretation* (Neukirchen-Vluyn: Neukirchener Verlag, 1981).

[19] Martyn, *History & Theology,* 61.

[20] Ibid., 73, n. 100.

Furthermore, with the expulsion as point of departure for our reading, the Gospel has become historically plausible as an etiological story which spoke for and gave shape to a community in exile. The conflict is thereby safely deposited in the distant past, as if it had never impacted our present. Consistent with this strict application of historical criticism, Martyn has therefore little to say concerning the meaning the Gospel holds for the present. Unless we comprehend the metaphysical project and the narrative logic of the Gospel, we cannot assess the depth of its antagonism. For theological/metaphysical ambitions and anti-Jewishness, this essay argues, are tragically interconnected forces in the Johannine narrative.

The Metaphysical Agenda

Let us begin not with the narrative minutiae but with an assessment of the macro-coordinates which circumscribe the narrative of the Fourth Gospel. In the broadest perspectives, the Gospel alludes to a heavenly descent *(katabasis)* of the Logos, narrates his earthly mission, which is marked by the performance of seven signs and four journeys into the city of Jerusalem, dramatizes an apotheosis at death, and anticipates a heavenly ascent *(anabasis) (20:17)*. While descent, incarnational career, and ascent constitute defining elements, all three features are fraught with unexpected difficulties which make for a complex and double-faced narrative.

1. That Jesus' incarnation is perceived as a descent is intimated for the first time in his conversation with Nicodemus (3:13) but is never the subject of the Gospel's narrative. The prologue's focus lies on the Logos in the beginning *(Logos en archē)* and on his coming into the world (1:9: *erchomenon eis ton kosmon)*. Reaching back to the beginning of beginnings, to the outside of time and to a state prior to the world, the prologue lodges the *Logos* in foundational primordiality. In what appears to be a strikingly logocentric gesture, the Gospel shows forth its metaphysical ambitions. Yet the noteworthy feature of the metaphysical *Logos is* his status of ambiguity. For the index of his authority is not absolute transcendence and unambiguous identity. Rather, in being both "with God" (1: 1: pros *ton theon)* and "God" (1:1: *theos ēn)*, the *Logos* manifests his identity in difference. Inscribed in the logic of identity is the irrepressible

nature of difference.[21] From the beginning, therefore, the Gospel creates a dilemma for the *Logos* which has a critical bearing on the subsequent narrative and on its readers as well.

2. As the *Logos* embarks upon his earthly career, he adopts a worldly status which enlarges his difference from divinity. But inasmuch as he differs, he simultaneously seeks to retain his identity from above. The *Logos* who enters into the flesh does so for the purpose of manifesting his glory, and the Jesus who submits to spatio-temporal standards never tires of insisting on his unity with the heavenly Father. In principle, therefore, the *Logos,* once descended and incarnated, acts out a problematic which was inscribed already in the beginning *(en archē).* But the transfer to earth has magnified the dilemma into one of above versus below and transcendence versus contingency. His status, initially described as being God who was with God, is now more accurately defined as divinity incarnated, yet never fully naturalized in the flesh.

3. The dual aspiration to enact identity in difference, and to dramatize difference in identity, reaches a paradoxical culmination in the narration of Jesus' death. The cross, experience of extreme difference, is also the hour of glorification that is said to bring knowledge of his identity (12:27-33; 3:14; 8:28). Linguistically effected through the double entendre of "lifting up" *(hypsōthēnai),* death and glory appear to be synchronized in "the noiseless hush of *Aufhebung."*[22] With flesh being subsumed under glory, are we then to assume that death actualizes *anabasis* which brings restoration of full identity insulated from difference? Not quite, because the ascensional "lifting up" on the cross is held in distinction from the post-resurrectional Jesus' own anticipation of ascension in the traditional sense (20:17: *oupo gar anabebēka pros ton patera),* an anticipation left unfulfilled in the narrative. In the end, Fernando Segovia rightly concludes, "one does fail to find a direct description or portrayal of the

---

[21] In an earlier essay ("In the Beginning Were the Words: The Apotheosis and Narrative Displacement of the Logos," *JAAR* 58 [1990] 69-98) I argued that "the Logos signifies *the* quintessential logocentric gesture," e.g., a "posture of underived origin and transcendental presence" (522). *I* have come to realize that in John 1:1, difference is already built into identity. It is this metaphysical ambiguity, not the logocentric posture *per se, which* creates the pre-eminent philosophical problematic of the Gospel.

[22] J. D. Caputo, *Radical Hermeneutics. Repetition, Deconstruction, and the Hermeneutic Project* (Bloomington and Indianapolis: Indiana University Press, 1987) 6.

return of the Word of God from the world of human beings to the world of God, that is to say, a formal closure" to the narrative and especially to the problematic introduced in the prologue.[23] The readerly expectations with regard to the fate of the principal character are thus left in a state of abeyance. Jesus' circuit is not completed.

It is hard to escape the impression that the traditional motifs of descent and ascent belong entirely to discourse, not to narrative. Despite familiarity with the traditional motifs, the Fourth Gospel seems to be adverse to mapping out a cosmology of heavenly journeys. The one ascent which is narrated, e.g., the "lifting up" on the cross, is a thoroughly demythologized version of the ascent genre. In the absence of a mythology of heavenly journeys, the discourses on descent and ascent serve to secure the heavenly profile of the Son of Man. "The reader cannot really know who Jesus is unless Jesus is understood in terms of his 'whence' and 'whither.'"[24] Insulated from narrative and severely demythologized, descent and ascent constitute a set of coordinates in reference to which Jesus' heavenly identity is formulated. It is as man from heaven that he walks the earth, discharges the functions of his mission, and proleptically announces his return.

Etched into this seemingly commonplace scenario is an issue of metaphysical proportions. At the very beginning, the reader is confronted with obscurity, indeed forthright opaqueness. The authority of the *Logos* is defined both by oneness with God and difference from God. This ambiguous identity of the *Logos* sets the agenda for what is to come. Descent, articulated as embodiment in the flesh, inevitably enlarges the issue of separateness from divine originality. In inhabiting the human flesh, the *Logos* must carry the burden of human communication. And yet, John the baptizer reminds his disciples that "he who comes from above is above all, he who is of the earth is from the earth and speaks of the earth" (3:31), implying that the heavenly man, while on earth, speaks the language from above. Indeed, the *Logos* presents himself as the man from heaven: "I am not of this world" (8:23), he tells the Jews unequivocally.

---

[23] F. F. Segovia, "The Journeys) of the Word of God: A Reading of the Plot of the Fourth Gospel," *Fourth Gospel from a Literary Perspective*, 46.

[24] R. A. Culpepper, "The Johannine *Hypodeigma:* A Reading of John 13," *Fourth Gospel from a Literary Perspective*, 136.

On the one hand, he is obliged to concede that the Father is greater than he (14:28), while at the same time he continues to state his unity with be Father (10:30, 38; 14:11; 17:21, 23). Jesus' ascent, whether on be cross or anticipated in the future, fails to resolve the dilemma. If anything, the duality of his ascents complicates matters further. Neither the characters in the narrative nor the readers of the narrative are encouraged to undertake an ascent to heaven. Their ascent is in fact discouraged, because where Jesus goes they cannot follow (13:36). We thus conclude that the macro-coordinates circumscribe and enact the principal Johannine dilemma of a complex and duplicitous narrative: to secure the heavenly profile of the One who embarked upon a journey in the flesh.

The Metaphorical Process

We have seen that the narrator of the Fourth Gospel has devised for himself and for others a problem of perplexing philosophical intricacy. How, we must ask, does the Gospel take up its central dilemma, deal with it, negotiate it, and attempt to resolve it? Negatively, John does not "resolve" the issue by resorting to the discourse of reason. For such is the problem that it does not submit to dialectical reasoning or to logical resolutions. Heaven and earth, John the baptizer assures us, are not negotiable terms (3:31). How can there be a rapprochement between be above and the below? John's principal tool of persuasion is a dualistic structuring of language which is deliberately integrated into the Gospel's narrative and discourse sections. Upon entering into the condition of the flesh, the Logos speaks words which are both in conformity with wordly intelligibility and in excess of it. Throughout his mission on earth, his words connote tension between apparent and intended meanings.[25] It is this well-known feature of the double-entendre which is employed to deal with the metaphysical agenda.

One of the best known cases of double-entendre is acted out in Jesus' discourse with Nicodemus (3:1-21). In response to this Pharisee's confessional statement (3:2), Jesus solemnly announces, "Truly, truly, I say to you, unless one is born *anōthen,* one cannot see be kingdom of God" (3:3). It is the word

---

[25] H. Leroy, *Rätsel und Missverständnis. Ein Beitrag zur Formgeschichte des Johannesevangeliums* (Bonner Biblische Beiträge 30; Bonn: Peter Hanstein Verlag, 1968).

anōthen which proves to be a stumbling block in the conversation between Jesus
and Nicodemus. While Nicodemus understands the birth *anōthen* in the sense of
being born again, and queries about the impossibility of a second biological birth
(3:4), Jesus intends to speak of a birth from above or in the Spirit (3:5-8).

Further misunderstandings arise in the conversation between Jesus and the
Samaritan woman (4:7-26). What initially unites them is their joint concern for
water. Jesus, fatigued from his journey, is sitting by the well when the woman
comes to draw water from it. But soon a dissonance arises over the meaning of
the word "living water" *(hydōr zōn).* Whereas the woman speaks of water and
well in the literal sense, Jesus has in mind not ordinary running water, but the
kind of water that will quench thirst forever (4:14). In spite of her tentative
comprehension of Jesus' identity (4:29), the woman is never able to grasp the
intended meaning of "living water." Even the readers remain in the dark until a
narrative aside following Jesus' speech on the last day of the feast of tabernacles
brings them enlightenment (7:37-38). Only at that point are they informed that
the living water welling up from one's innermost being was meant to be the Spirit
(7:39). In "one of Jesus' few private conversations" with the disciples "outside
of the farewell speech" (4:31-34),[26] he speaks mysteriously of food in his
possession which is unknown to them (4:32: *egō brōsin echō phagein hēn
hymeis ouk oidate).* This takes the disciples by surprise because they had just
gone to the city to buy food (4:8). Food *(brōsis* or *brōma)* is the double-entendre
which evokes misunderstanding. Whereas the disciples understand the word to
mean physical nourishment, Jesus interprets it in terms of his mandate to do the
will of the One who sent him (4:34). Yet another semantic controversy surrounds
the meaning of the word "death." Jesus assures the Jews that "anyone who keeps
His words [he] shall never see death" (8:51: *thanaton ou mē theorēsē). As* far as
the Jews are concerned, death signals the termination of life (8:52-53), but what
Jesus has in mind is a cessation of living in sinfulness and the experience of new
life in the Spirit (5:24; 6:48, 68; 7:38).

"To be born *anōthen,"* "living water," "food," "death," and many other terms
denote double meanings. In all instances, the apparent meaning is deemed
inadequate, while the less obvious but intended meaning carries the blessing of

---

[26] G. R. O'Day, *Revelation in the Fourth Gospel. Narrative Mode and Theological
Claim* (Philadelphia: Fortress Press, 1986) 77.

the narrator. It is noteworthy that John's linguistic bipolarity creates an awareness that truth is not directly accessible. The deliberately crafted double-entendres cause extension of meaning at the very least and displacement of meaning at the very most. They beget misunderstandings and thereby complicate, and indeed inhibit, communication. In effect, the Johannine language of double-entendres opens up the gap of difference. This needs to be recognized before one dwells on revelation and identity.

This observation of the Johannine double-entendre can be extended to the whole semiology of symbols and signifying features which characterize Johannine language.[27] Miracles enacted as signs reinforce pressure on readers to differentiate appearance from intended significance.[28] Initially at least, signs are obstacles to immediacy. Metaphors and irony likewise institute difference through various configurations of double meaning.[29] For whether metaphor inclines more toward resemblance of meanings, or irony toward the clash of meanings, both forgo the sweet taste of presence. Both enlist readers in the task of tracking down the detours words are taking away from the straight route of literalism. Insofar as "the entire Gospel of John might be considered an extended metaphor,"[30] or as a book in which "narrative and discourse" were "bound together by an intricate network of symbolism,"[31] it communicates the differential quality of language, opening up the gap between what is said and what is meant. This needs to be recognized before one dwells on revelation and identity.

While Jesus' metaphorical discourses and symbolic actions engender

---

[27] R. A. Culpepper, *Anatomy of the Fourth Gospel. A Study in Literary Design* (Philadelphia: Fortress Press, 1983) 180-202; E. Richard, "Expressions of Double Meaning and Their Function in the Gospel of John, " NTS 31 (1984-85) 96-112.

[28] R. E. Brown, *The Gospel According to John* (2 vols; AB 29-29a; Garden City, NY: Doubleday and Company, 1966-70) 1:525-32.

[29] P. D. Duke, *Irony in the Fourth Gospel* (Atlanta, GA: John Knox, 1985); R. Kysar, "Johannine Metaphors-Meaning and Function: A Literary Case Study of John 10:1-8," *Fourth Gospel from a Literary Perspective,* 81-111; Culpepper, *Anatomy,* 165-80; O'Day, *Revelation.*

[30] Kysar, "Meaning and Function," 99.

[31] C. H. Dodd, *The Interpretation of the Fourth Gospel* (Cambridge: Cambridge University Press, 1953) 143.

difference, they likewise bespeak a desire for identity. A persistent longing
pervades the Gospel to rise above the terrestrial mundaneness of meanings. The
whole semiology of symbols and signifying tropes is enlisted into the service of
the highest aspirations. That signs are both imperative and capable of uplifting
readers above the literal meaning of the miraculous is a core conviction which
flows like an undercurrent from the wedding at Cana to the raising of Lazarus,
and on to Jesus' "lifting up" and Peter's good haul of fish. If signs in effect open
the gap of difference, they also labor to overcome it. While double-entendres
inhibit direct communication, they do so in the interest of negotiating ascending
moves from corporeality to transcendence. The climactic scene of crucifixion
both magnifies the central paradox and seeks to erase it by the figurative
movement of sublation or *Aufhebung*. In sum, the whole network of metaphors
and ironies brings dissimilarities into dramatic play with the aim of ensuring
Jesus' identity.

If the question is raised concerning the rationale of John's heavily symbolic
apparatus, one needs to recall the Gospel's principal project, e.g., its
metaphysical agenda. The dual potential of the sign to obstruct and to uplift, to
differentiate and to signify, is commensurate with the philosophical project of the
Johannine narrative. Whether metaphor communicates an intrinsic connection
between appearance and higher reality, or irony stresses dissimilarity in
similarity, both tropes are ideally suited for transacting the Johannine purpose: to
secure Jesus' identity in a thoroughly different world. As for Jesus' many
dialogues and virtual monologues, "the tactic of the Johannine discourse is
always for the answer to transpose the topic to a higher level."[32] In the ebb and
flow of the narrative, metaphoric language breaks open the human realm to
reveal the divine and invites readers to consider both the literal and the figurative
meaning. Thus, the deliberate ambiguity of language enacts the double-focused
dramatization. Signs and metaphors, in short, appeal to John because they take
one thing for another while simultaneously entertaining metaphysical
aspirations.

The Role of the Reader

The recent application of literary criticism, hailed widely as a Copernican

---

[32] Brown, *Gospel According to John,* 1:138.

turn in biblical studies, has focused more closely on the narrative text, what it is, and how it affects its readers. In the perspective of most contemporary literary practitioners, irony, metaphor, and the implied misunderstandings in John's narrative engage readers in the process of education. It is precisely due to the rhetorical function of the double-entendres, in whatever form they manifest themselves, that a course of illumination is set into motion. Through misreadings and symbolization the narrative enables the readers to grasp what the characters in the narrative fail to understand. The readers are thereby raised from the naivetés of literalism to the level of genuine enlightenment and invited "to ascend again and again to the higher plateau of meaning."[33] Thus the recurrence of misunderstandings which arise primarily over the ambiguities of language seem calculated to usher readers into the circle of privileged insiders. Theologically speaking, irony and metaphor operate as a mode of revelatory language.[34]

To be sure, literary critics of the Fourth Gospel are cognizant of the varying degrees of double-entendres and the multiple engagements of duplicitous language, of transpositions of meaning, and of perplexing distortions of time and space. Such are the demands the narrative makes on its readers that a few critics have advanced the idea of "the victimization of the implied reader"[35] Built into the narrative, Jeffrey Staley proposed, is "a strategy designed to humble those real readers who feel that they are on the inside track."[36] Although the readers may come face to face with uncomfortable conclusions concerning the person of Jesus, the opaqueness of his journey, the identity of the Beloved Disciple, and the meaning of many words and discourses, their disappointments, Staley assures us, are temporary and always in the higher interest of their readerly education. "So although the rhetorical strategy demands that the implied reader be occasionally placed in an inferior position as an outsider, the

---

[33] Culpepper, *Anatomy,* 199.

[34] O'Day, *Revelation,* 22-32.

[35] The phrase was introduced into Johannine studies by J. L. Staley, *The Print's First Kiss: A Rhetorical Investigation of the Implied Reader in the Fourth Gospel* (SBLDS 82; Atlanta: Scholars Press, 1988). Staley (95 n. 1) attributes it to J. McKee, *Literary Irony and the Literary Audience: Studies in the Victimization of the Reader in Augustan Fiction* (Amsterdam: Ropodi, 1974).

[36] Staley, *Print's First Kiss,* 105 n. 48.

implied reader does move onward and upward in his journey of faith."[37]

In some of my own studies on no Fourth Gospel, I have taken the position that in some instances at least the narrator lets irony and metaphor do their unsettling work on the characters in the narrative no less than on the readers of no narrative. In the cases of Jesus' discourse on no bread and his dialogue with the Samaritan woman, for example, I raised the question as no no advantage the readers truly have over the characters in the narration.[38] Stephen Moore, following up with a stronger reading, confessed an interest in what was within the control of the narrator no less than what might be out of his control.[39] He therefore disputed no very working hypothesis of literary criticism and reader-oriented exegesis that it was the aim of the narrative to lead "an audience through complications and deferrals to a climactic, completed understanding."[40] The reading Moore enacted suggested that the recipients of no story can well be the ultimate victims of irony.

And yet, critical readings of this kind which accord special attention to features resistant to meaning and to readerly comprehension are (still?) very much the exception. What is distinct about the bent of current literary criticism is to discern the Gospel's transparency, not its obstruction, and to affirm its coherence to the virtual exclusion of hidden contradictions. This particular literary outlook on the Gospel is concisely summarized in Culpepper's statement: "Never is the reader the victim of irony."[41] Inclusion, intimacy, and fellowship between readers and the implied author are said to be the strongest effects of Johannine double-entendres. "In the hands of others irony becomes a sword, but in the hands of our author it is more like a net in which readers are caught and drawn to the evangelist's theology and faith.[42] The general assumption is that the whole apparatus of symbolism and semiology works for the benefit of readers, enabling them to climb onto the roof and to take in the

---

[37] Ibid., 116.

[38] W. H. Kelber, "The Birth of a Beginning: John 1:1-18," *Beginnings and the Gospels (Semeia 52;* Atlanta: Scholars Press, 1990) 135-38; "In the Beginning," 88-89.

[39] S. D. Moore, *Literary Criticism and the Gospels. The Theoretical Challenge* (New Haven and London: Yale University Press, 1989) 159-70.

[40] Ibid., 160.

[41] Culpepper, *Anatomy,* 179.

[42] Ibid., 180.

whole view, if not at once, then certainly by degrees.

To keep our literary readings of the Gospel in proper perspective, we need to remind ourselves that the underlying theological, linguistic premises are in conformity with ancient, tradition-honored hermeneutical conventions. For what has typified the prevailing exegetical tradition in antiquity and through the Middle Ages was precisely the dichotomy of the literal versus the spiritual sense and the conviction that figurative language served the metaphysical welfare of the (or certain) readers. Even the two eminent theological adversaries who wrote the earliest commentaries on the Gospel, Heracleon, the disciple of Valentinus, and Origen, representative of "ecclesiastical" Christianity, were in agreement on these two principles.

To be sure, for Heracleon the literal level was theologically irrelevant, causing Origen to complain that the gnostic theologian failed to perceive "that those good words contain the shadow of future things."[43] Origen himself was persuaded that what was perceptible on the literal level required, in most instances, translation to the spiritual level.[44] Heracleon, moreover, felt that for the present the *psychics* were excluded from the privilege of full gnosis,[45] whereas Origen insisted on preaching the literal gospel, if necessary, to the common or somatic hearers, while the spiritual gospel was reserved for those capable of the highest level of insight.[46] However, notwithstanding the differences which separated Heracleon from Origen, we must not lose sight of the fact that both operated on the unchallenged assumption of the differential quality of Johannine (and all biblical) language, and both elevated certain readers to the status of privileged insiders. To be sure, both Heracleon and Origen searched for the higher meaning primarily by way of allegorizing, roaming freely through the wide world of Jewish and Christian traditions, and rarely derived the transcendental reading from the strictly intra-Johannine logic of signification and misunderstanding. But again what unites Heracleon and

---

[43] Origen, *Commentary on the Gospel According to John. Books 13-32* (The Fathers of the Church 89; Washington, D.C.: The Catholic University of America Press, 1993) 13, 61.

[44] Origen, *Commentary on the Gospel According to John. Books 1-10* (The Fathers of the Church 80; Washington, D.C.: The Catholic University of America Press, 1989) 1, 45.

[45] E. H. Pagels, *The Johannine Gospel in Gnostic Exegesis. Heracleon's Commentary on John* (SBLMS 17; Nashville & New York: Abingdon Press, 1973) 83-97.

[46] Origen, *Commentary on the Gospel According to John. Books 1-10,* 1, 43.

Origen with the modern literary critics is the metaphysical premise of the letter and the Spirit and its hermeneutical implications for the readers, a premise deeply etched into the agenda of the Gospel and shared by a multitude of Christian readers through the ages.

Given the metaphysical and metaphorical readings, past and present, we must return to the modern insistence on the benign effects of Johannine double-entendre and symbolic language. Heracleon and Origen, we remember, were less generous about the fate of all the readers. Both claimed that the spiritual meaning was not open to just anyone. Even if we were to agree with the current literary mode that the "gospel's use of irony sweetens and spices the fellowship between reader and narrator,"[47] we need to realize that John employs the language of ambiguity not only to include readers among the circle of believers but also to exclude other characters in the narrative. In the philosophical tradition it was Kierkegaard who had viewed irony less as a catalyst of illumination and more as a tool of limitation, indeed of destruction.[48] That truth was never fully transparent and irony the last word on it was, in Kierkegaard's view, the message of Socrates. The last effect of Socratic irony was to destroy at their deepest roots the pretensions, corrupt anticipations, and misunderstandings perpetrated by classical Hellenism. Because "truth demanded a silence before again lifting up its voice," Socrates "was exclusively negative"[49] in carrying out his "destructive activity."[50] "Thus irony is the brand, the two-edged sword, which he wielded over Hellas like a destroying angel."[51] Kierkegaard could go so far as to compare the role of irony to the Christian, Pauline skepticism of the Law which purports to consume and burn away the natural man. If the example of Kierkegaard seems far-fetched, it may serve to make us mindful of irony's potential in functioning not only as the midwife of truth but also as the perpetrator of negativity, of cruelty even.

---

[47] Culpepper, *Anatomy*, 180.

[48] S. Kierkegaard, *The Concept of Irony, With Constant Reference to Socrates* (trans. L. M. Capel; London: Collins, 1966).

[49] Ibid., 232.

[50] Ibid., 236.

[51] Ibid., 234.

The Victimization of the Jews

We have taken pains to sketch the Gospel's linguistic implementation of its metaphysical agenda, because this other legacy it has bequeathed to Christianity, anti-Judaism, plays itself out in this philosophically ambitious and linguistically intricate narrative. "The Jews" are the ultimate victims in John's thoroughly dichotomous dramatic world. Their marginalization is coexistent with the theological aspirations of the narrative. Whether the protagonist strives to carry the burden of the flesh while aspiring to manifest glory, or whether the discourses address audiences from below while seeking to communicate a presence from above, or whether the narrative runs the course of signifying differences while thirsting after the metaphysical signified—the narratological, linguistic, and theological dramatization of the Johannine agenda thrives on the marginalization, indeed demonization, of the Jews.

On his first journey to Jerusalem, Jesus performs a powerful deed of purification in the temple (2:13-22) which elicits a response both from the disciples and the Jews. The disciples, relying on their scriptural memory, think they have the clue to what transpired in the temple, but their insight does not penetrate to the deeper significance of the event (2:17). The Jews ironically introduce the notion of the sign (2:18), unaware, it seems, of its inherent potential for ambiguity. What they are asking for is in effect "an authorisation which will show the lawfulness of his [Jesus'] action."[52] The Johannine Jesus promptly responds with a saying of the temple's destruction and reconstruction, forcing the double meaning of the temple and playing it out against the Jews (2:19). Pondering the saying on the literal level, the Jews stumble over the significance of the temple's rebuilding in three days (2:20). Instead of reaching for a different, a figurative, meaning, they remain stuck on the literal level whose implausibility they readily acknowledge. It is true, the disciples themselves fail to catch the double-entendre. But we the readers are admitted into the special meaning of Jesus' saying (2:21), and we are assured, moreover, of the disciples' eventual enlightenment (2:22). It is the Jews who are left out and behind.

On his second journey to Jerusalem, Jesus performs the first sign in the south

---

[52] R. Bultmann, *The Gospel of John. A Commentary* (trans. G. R. Beasley-Murray et al.; Philadelphia: Westminster Press, 1971) 124.

by healing a lame man at a pool near the sheep gate (5:1-18). The questions
raised do not pertain to the cure itself but rather to the timing of the healing on a
Sabbath day. Initially, therefore, the dispute triggered by the Jews is over the
sacred status of the Sabbath (5:9b-10). But it is soon evident that the offense
caused by the sign exceeds by far the issue of Sabbath violation. Jesus' own
interpretation makes the point that the healing is meant to reveal the working of
the Father as well as that of himself (5:17). The Jews take this statement to be
problematic to the core because it unmasks Jesus' claim to divinity (5:18: *ison
heauton poiōn to theō*). To them the healing constitutes not only a transgression
of the Law but the far more serious offense of the abrogation of monotheism.
This time, the Jews fully recognize the extraordinary implications of the sign,
and they repudiate Jesus' metaphysical postulation as utter blasphemy.

In the case of Jesus' feeding of the five thousand on a Galilean mountain at
Passover, we the readers have the narrator's assurance that the people recognized
its character as a sign (6:1-13, 14). And yet, the crowd's interpretation falls short
of the narrator's intended meaning, for when in response to the feeding the
people identify Jesus as the expected Mosaic Prophet-Messiah (6:14-15),[53] their
interpretation is inadequate at best and inappropriate at most. In the subsequent
discourse (6:25-51), Jesus proceeds to spell out the implications of the feeding
sign. One must learn, he asserts, to draw a distinction between perishable and
imperishable food (6:27: *tēn brōsin ten apollymenēn-tēn brōsin tēn menousan*),
for only the latter is capable of granting eternal life. It is a distinction not without
interest to the Jews, for they have a clear recollection of the heavenly bread their
fathers received and ate in the wilderness (6:31). But when Jesus identifies
himself as the heavenly bread (6:35-40), they are scandalized (6:41). Their
familiarity extends to the manna in the wilderness and to Jesus, the son of Joseph,
whose father and mother they know (6:42), but they cannot apprehend the ironic
transference of the meaning of bread and follow Jesus onto the higher ground of
his identification with the heavenly bread.

As if the metaphorical equation of Jesus with the heavenly bread were not
paradoxical enough, the bread he offers is further specified to be his own flesh,

---

[53] W. A. Meeks, *The Prophet-King. Moses Traditions and the Johannine Christology*
(NovTSup 14; Leiden: E. J. Brill, 1967) 87-91; Martyn, *History & Theology,* 123-28.

and the eating of his flesh (and the drinking of his blood) is recommended in starkly cannibalistic terms (6:53-54). No sooner is the audience introduced to the difference between material versus spiritual food than it is confronted with the identity of Jesus with the heavenly bread; and no sooner is the audience confronted with Jesus the heavenly bread than it is asked to commune with Jesus in terms of his flesh and blood. Earthly and heavenly dimensions, corporeal and spiritual aspirations, difference and identity are intermingled to the point of producing highly contradictory effects. Little wonder that not only the Jews are scandalized (6:52), but many of the disciples cease following Jesus (6:60-61). The more metaphor and irony are allowed to do their divisive work, the more the characters in the narrative are marginalized.

While in Jerusalem at the feast of tabernacles, Jesus announces that "For a little while longer I am with you, then I go *(hypagō)* to Him who sent me" (7:33). This statement about his intended departure leaves the tees in a state of puzzlement. Incredulously they ask whether he was going *(poreuesthai)* into the diaspora to teach the Greeks (7:35). The tension is between the transcendental meaning of going *(hypagein)* to the Father and the literal meaning of going *(poreuesthai)* into the diaspora. At a later point, sensing the metaphorical implications of Jesus' language about "going," they speculate on suicide (8:2122). That "to go" in Jesus' vocabulary connotes his return to the Father is forever concealed to them.

To be sure, Peter himself falls victim to a similar misunderstanding. When Jesus announces to his disciples that he was going *(hypagein)* where they could not come (13:33), Peter insists on following him *(akolouthesai)* immediately. He, no less than the Jews, fails to grasp the meaning of Jesus' going to a place where nobody on earth can follow him. But whereas Peter is rehabilitated (21:15-19), the tees are not.

The narrative leaves no doubt about the fact that there are those among the Jews who came to believe in Jesus (8:31). But even they, it seems, remain subjected to the ambiguities of Jesus' language. When he speaks to them about the observance of his words, about knowledge of truth and the acquisition of freedom, a misunderstanding arises above all over the ambiguous meaning of freedom (8:31-39). "The truth," Jesus maintains, "shall make you free" (8:32: *he alētheia eleutherōsei hymas)*. The Jews respond by pointing out that they were Abraham's offsprings and hence enslaved to no one. They clearly take freedom to mean liberation from the social and political forces of oppression, whereas Jesus thinks of what he perceives to be the "truly" (8:36: *ontōs*) liberating experience of freedom from sin. To the Jews the metaphorically extended meaning of freedom remains incomprehensible.

When in the ensuing discourse the Jews appeal to the fatherhood of Abraham, their claim runs into a challenge of unprecedented hostility. If they were truly Abraham's children, the Johannine Jesus states, they would be furnishing proof by recognizing him (Jesus) instead of seeking to kill him. Since they fail to acknowledge him who told them what he had seen with and heard from God, they must be the children of the Devil rather than of God. Their father does not know the truth; he is "the father of lies" (8:44: *pseustēs estin kai ho patēr autou*) and "a murderer from the beginning" *(anthrōpoktonos ēn ap' archēs)*. At this point, the Gospel's animosity toward the Jews has reached an unparalleled level of intensity, which in itself turns out to be profoundly paradoxical. After the narrative has typified the Jews as those who fail to rise above literalism to the metaphysical level of meaning, it proceeds to trace this very proclivity to its own metaphysical origin. Their inability to comprehend the signs, to hear the language from above, and to recognize identity in difference is itself claimed to be metaphysically rooted in the primordial Father of lies. Manifestly, the narrator has resorted to a metaphysical dualism which purports to demonize the Jews and to challenge, "their status as God's people."[54]

The last of the signs, the raising of Lazarus (11:1-44), unquestionably meets with the most positive response among the Jews. Many of the them who learned of the events surrounding Lazarus come to believe in Jesus (11:45; 12:9-11). While it remains unclear whether they grasp the fuller christological implication of the raising which signifies Jesus himself as the resurrection and life (11:25), they come to meet him and bear witness to him as he enters Jerusalem riding on a donkey (12:17-18).

But if we have thought that the narrative drift toward the exclusion of the Jews was being reversed, we are soon to be disappointed. For in anticipating the crucifixion, the narrator takes pains to make the point that the Jews are barred from the central event of *Aufhebung*. Three times the Johannine Jesus speaks in mysteriously metaphorical language about his being "lifted up." Nicodemus is

---

[54] Brown, *Gospel According to John*, 1:363.

the first person who is informed that the "Son of Man must be lifted up" (3:14: *hypsōthēnai dei ton hyion tou anthrōpou*). Speaking in the temple of Jerusalem, Jesus tells the Jews that they are the ones who will lift him up (8:28). Finally, in his last public speech, he once again anticipates the event of being lifted up (12:32). At this point, the veil of obscurity is lifted ever so slightly to allow readers a glimpse of the kind of death Jesus was to die (12:33). As the double meaning of *hypsōthēnai* dawns on the readers, they can have imaginary access to the transcending ascent which is being acted out in the moment of fatal obstruction. To the multitude of the Jews, however, the act of "lifting up" remains unintelligible. Since the Christ is to remain forever on earth, his presence is unambiguously terrestrial, and the thought of his death, let alone the paradoxical sublation of his death on the cross, is irreconcilable with the identity of the Messiah (12:34).

Following Jesus' last public speech, the narrator reemphasizes the unbelief of the Jews. In spite of the demonstration of the many signs, "they did not believe in him" (12:37: *ouk episteuon eis auton*). Not content with this rather pessimistic comment at the closing of Jesus' public ministry, the narrator feels compelled to offer a rationalization for the ineffectiveness of the signs. Citing Isaiah's words concerning the blinding of eyes and the hardening of hearts, the narrative attributes the fate of the Jews to divine causality (12:40; Isa 6:10). The negative purpose clause, *hina mē*, leaves no doubt that the Jews were struck with incomprehension so as not to be able to experience healing. "In John's rendition it is God who has blinded the eyes of the people."[55] Whereas earlier the negativity of the Jews was reinforced by attribution to the *archē* of the Devil, here at the close of the public ministry it is traced to the realm of divine will and causality. In either case, the fate of the Jews is presented as being predetermined and unalterably fixed in metaphysical primordiality.

Divine causality aside, the Jews are portrayed as people who have no place in the set of theological longitudes and latitudes which define the ministry of Jesus. They do not know where he is from, what the significance of his signs is, and where he is going. Jesus' heavenly *katabasis* (8:14; 9:29), the signification of the *semeia* (12:37), the apotheosis on the cross (12:34), and his anticipated heavenly *anabasis* (8:14) remain closed to them. They are being shut out from

---

[55] Ibid., 1:486.

the macro-coordinates which circumscribe the narrative world of the Fourth
Gospel. To be sure, the difficulties enscribed in John's metaphysical agenda
affect all characters in the narrative and the readers as well. But no one
encounters greater obstacles than the Jews because the metaphorical dynamics
entailed in John's metaphysical agenda are primarily played out against them. Or,
in different words, the marginalization of the Jews is a growing co-presence in
the narrative development of signification, metaphor, and irony. Perceived to be
from below (8:23) and unwilling to seek the glory from above (5:44), they live,
in Culpepper's perceptive formulation, "on the wrong side of John's dualism."[56]

Epilogue

Theologically, the gospel has been read and is being read in the classic sense
as advocate of love, manifested in the sending of the Son, and as champion of
truth, consummated in the fullness of metaphysical presence. So deeply rooted is
this comprehension in the Christian tradition that the so-called Copernican
revolution brought about by literary criticism has by and large merely succeeded
in reinforcing the ethically and metaphysically sanctioned reading of the Gospel.

The narrative has set high standards for love as a self-giving on behalf of
brothers and sisters. "Greater love has no one than this, that one lay down his life
for his friends" (15:13). It is, however, more than a matter of practical
observation that love fulfills itself in the inner circle of friends. This is in fact the
meaning of the *new commandment* (John 13:34: *entolē kainē;* cf. also 15:12)
that the members of the Johannine community love one another as Christ loved
them. Conspicuously absent is the counsel to love God, which is the great
commandment in Deut 6:4-9, and to love one's neighbor, which is set forth in
Lev 19:18. This is all the more striking since the Synoptics have combined love
of God and love of neighbor into the treat Commandment (Mark 12:28-34; Matt
22:34-40; Luke 10:25-28) . Absent from the Johannine narrative is also the love
of strangers, e.g., foreigners, which is commanded in Lev 19:34, and the love of
the enemy, which is enjoined in Exod 23:4-5 and in Prov 25:21, as well as in
Matt 5:44 and Luke 6:27, 35. In the Fourth Gospel love is strictly limited to the
selfless giving of one's self within the community of believers.

---

[56] Culpepper, *Anatomy*, 129.

The same narrative which upholds love as the standard for intra-Christian conduct increasingly dramatizes the status of the revs as the demonic other. It is easy to discern that the Gospel shapes and sanctions a cultural identity vis-à-vis the synagogue. But the depth of Johannine anti-Jewishness is not fathomable on the historical, sociological, or rhetorical level. Literary criticism, no less than historical criticism, has failed to confront us with the theological and ethical crux of the dilemma. Historical criticism has neutralized the Gospel's violently exclusionary features and tranquilized our memory of their appropriation for further hatred. No doubt, in reader-oriented approaches to the gospels, "the reader emerges as the hero or heroine whose actions and progress are central."[57] It is, however, noteworthy that ethical concern for intratextual characters is alive and well in other branches of critical theory. Feminist criticism, for example, has exposed gender construction in literature and interpretation and sharply raised our consciousness about the marginalization of the female as the dominated "other."[58] But we have as yet not applied ourselves to scrutinizing the literary construction of the "Jews" with a theoretical sophistication equal to the best in feminist criticism. Hence, keen interest in the metaphysical welfare of the reader has clouded our conscience and repressed awareness of the enforced closure toward the Jewish other. Above all, we tended to suppress the fact that metaphysics and repudiation of the other are tightly knotted and calamitously intertwined in John's narrative.

What is at stake, finally, is metaphysics and ethics, or perhaps more to the point, the exclusionary implications of metaphysics. Having constructed the dilemma of difference and identity, the narrative ultimately desires *Aufhebung* of difference in transcendental unity. To this end, it sets into motion a metaphorical process which enforces the metaphysical distinction of the letter and the Spirit. But the language of double-entendre, while allegedly working well for the readers, plays havoc with the welfare of others. For in this intricately metaphorical and ambitiously metaphysical narrative the Jews are

---

[57] Moore, *Literary Criticism and the Gospels,* 83.

[58] K. G. Cannon, ed., *Interpretation for Liberation (Semeia* 47; Atlanta: Scholars Press, 1989); *L.* M. Russell, ed., *Feminist Interpretation of the Bible* (Philadelphia: Westminster, 1985). As regards the Gospel of John, see the contribution by Sandra M. Schneiders in the present volume.

made to play the role of the letter—the letter which must be overcome in the interest of the Spirit. Put bluntly, the Gospel has taught us to think of the other by way of negation. It has been a contributor to the fateful premise that Judaism was in carnal servitude to the letter, "taking signs of spiritual things for the things themselves."[59] Philosophically, the narrative has not been able to tolerate the pressures of sustaining difference in identity. An insatiable longing for identity endeavored to override the nature of difference. Morally, the Gospel's quest for life beyond difference has been neglectful of the condition it has created for the other. In its passion for self-identity it has trampled upon alterity.

---

[59] Augustine, *On Christian Doctrine* (trans. D. W. Robertson. Jr.; New York: Macmillan, London: Collier Macmillan, 1958) 3.6.

Chapter Seven

John 20:11-18:

The Encounter of the Easter Jesus
with Mary Magdalene—A Transformative Feminist Reading

SANDRA M. SCHNEIDERS

Let me begin this paper by fulfilling the primary instructions that the contributors to this project received from Professor Fernando F. Segovia, namely, to be "up front about our perspective, objective, and strategy" so that the role of the reader/interpreter in the reading offered will be clear. My perspective on the biblical text in general and the johannine Gospel in particular is that of a believing feminist interpreter who regards the text as potentially revelatory and revelatory experience as personally transformative. I take completely seriously the original conclusion of John's Gospel in 20:30-31, which says that this text was written to enlighten and strengthen the faith of the reader in order that the believer may be transformed, that is, might have eternal life. My objective as an interpreter is to collaborate with and to serve that basic intent of the literature itself by interpreting the text in such wise that it is able to exercise its transformative power on the reader.

My strategy for achieving a transformative interpretation involves two conscious commitments. First, I aim to achieve *a* (not *the*) complete or integrated reading of the whole text rather than an exegesis of fragments, which means that my reading of the Mary Magdalene episode should make sense of that episode in itself but also in the context of the whole of the Resurrection narrative in John (chap. 20) and eventually within the whole of the Gospel. This integrated reading, if it is to be a transformative one, should be both faithful to the text and creatively interactive with contemporary religious concerns. Secondly, I am concerned to expose patriarchal and androcentric bias in the text when such is evident and in the history of interpretation where it is rampant and to counteract this bias by a consciously feminist approach to the text. In actual practice, my strategy is interdisciplinary, making use of historical, literary, and theological methods in the service of an agenda of transformation. In other words, the overarching perspective from which I am reading the biblical text is feminist spirituality and my methodology is essentially interdisciplinary.

Placing the Mary Magdalene Episode within John 20

The Mary Magdalene episode includes vv. 1-2 and vv. 11-18: the former recount Mary's discovery of the empty tomb on Easter morning and her report to Simon Peter and the other disciple (immediately identified in an obvious redactional move as the Beloved Disciple) that (the body of) the Lord had been taken away; the latter recount the appearance of the glorified Jesus to Mary. This account must first be situated within John 20 as a whole, which is the johannine Easter narrative. As has often been remarked by commentators, the Fourth Gospel does not need a resurrection narrative[1] in the same sense that the synoptic Gospels do, because in John the death of Jesus, his lifting up on the cross, is his glorification[2] and he does not, therefore, require divine vindication after a shameful execution. In fact, as I will try to show, the primary purpose of chap. 20 is not to tell the reader what happened to Jesus after his death but to explore, through the paradigmatic and foundational experiences of the disciples, the effect on and meaning for believers of Jesus' glorification. Elsewhere I have suggested that there are two sides to the pascal event in John: *glorification* is what happens to Jesus on the cross; resurrection is the communication to Jesus' disciples of his pascal glory through his return to them in the Spirit.[3] When Jesus says in 11:25, "I am the Resurrection" rather than I am the resurrected one or the one who will rise, he describes the role of his glorification in the life of believers whom he indwells rather than something which occurred in his own life.

---

[1] See, e.g., C. F. Evans, *Resurrection and the New Testament* (Studies in Biblical Theology, 2nd series 12; London: SCM, 1970) 116.

[2] See John 3:14; 8:28; 12:32, 34 on the "lifting up" and 12:16, 23, 28; 13:31-32 on the "glorification."

[3] S. M. Schneiders, *The Johannine Resurrection Narrative: An Exegetical and Theological Study of John 20 as a Synthesis of Johannine Spirituality* (Ann Arbor: University Microfilms International, 1982) 97-141.

Chap. 20 is divided into two parts. The first, vv. 1-18, takes place in the garden of the tomb before dawn on Easter morning; the second, vv. 19-29, takes place somewhere in Jerusalem where the community of Jesus' disciples is gathered on Easter evening and the following Sunday. The first part is governed by the question, *"Where* is the Lord?" while the second part is concerned with forming and missioning the community of the New Covenant once that all important question has been satisfactorily answered.

The theme of Part I is announced by Mary Magdalene in v. 2. Having seen that the stone has been removed from the tomb, she runs to Simon Peter and his companion and announces that "the Lord has been removed" and that "we do not know *where"* he is. As Donatian Mollat pointed out many years ago, the adverbs *pou* and *hopou* ("where") have a thematic importance in John's Gospel.[4] Both occur very frequently (18 and 30 times, respectively) and most often in theologically important contexts. The first question addressed to Jesus in John is that of the first two disciples, "Rabbi, where do you dwell?" (1:38). A principal difference between Jesus and his enemies in John is that he knows where he is from and where he is going and they do not (see 8:14). His enemies cannot go where he goes (e.g., 7:34, 36; 8:21, 22), but his true disciples and servants can (e.g., 14:3, 4; 17:24). In the Last Discourse(s)[5] the question of where Jesus is going becomes central (14:5). While Jesus is in the world, he is the Light of the world and those who follow him walk securely, knowing where they are going, but in the dark hour of the passion, his disciples do not know where Jesus has gone or how to follow him (9:4). Mary Magdalene voices the question of all disciples caught in the pre-dawn darkness of the scandal of the cross, "Where is the Lord?" In fact, the "where" of Jesus in John is not primarily spatial or geographical location. It denotes indwelling, the communion between Jesus and God and between Jesus and his disciples. Where Jesus is is in the bosom of the Father. He comes into the world to give the power of divine

---

[4] D. Mollat, "La découverte du tombeau vide (Jn 20, 1-9)," *Assemblées du Seigneur* 221 (1969) 90-100.

[5] Fernando F. Segovia in *The Farewell of the Word: The Johannine Call to Abide* (Minneapolis: Fortress Press, 1991) has made a strong case for the unity of John 13-16 which many commentators have treated as a composite of disparate discourses. Although I find Segovia's position persuasive, I am not taking a position on the question here since it is not significant for my own argument.

filiation to his disciples. He then departs again to resume his primordial glory in the presence of God and returns to initiate his disciples into that glory. Until the final phase, that is, until Jesus returns to his own, the darkness of the hour envelops all.

The answer to the question "Where is the Lord?" is given in two stages in Part One of chap. 20. In vv. 3-10 the Beloved Disciple, upon seeing the sign, the face cloth of the New Moses definitively rolled up and laid aside, comes to believe in the glorification. Unlike Simon Peter, who remains uncomprehending with regard to what he sees in the tomb, the Beloved Disciple "sees and believes" (20:8), a virtually certain linguistic indication of the presence of a *sēmeion* (a revelatory sign) in John.[6] The Beloved Disciple knows that Jesus' historical presence among them has ended in his definitive ascent into the presence of God through his glorification on the cross. The glory of Jesus is no longer veiled in his earthly humanity or in the ambiguity of his physical death. A new dispensation has begun. But neither disciple yet understands the Scripture about Jesus' resurrection (see 20:9), that is, Jesus' return to his own. The first part of the answer to the question "Where is the Lord?" is that Jesus is in God. His glorification is his return to the Father, his repossession of the glory that he had with God before the world was made (17:5). The second part of the answer, however, is that Jesus who is glorified in God has also returned to his own. "I go away and I come to you," he had promised in 14:28.[7] The resurrection, the return of Jesus to his own, is revealed in the encounter between Jesus and Mary Magdalene in vv. 11-18.

The Structure of John 20:11-18 and Its Position in the Tradition

Two preliminary considerations which are important for the interpretation of the Mary Magdalene scene concern the literary structure of the pericope and the place of the Johannine account in the theological tradition history of the

---

[6] I presented this exegesis in greater detail in the article, "The Face Veil: A Johannine Sign (John 20:1-10)," *BTB* 8 (1983) 94-97.

[7] It is important to note that both verbs in this text are in the present: *hypagō kai epchomai pros hymas*. It could perhaps be paraphrased as follows: "My going away [by glorification on the cross] is my coming to you [in resurrection or as the resurrection and the life]."

resurrection appearances.

Structurally, the episode can be divided into three sections, each governed by a thematic participle. The first section, vv. 11-15, stands under the sign of *klaiousa*, "weeping," which occurs at the very beginning of that section. Mary stands outside the tomb, weeping.[8] The second section, v. 16, is governed by *strapheisa*, "turning," which occurs exactly in the middle of the verse as the pivot between Jesus' address to Mary and her response to him. This turning, as we will see, is not a physical action but a conversion of the pre-Easter disciple away from the "things that lie behind" and toward the glorified Jesus, the only true Teacher. The third section, vv. 17-18, culminates in *aggelousa*, "announcing," which occurs at the end of the scene when Mary goes to the community to proclaim that she has seen the Lord and to deliver the easier kerygma that he has entrusted to her. We will take up each of these sections in more detail shortly. But first, it is necessary to situate this pericope theologically and ecclesiologically.

Until quite recently, post-patristic commentators have, virtually to a man (and I use the word designedly), treated the appearance to Mary Magdalene as a minor, private, personal, or unofficial encounter between Jesus and his (hysterical?) female follower, in which he kindly consoles her before making his official and public Easter appearances to male witnesses and commissioning them to carry on his mission in the world.[9] More recently, commentators, under the influence of feminist scholarship, have tended to recognize the raw sexism of this traditional interpretation, which ignores the plain content and intent of the johannine text, because patriarchal bias and the ecclesiastical power agenda blinded the interpreters to the apostolic identity of a woman witness and its potential repercussions on contemporary Church order.[10]

---

[8] "Wept" or "weeping" occurs four times in the five verses of this section: v. 11 (2); v. 13; v. 15.

[9] See, e.g., R. E. Brown, *The Virginal Conception and Bodily Resurrection of Jesus* (London and Dublin: Geoffrey Chapman, 1973) 101, n. 170; X. Leon-Dufour, *Resurrection de Jesus et message Pascal* (Parole de Dieu; Paris: Seuil, 1971) 272; A. George, "Les récits d'apparitions aux onze à partir de Luc 24, 26-53," in *La Resurrection du Christ et l'exégèse moderne* (Lectio Divina 50; Paris: Cerf, 1969) 76.

[10] For a summary of the tradition of interpretation and an excellent marshalling of the data for reinterpretation, see G. O'Collins and D. Kendall, "Mary Magdalene as Major

Although I cannot mount the entire argument in this brief presentation, it should suffice to point out that the tradition that the first appearance of the risen Jesus was to Mary Magdalene, either alone or with women companions, is attested in Matthew 28:9-10, in the Markan appendix of 16:9-10, as well as in John. It is most likely that John and Matthew, at least, represent literarily independent traditions, while Mark conflates a variety of traditions. In conjunction with the agreement of all four Gospels that women were the primary and/or exclusive witnesses of the death, burial, and empty tomb,[11] the multiply attested tradition that the first resurrection appearance was to Mary Magdalene must be judged as probably authentically historical.[12] This is especially so because the Mary Magdalene tradition rivaled the Lukan and Pauline tradition to the effect that the Easter protophany was to Peter and would surely have been suppressed if that had been possible.

The rivalry between Peter and Mary Magdalene is vividly detailed in the extra-canonical literature of the first Christian centuries, such as *The Gospel of Peter, The Secret Gospel of Mark,* the Coptic *Gospel of Thomas, The Gospel of Mark, The Wisdom of Jesus Christ,* and others which François Bovon reviewed in a 1984 article in *New Testament Studies.*[13] Bovon suggests that this literature was declared heterodox less because of its doctrinal content than because of the embarrassing priority among the disciples, and especially in relation to Peter, that it assigns to Mary Magdalene. In any case, it is clear from the text itself that the Fourth Gospel intends to present Mary Magdalene as the recipient of the first Easter christophany upon which the pascal faith of the johannine community was based, as Luke's community's faith rested on the appearance to Peter, the Gentile churches on that to Paul, and the Jerusalem community's on the appearances to James and the Eleven. According to John, it is Mary

---

Witness to Jesus' Resurrection," *TS* 48 (1987) 631-646.

[11] Matt 27:55-56, 61; 28:1-8. Mark 15:40-41, 47; 16:1-8. Luke 23:49, 55-56; 24:1-10. John 19:25-30; 20:1-2. Interestingly enough, John is the only Gospel that does not explicitly state that the burial was witnessed by the woman/women, although this is clearly implied by the fact that Mary Magdalene knows the location of the tomb on Easter morning.

[12] Brown, even in his early and already cited work *(Virginal Conception,* 101 n. 170), suggests that the tradition of the appearance to Mary Magdalene, although "minor" and not the basis of apostolic witness, was very possibly historical.

[13] F. Bovon, "Le privilège pascal de Marie-Madeleine," *NTS* 30 (1984) 50-62.

Magdalene to whom the glorified Jesus entrusted the pascal kerygma in its characteristically johannine form, whom he sent to announce that Easter message to the community of disciples, and who fulfilled successfully that apostolic commission so that the disciples in John, unlike those in Luke who dismissed the testimony of the women returning from the empty tomb (Luke 24:11), were fully prepared to recognize and accept Jesus' appearance in their midst that evening (John 20:20). From every point of view and according to every criterion developed in the New Testament, Mary Magdalene is, in town's Gospel, the apostolic witness upon whom the pascal faith of the community was founded.

SECTION 1: HOPELESS SUFFERING AND SPIRITUAL BLINDNESS

Let us turn now to the first section of the Mary Magdalene episode. This is a highly symbolic scene. It is still dark: the pre-dawn obscurity noted in v. 1 seems still to preside at least over Mary's inner landscape if not over the garden itself.[14] Only John places the tomb of Jesus in a garden and describes Mary's ironic mistaking of Jesus for the gardener. His address to her as "woman" and her action of "peering" through her tears into the tomb expressed by *parekypsen*—a word that occurs rarely in the New testament[15] and, strikingly, in the LXX of the Canticle of Canticles 2:9 in describing the search for the Beloved—alerts the reader to the fact that this garden setting is intended to evoke both the creation account in Genesis, where God walks and talks with the first couple in the garden (Gen 2:15-17; 3:8) and promises salvation through a woman (Wen 3:15), and the Canticle of Canticles, which, by the time this Gospel was written, was understood to be the hymn of the covenant between Israel and Yahweh. In this garden of new creation and new covenant, Jesus who is both the promised liberator of the New Creation and the spouse of the New Israel encounters the woman who is, symbolically, the johannine community, the Church, the new People of God.

---

[14] See C. Combet-Galland, "L'Aube encore obscure: Approche sémiotique de Jean 20," *Foi et Vie* (Cahier biblique 26; Septembre 1987) 17-25.

[15] Actually, it occurs only here and in 20:5, where it describes the Beloved Disciple looking into the tomb before the arrival of Simon Peter, as well as in Luke 24:12 which is a western non-interpolation very possibly dependent on John or on a common source.

But Mary is distraught, overcome with hopeless sorrow. She is so fixated on the loss of the body of Jesus, which she obviously identifies exhaustively with Jesus himself, that she does not even register surprise at being addressed by angelic messengers. Like the cherubim in Exod 25:22 and 38:7-8 who sit one on either end of the mercy seat of the Ark of the Covenant, these angels in white sit "one at the head and one at the feet where the body of Jesus had lain" (v. 12). Mary is seeking Jesus, a quintessentially positive enterprise in John's Gospel, but her grief has spiritually blinded her, rendered her incapable of revelation even when Jesus himself stands before her and speaks to her. She does not recognize him. The evangelist indulges in delicious irony in having Mary identify Jesus as precisely who he is, the gardener, while completely missing the symbolic point of her own materially correct identification. Jesus challenges her weeping, trying to re-focus her distraught attention from his physical body to his person with the question, "Whom [not what] do you seek?" (v. 15). But Mary remains fixed in her obsession, again interchanging "him" who is missing with the "body" which is missing just as she had interchanged "the Lord" and "the stone" in reporting the body missing in v. 2. In this first section of the pericope, under the sign of *klaiousa,* that is, blinding spiritual sadness and hopelessness, the evangelist dramatically prepares the reader to accept a new mode of Jesus' presence. To do this one must surrender the obsessional fixation on the physical presence of the earthly Jesus and prepare to cross the threshold from the economy of history into that of the resurrection.

SECTION 2: CONVERSION

The second section of the pericope is comprised of a single verse, one of the most moving in the New Testament. The utter simplicity and symmetry of verse 16 makes the point with lapidary eloquence. "Jesus said to her, 'Mary.' Turning [*strapheisa*] she said to him, in Hebrew, 'Rabbouni.'" The turning, as has been said, is obviously not physical. Already in v. 14, after Mary responded to the angels with a repetition of her lament that "they have taken away my Lord," we are told, "And saying this she turned back (*estraphē eis ta opisō*) and saw Jesus standing." Two things are to be noted. First, the phrase usually translated "around" or "back" (*eis ta opisō*) means literally "toward the things that lie behind" or "backwards." Second, as she turns away from the angels, she faces Jesus and speaks with him. Consequently, when Jesus speaks her name, she is already face to face with him. Her "turning" in v. 16 in response to his address, now not qualified as "backwards" or "around" but simply as turning, is the second member of the "turning and turning again," the "turning away" and "turning back," the apostasy and conversion, that the word *šûb* in the book of Jeremiah captures so well.[16]

What Mary does, spiritually, by insisting that the absence of Jesus' dead body constitutes the absence of the living person of Jesus, is to turn back, or to turn toward what lies behind, namely the dispensation which came to a close with the glorification of Jesus on the cross. In the historical context of the johannine community, it is probably also to turn back toward the synagogue, toward religious experience governed by the coordinates of Judaism, toward Moses as teacher of the way. When Jesus speaks her name, as most commentators have recognized, he is calling his own by name (10:3). Mary did not, as some have suggested, recognize Jesus by the sound of his voice in the ordinary sense of the word, for she had already spoken with him, heard his physical voice, without recognizing him (v. 15). It is being called by name that effects the conversion. Jesus knows his own as the Father knows him and he knows the Father (10:14-15). He calls his own sheep by name and they know his voice and they follow him (10:3-5). Consequently, the evangelist makes certain that the reader does not miss the significance of Mary's response, "Rabbouni." He tells us she spoke in Hebrew and that the word means, "Teacher." Throughout the Fourth Gospel, beginning with the Prologue in which the reader is told proleptically that the Law came through Moses but that grace and truth came through Jesus Christ (1:17), a major question is "Who is the true teacher of the way of salvation?" "Of whom are you (the reader) a disciple?" "Do you look to Moses or to Jesus?" A choice must be made, as was dramatically presented in the story of the Man Born Blind, who asks his Jewish questioners, "Do you also want to become his [Jesus'] disciples?" and they emphatically choose Moses while the healed man chooses Jesus (9:27-34) and

---

[16] The standard exploration of this theme is the monograph of W. L. Holladay, *The Root ŠÛBH in the Old Testament, with Particular Reference to its Usages in Covenantal Contexts* (Leiden: Brill, 1958). D. Mollat ("La conversion chez saint Jean," in *L'espérance du royaume* [Parole de Vie; Tours: Marne, 1966] 55-78), explored the relevance of this to John's Gospel.

his parents try to remain neutral (9:20-21). Here, Mary, symbolic representative of the New Israel, the johannine community and the readers, makes the salvific choice: Jesus, and Jesus alone, is the Teacher, even—according to John—for the Jews.[17]

The third section of the Mary Magdalene pericope contains the notoriously difficult v. 17, which begins with Jesus' prohibition, *mē mou haptou,* translated most often as "Do not hold on to me" (cf. NRSV and NIV) or "Do not cling to me," followed by the even more difficult reference to Jesus' ascension to the Father. If one puts aside, as I think we must, the temptation to interpret this text in John in the light of Matt 28:9, where the women clasp the feet of the risen Jesus and worship him, and stick to what the text actually says rather than imagining Mary's psychological responses, we should. read, "Do not continue to touch me," or even more literally, "Not me (emphatic) continue to touch" but "Go to my brothers and sisters." The emphatic placement of the "me" at the beginning of the command and closest to the negative, which thus seems to govern the pronoun "me" rather than the verb "touch," suggests that what Jesus is forbidding is not so much the touching itself but Mary's selection of the object to touch, namely, the Jesus who stands before her as an individual. What Mary is told not to do is to try to continue to touch Jesus, that is, to encounter him as if he were the earthly Jesus resuscitated. The time for that kind of relationship is over. The negative present imperative of "touch" does not really mean "cling" or "hold," for which there is a perfectly good Greek word, *krateō,* which John uses in 20:23 and Matthew in 28:9. Furthermore, "to touch" often means not simply or even primarily the physical gesture of laying one's hands on a person but rather interpersonal relating, such as being deeply touched by a person's kindness or touched by the Evil One as in 1 John 5:18, which is the only other place the word occurs in the johannine corpus. In other words, I would suggest that what Jesus is really doing is redirecting Mary's desire for union with himself from his physical or earthly body (which in any case no longer exists because it is the glorified Lord who stands before her in an

---

[17] For the problem this johannine perspective creates for the contemporary reader because of its anti-Jewish and potentially anti-Semitic cast, see the studies by R. Alan Culpepper and Werner Kelber in this volume.

appearance which is temporary) to the new locus of his presence in the world, that is, the community of his brothers and sisters, the disciples.

What then are we to make of the reason Jesus seems to offer, "I am not yet ascended to my Father"? If anything, this seems less a reason for not touching him than a contradiction. If Jesus is not yet ascended, i.e., if he is still present in the earthly sphere, it would seem that Mary, like the pre-Ascension disciples in Luke 24:29, could be invited to touch him and verify his bodily reality. But, as most commentators have pointed out, the entire mystery of Jesus' glorification takes place in the Fourth Gospel when he is lifted up on the cross. It is virtually impossible, theologically, to understand Jesus in this scene as being somewhere in between (whether ontologically, spatially, or temporally) his resurrection and his ascension. The Jesus Mary encounters in the garden is clearly the glorified Jesus. Although it would take us too far afield to develop the thesis here, I would propose to translate this part of Jesus' address to Mary not as a declarative sentence, "I am not yet ascended to my Father," as if this supplied some reason why she should not or could not touch him, but as a rhetorical question expecting a negative reply, that is, "Am I as yet (or still) not ascended?" The proper answer to the question is, "No, you are indeed ascended, that is, glorified." The grammar and syntax of the sentence allows its translation as a question,[18] and, in my opinion, that makes much better sense of the passage because Jesus' ascension to the Father, i.e., his glorification, is precisely the reason Mary will now encounter him in the community of the Church rather than in his physical or earthly body, which may appear to be resuscitated but is not. In brief, a paraphrastic translation of v. 17 would proceed as follows: "It is no longer in and through my physical or earthly historical individuality that you can continue to relate to me. After all, am I still unascended to my Father? Rather, go to the community, the new locus of my earthly presence."

Jesus continues by commissioning Mary Magdalene to announce to the

---

[18] I am applying to this verse the theory A. Vanhoye developed in "Interrogation johannique et exégèse de Cana (Jn 2,4)," *Bib* 55 (1974) 157-167. Vanhoye proposed that John uses double-meaning or ironical questions whose answer is both positive and negative to lead the reader into theological reflection. In this case, Jesus appears to be not yet ascended because he is interacting with Mary, but what she (and the reader) must realize is that in reality he is now in a very different state, that is, glorified.

disciples what is clearly the johannine version of the Easter kerygma. The message is not "I have risen" or "I go before you into Galilee"; the message rather is that all has been accomplished. The work of the Word made flesh is complete and its fruits available to his disciples. In the Prologue the reader was told that the Word became flesh to give the power to become children of God to those who believed in him (1:12-14). Now that the work of Jesus is completed by his glorification, those who believe in him have become children of God. They are Jesus' brothers and sisters; his Father to whom he ascends is now their Father. It is important to note that 20:17 is the first time in John's Gospel that the disciples of Jesus are called *adelphoi*, that is, siblings. Since it is abundantly clear in this Gospel that the circle of the disciples is not limited to males and Mary is sent not to the Apostles (a term not used for Jesus' disciples in John) or to "the Twelve" (which is a term the evangelist does use, e.g., in 6:70 and 20:24) but precisely to the disciples, the plural of "brother" in this verse is evidently a collective noun in masculine form, inclusive of male and female siblings, as our English masculine collective "brethren" once was considered inclusive. We can regret the masculine form in the text which reflects the androcentric character of the Greek language and the culture of the times, but in reading and translating it we should honor its obviously inclusive meaning.[19]

The message Jesus sends to his disciples is hauntingly reminiscent of the Old Testament. My ascension, he says, "is to my Father and your Father, my God and your God." It recalls the words by which the foreigner, the Moabitess Ruth, entered into the covenant people of her mother-in-law, Naomi: "Your people will be my people and your God will be my God" (Ruth 1:16). It echoes also the prophetic promise that in the time of the New Creation God will make a New Covenant with a renewed people to whom God promises, "I will be your God and you will be my people" (Jer 31:31-34). The conclusion of this scene, which takes place in a garden reminiscent of both Genesis and the Canticle of Canticles and in which Jesus, the true Gardener and the true Beloved, encounters the one who is searching for him, is the announcement that the work of Jesus is now complete. He ascends to the God he calls, by right, his Father. For his disciples this means that they are the first to participate in the salvation of the New

---

[19] It is unfortunate that the NRSV and the NIV both retain the translation "brothers."

Creation, the first to be born not of blood, nor of the will of the flesh, nor of the desire of a man, but of God (1:13). They are now truly his sisters and brothers, members of the New Israel with whom God, through Jesus the new Moses, has sealed a New Covenant. The gift of God in Jesus, according to John, is divine filiation, eternal life in the Spirit springing up from within the believer (4:10-11) and flowing forth for the life of the world (7:37-39 and 19:3437).

In v. 18 Mary Magdalene, now again given her full name as in v. 1, goes to fulfill her apostolic mission. She comes "announcing" *(aggelousa).* This is the third thematic participle. Mary, who began this episode in the depths of spiritual darkness and sorrow, *weeping,* has been converted, turning away from the dispensation that lies behind to the new life offered to her in the glorified Jesus who lives now with God and in the temple of his body (2:21-22) which is the community, and she goes joyfully *announcing* that which has been revealed to her.

There is an evident redactional seam visible in this verse which the evangelist could scarcely not have noticed and must have left for a reason. The verse says literally, "Mary Magdalene went and announced to the disciples, 'I have seen the Lord' and he said these things to her." In other words, the sentence goes from first person direct discourse to third person indirect discourse without transition or explanation. Apparently, the source verse with which the evangelist was working was "Mary Magdalene went and announced to the disciples that he had said these things to her." The evangelist has opened up the sentence and inserted, in direct address, "I have seen the Lord." This is precisely the witness of the disciples to Thomas in v. 25, "We have seen the Lord," a testimony which Thomas evidently was expected to accept as the Easter kerygma. In John's Gospel, bearing witness is always based on what one has seen and heard. Jesus bore witness to what he had seen and heard with God (3:11). The Beloved Disciple bore witness to what he saw on Calvary (19:35). In other words, to claim to have seen and/or heard is to claim to be an authentic and authenticated witness. It is, quite simply, a credential formula. In the early Church it seems to have been particularly the credential statement for resurrection witnesses. Paul's ultimate self-vindication as an apostle is, "Have I not seen Jesus our Lord?" (1 Cor 9:1), which is not a reference to the earthly Jesus whom Paul had never met but to his experience of the risen Jesus on the road to Damascus.

In other words, Mary Magdalene, contrary to what generations of condescending male commentators would have us believe, is by all accounts an official apostolic witness of the resurrection. She is the one who, in the johannine community, takes Peter's role of confirming the brothers and sisters once she herself has been converted (Luke 22:31-32). She is the only person, in this Gospel, to receive an individual appearance and a personal and individual commission from Jesus. The meaning and particular johannine formulation of the Easter message is given only to her and she communicates it to the Church. Jesus does not repeat it when he appears to the disciples on Easter evening (20:19-23). He presumes it and, on the basis of Mary's confirming of the disciples, he commissions them to live out what he has accomplished in and for them by extending to all his work of taking a way of the sin of the world (1:29 and 20:23).

Conclusion

I have tried to establish two points in my interpretation of the encounter between the glorified Jesus and Mary Magdalene. First, Mary Magdalene is presented by the Fourth Evangelist as the official Easter witness in and to the johannine community. She is symbolically presented, by means of Old Testament allusions, as the beloved of the Lover in the Canticle, the spouse of the New Covenant mediated by Jesus in his glorification, the representative figure of the New Israel which emerges from the New Creation. Symbolically, she is both the johannine community encountering its glorified Savior and the official witness to that community of what God has done for it in the glorification of Jesus.

Second, the answer to the question, "Where is the Lord?", is that Jesus is with God, face unveiled, in the glory which he had with God before the world was made, and he is intimately present within and among his own of the first and all later generations to whom he has returned, as he promised, to fill them with a joy no one can take from them. By the time the first Easter ends in John's Gospel, the promise made in the Last Discourse(s) by the departing Jesus has been fulfilled: "I will not leave you orphaned; I am coming to you. In a little while the world will no longer see me, but you will see me; because I live, you also will live. On that day you will know, that I am in my Father, and you in me, and I in you" (14:18-20). And this saving revelation comes to us as it did to the first disciples-through the word of a woman bearing witness.

Chapter Eight

Prolegomena to a Canonical Reading
of the Fourth Gospel*

D. MOODY SMITH

My favorite story about theological controversies over infant baptism concerns an empirically oriented Christian, who when asked whether he believed in it responded, "Believe in it? I've seen it!" His comment raises questions about seeing and believing that are important also for the Gospel of John. But I cite it because it applies particularly to canonical readings of John, or of the New Testament generally. I have seen, or heard, such readings. Probably you have too.

John Dominic Crossan has recently written a book on Jesus which, because of the content as well as the title, has attracted a good bit of attention.[1] In due course Crossan appeared on the Larry King television interview show, gave a brief synopsis of his work, and answered questions phoned in by viewers, most of whom of course had not read the book. A good many of them simply wanted to set Crossan straight. If you really want to know who Jesus was and what he thought, just read the Bible. Doesn't Jesus say that he and the Father are one (John 10:30)? Doesn't he say that he is the way, the truth, and the life, etc (John 14:6)? In other words, such questions as Crossan was seeking to answer through scholarly investigation are already answered in the Gospels, particularly in the

---

* To Frederick Herzog on his seventieth birthday, a token of esteem, friendship, and gratitude for his stimulation as a colleague and fellow reader of the Gospel of John. His *Liberation Theology: Liberation in the Light of the Fourth Gospel* (New York: Seabury Press, 1972) raised for me in an acute way the question of how we should read that Gospel and made me aware for the first time of the importance of the question of who is reading.

[1] J. D. Crossan, *The Historical Jesus: The Life of a Mediterranean Jewish Peasant* (San Francisco: Harper Collins, 1991).

Gospel of John. The callers were interpreting the Synoptic Gospels' portrayals of Jesus in light of the Gospel of John. "That's theology," said Crossan, "but I'm interested in history." We know what Crossan was saying, and would probably agree with him. But the callers were greatly perplexed. Following the lead of scripture, the canon, they were answering questions arising out of the Synoptic Gospels by drawing upon the Fourth Gospel. That has ancient precedent! Clement of Alexandria saw in John a spiritual gospel, written in full cognizance of the other three. Calvin professed that he found in the Gospel of John a key to the other three. The church, in listing the authoritative Gospels and then putting them together into one codex, usually placed the Gospel of John last, after the other three. The implication was clear enough. John was to be read last, presumably to clarify christological questions the others raised.

John and the Synoptics

The Common Lectionary seems to break with the order of the canon by distributing readings from the Gospel of John through the three years of the lectionary cycle. Yet the effect is to encourage a canonical reading of John in that readings from the Fourth Gospel are interspersed among the other three. John is read and preached not continuously, that is, straight through, as the other Gospels are, but along with them. One wonders what the effect on the preaching of the Gospel of John, and the others, may be.

In teaching a course on preaching from the Gospel of John with a colleague in homiletics, we have found that there is often a tendency for a synoptic-like characterization of Jesus to slip into the sermon based on a Oohannine text. (The obverse also occurred last semester when we taught Mark.) Sometimes it is simply a matter of the historicist assumption—inappropriate enough with the Synoptics—creeping into the interpretation of John. Naturally, my colleague and I frown gently on this when it happens. Often it is simply an expression of naiveté. But it is partly something more or other than that. John, like the Synoptics, tells the story of Jesus, and that story is laid alongside the others in the New Testament. The readers, or preachers, naturally merge the narratives together in their consciousness. In other words, the naiveté of the reader or preacher is the natural result of the shape and character of the canon. It was mainly modern and historical-critical exegesis that taught us to read the Fourth

Gospel, and other Gospels, the way we do, independently of one another except where literary-historical considerations dictate otherwise.

Moreover, on one reading of the John-Synoptics relationship, namely the one dominant until mid-century, the exegete could legitimately claim that John should be read in light of the others, because it was written in cognizance of them and intended to be so read. This is, in fact, the position of Frans Neirynck and of an increasing number of scholars.[2] Perhaps the most skillful, persuasive, and finely nuanced presentation of this position was set out by Sir Edwin Hoskyns in his commentary on the Fourth Gospel, which was written essentially in the 1930s.[3] Hoskyns took the position that the Fourth Evangelist presupposed, if not the Synoptic Gospels in the form we have them, certainly their substantial content or tradition. There is something essentially correct in this, as most serious readers of John, including Clement and Calvin, will attest.

John's historical and literary relationship to the Synoptic Gospels is, however, complex, and it is difficult to explain because the evidence points in opposite directions. One might simplify the problem in a way that is not misleading by saying that, on the one hand, the theology of John agrees fundamentally with the Synoptics. That is, there are no outstanding contradictions, and for the most part John seems to accentuate, amplify, or make explicit what is found or suggested in the Synoptics. On the other hand, John presents other kinds of problems for the reader who knows the synoptic accounts.

Not only is he alone in portraying a three-year ministry, mostly in Judea, but he has a different chronology or calendar of the last supper and passion. One could go on to enumerate the sheer differences in content as well as in the work and attitude of Jesus himself. Seemingly, in relation to the Synoptics, John

---

[2] Neirynck, now Professor Emeritus at Louvain University, has devoted much of his attention to Gospel relationships and in recent years to the relationship of the Gospel of John to the Synoptic Gospels. His works are too numerous to cite here. Representative of his position and the present state of scholarship is his *Forschungsbericht,* "John and the Synoptics: 1975-1990," in *John and the Synoptics* (ed. A. Denaux; BETL 101; Leuven: Leuven University Press, 1992) 3-62. Neirynck's paper, along with the others collected in this volume, was presented at the 1990 Louvain Colloquium on John and the Synoptics.

[3] E. C. Hoskyns, *The Fourth Gospel* (ed. F. N. Davey, rev. ed.; London: Faber & Faber, 1947).

creates fewer difficulties for the theologian than for the student of the gospel narratives.[4]

Yet, to say that last is indeed an oversimplication, for at some points John seems to presuppose what we read in the Synoptics. Even the way the name of Jesus Christ is introduced in the prologue (1:17) may suggest that the reader already knows who he is. Actually, "Jesus Christ" occurs only here and in 17:3 in John. To judge from Acts and Paul, it virtually functioned as a proper name. Of course, the prologue prepares for the naming of the name, but the prologue would be particularly meaningful only to one who already knew the story and the name, as we do. (The now increasingly common view that the prologue was added to the penultimate form of the Gospel fits this view of how it would have been reads) If the Fourth Gospel presupposes the Synoptic)), the prologue would also be read in light of them. But such a presupposition is not, strictly speaking, necessary. Possibly the prologue was intended to be read against the background of Paul, or of commonly known Christian belief and tradition. Of course, when read for the first time, it unfolds an intriguing mystery. But the mystery is not resolved by the naming of Jesus (1:17), unless one already knows something of who Jesus is.

Canonical Reading

Actually, this discussion illustrates the problem. If one asks from a historical-critical point of view exactly what is presupposed by the prologue, a definitive answer is scarcely attainable. It makes good sense to view the prologue as a hymn that extols and places in a cosmic setting what is already known, namely, that when the time had fully come, God sent forth his Son (Gal 4:4). This

---

[4] On the recent history of the problem of John and the Synoptics, see D. M. Smith, *John Among the Gospels: The Relationship in Twentieth-Century Research* (Minneapolis: Fortress Press, 1992).

[5] See, for example, J. Ashton, *Understanding the Fourth Gospel* (Oxford: Oxford University Press, 1991) 84, 286-87. The most consistent representative of this position on the North American scene has been R. T. Fortna. See his *The Fourth Gospel and Its Predecessor: From Narrative Source to Present Gospel* (Philadelphia: Fortress Press, 1988), 28-29, where he maintains his earlier position in *The Gospel of Signs: A Reconstruction of the Narrative Source Underlying the Fourth Gospel* (SNTSMS 11; Cambridge: Cambridge University Press, 1970).

reading of the prologue makes excellent sense, not only in the light of the rest of the Gospel of John, but also in light of the New Testament generally. This is what we mean by a canonical reading. When the prologue is read before a Christian congregation on Christmas Eve or Christmas Day as the appointed reading, this is the way it is heard. Whether or not the evangelist intended it to be heard in this way, I believe he would nevertheless have applauded and approved this reading and hearing.

Now to return to the question of what the Gospel of John actually presupposes historically. At the conclusion of the Temple Cleansing (2:22), the author refers to Jesus' resurrection as if it were something already known to the reader. The coming of the Spirit is similarly referred to during the narrative of Jesus' appearance at Tabernacles (7:39). The repeated references to Jesus' glory, or the coming hour of his glorification (7:39; 2:4, 12:23), seem to presuppose that the reader knows of Jesus' death and needs to be guided into a more profound understanding of its meaning. Smaller items: Jesus' encounter with the Baptist is recounted in retrospect by John; Mary and Martha are mentioned in 11:1 as if they are already known; the trial before Caiaphas, reported in the Synoptics, is alluded to, but not narrated; in the trial before Pilate the Jewish condemnation seems to be assumed without having been reported. In other words, John appears to presume knowledge of the story of Jesus as well as early Christian tradition. All this comports well with the view that John is the last of the canonical Gospels and written with the others in view. Again, while such a view makes perfectly good sense in many respects, it is not a necessity. But at least the Gospel presupposes knowledge of the Christian kerygma and story, if not necessarily the documents that we have in the New Testament. Yet, the question of a canonical reading does not depend on canonical knowledge, that is, John's knowledge of other canonical books. Canonical reading is a given for us, whatever the intention or knowledge of the author and his intended readers.

A canonical reading of John is now natural for anyone who falls under Christian cultural influence, what used to be called Christendom. Thus Harold Bloom, in the introduction of his edited volume of essays on the literary interpretation of the Gospels, seems to view John as the epitome of what offends, while at the same time stimulates, in the New Testament.[6] As a strong misreading of the Hebrew Bible, John surpasses Paul, although Paul is on the same track, not to mention the other Gospels. This negative canonical reading of John is quite understandable, particularly given the role that the Fourth Gospel has occupied in Christian canonical interpretation of the New Testament.

Canonical reading is also a common phenomenon outside the realm of biblical interpretation. Recently, Garry Wills has made us aware of how one document can influence the interpretation of another and thus change or define the course of American constitutional interpretation. (Not coincidentally, the field of constitutional law affords interesting and informative parallels to biblical interpretation.) In a recent article on Lincoln and the Gettysburg address, Wills maintains that "Abraham Lincoln transformed the ugly reality [of the bloody battle of Gettysburg] into something rich and strange—and he did it with 272 words."[7] Lincoln's immediate purpose was largely practical and political. But Lincoln also "knew the power of his rhetoric to define war aims. He was seeking occasions to use his words outside the normal round of proclamations and reports to Congress."[8] So his own purposes were more than momentary and local. Lincoln was "a student of the Word," as Wills calls him; he knew and intended that this address should have a broader resonance. Yet, he scarcely could have anticipated its long-term effect.

Lincoln's Gettysburg Address became a kind of canonical event (my word, not Wills'). Afterward, our speech changed and the nation's primary documents were read differently. (For one thing, and perhaps tellingly, after Gettysburg "the United States" became a singular, no longer a plural, term.) Lincoln's theme at the outset was the new nation "conceived in liberty, and dedicated to the proposition that all men are created equal." The speech ended with the hope "that this nation under God shall have a new birth of freedom—and that government of the people, by the people, for the people, shall not perish from the earth." Lincoln, writes Wills, was a revolutionary: "He not only presented

---

[6] See Bloom's introductory article in the book he edited, entitled *The Gospels, Modern Critical Interpretations* (New York: Chelsea, 1988) 1-15.

[7] G. Wills, "The Words that Remade America: Lincoln at Gettysburg," *The Atlantic Monthly* 296:6 (June 1992) 57-79. The quotation is found on p. 57.

[8] Ibid., 58.

the Declaration of Independence in a new light, as a matter of founding law, but put its central proposition, equality, in a newly favored position as a principle of the Constitution,"[9] (although the Constitution never uses the word!). Through his Gettysburg Address Lincoln accorded a new status to the Declaration of independence and changed the way people thought about the Constitution, much to the annoyance of States' Rights advocates and strict constructionists ever since.

Perhaps the Gettysburg address is best described as a crucial hermeneutical event rather than a canonical one, but the two are not unrelated. In fact they are importantly related. The establishment of the canon was the crucial hermeneutical move shaping the way the early Christian writings that makeup the New Testament were to be read. Moreover, the inclusion of the Gospel of John in the Gospel canon exerted an important influence on how the other Gospels and the rest of the New Testament were read.

It would perhaps be unwise to argue, or to attempt to demonstrate, that the Gospel of John is to the New Testament as Lincoln's Gettysburg Address is to the United States Constitution. For one thing, John is a part of the New Testament in a way the Gettysburg Address is not part of the Constitution. Yet one might consider that the Gettysburg Address is a part of the national canon of Scripture, including also the Declaration of Independence and the Constitution, by which the nation thinks to live. As such, it plays a central role in the national consciousness. Similarly the Gospel of John has played a crucial

---

[9] Ibid., 79. See also Wills' more extensive treatment of the Gettysburg Address: *Lincoln at Gettysburg: The Words that Remade America* (New York: Simon & Shuster, 1992), from which the *Atlantic* article is largely excerpted.

Students of the prologue of the Gospel of John will also be interested in Wills' observation about the form and style of the Gettysburg Address *(Lincoln at Gettysburg,* 172-174). In reproducing the text of the Address, he uses bold face, italics, and underlining to show that "each of the paragraphs ...is bound to the preceding and the following by some resumptive [word or] element ...." Moreover, "by this reliance on a few words in different contexts, the compactness of the themes is emphasized ....The spare vocabulary is not impoverishing because of the subtly interfused constructions ....`Plain speech' was never less artless." All these observations are equally true of the Johannine prologue. Wills elsewhere shows Lincoln's indebtedness to classical and biblical style. One wonders whether the Gettysburg Address was subtly influenced by the prologue of John's Gospel!

role in Christian consciousness and in defining what being Christian is to countless millions of people who through the centuries have considered themselves followers of Jesus. The words of John and of the Johannine Jesus determine the way Christians understand themselves and their Lord.

> -The Word became flesh and dwelt among us. (1:14)
> -God so loved the world that he gave his only Son .... (3:16)
> -You will know the truth and the truth will make you free. (8:32)
> -I came that they may have life and have it abundantly. (10:10)
> -I am the resurrection and the life; he who believes in me, though he die, yet shall he live .... (11:25)
> -I am the way, the truth, and the life, no one comes to the Father but by me. (14:6)

Whatever else Jesus Christ may mean to Christians, to many if not most of us he is defined by such sayings as these. The confidence that Jesus in John brings to full expression what the synoptic Jesus represented, while it cannot perhaps be demonstrated exegetically, need not be dismissed as simply uninformed. Within the Christian community it can scarcely be dismissed, so deeply is the historic Christian consciousness imbued with the Gospel of John. In becoming a part of the canon, John quickly assumed a key role, not only in determining how believers and preachers would understand Jesus in the other Gospels, but also how he would be understood in the development of church doctrine. The language of the Nicene Creed and the issues addressed in the Creed of Chalcedon hark back to the Gospel of John in remarkable ways. (Thus John affects not only the canon of faith as regards its New Testament parallels and antecedents, but also the canon of faith that was instituted in the creeds.)

Gospel of John as Central Canonical and Hermeneutical Event

All that we have been discussing seems to point in the direction of the central role of John as a hermeneutical instrument in the formation of the canon. Even those modern exegetes who doubt John's dependence on other Gospels or his knowledge of such germinal predecessors as Paul tend to regard this Gospel as somehow centrally located in its presentation of the mission of Jesus and the message of early Christianity. I am thinking, of course, of the two great mid-twentieth century interpreters of the New Testament, Rudolf Bultmann on the Continent and C. H. Dodd in England.

It is clear that for Bultmann the Johannine literature (Gospel and Epistles) represented the essence of the New Testament presentation of the revelation of God in Jesus Christ. Appropriately, John appears as the third of four major parts of Bultmann's *Theology of the New Testament;* the final part is devoted to the development toward early Catholicism. Moreover, Bultmann's theological, as well as exegetical, magnum opus is his commentary on the Gospel of John.[10] It is John who understands most clearly that what has happened is precisely revelation, a making known of God as the light and life-giver—and of humankind in the precariousness of existence before God or nothingness. It would be wrong to speak of a zenith of the development of New Testament theology, for Bultmann eschews both the concepts of development and the notion that John stands on the shoulders of his predecessors. Rather, in retrospect, toward the end of the first century, John presents his pristine understanding of the New Testament preaching with respect to its theology and its inseparably related anthropology. Thus John becomes the canon within the canon. Bultmann has often been criticized for advocating such a thing or allowing it to happen, but in this respect he belongs in a venerable tradition of Christian theology and piety.

Something similar could be said, *mutatis mutandis,* of C. H. Dodd. Dodd's project was perhaps not so explicitly theological as Bultmann's. Yet Dodd turns to the Fourth Gospel at crucial points to confirm his view of the essence of the New Testament message. Thus in his programmatic book, *The Apostolic Preaching and its Developments,* Dodd saw in the Gospel of John not only the culmination of theological development in the New Testament, but the best, and historically most felicitous, view of Jesus' eschatology.[11] Jesus did not announce an imminent, apocalyptic kingdom, but rather the presence of the kingdom in his own ministry. Dodd's assessment of John's importance is also reflected in the weight of his own scholarly publications, which culminated in two

---

[10] R. Bultmann, *Theology of the New Testament* (trans. K. Grobel; New York: Scribner's, 1955) 2:392 ("The Theology of the Gospel of John and the Johannine Epistles"); also, *The Gospel of John: A Commentary* (trans. G. R. Beasley-Murray, R. W. N. Hoare, and J. K. Riches; Philadelphia: Westminster Press, 1971).

[11] C. H. Dodd, *The Apostolic Preaching and Its Developments* (New York: Harper, 1936) 65-78.

monumental volumes, one on the interpretation of John's Gospel, the other on the question of historical tradition in that document.[12] For Dodd, as well as Bultmann, the Gospel of John is an implicit canon within the canon. They are not by themselves, as some other treatments of the theology of the New Testament confirm.[13]

There is another side of the picture, however, and that is the role the other Gospels, and other New Testament writers may, or should, play in the interpretation of the Fourth Gospel. This role is not something that belongs in the realm of the purely hypothetical or within the ambience of some now passe liberal theology. It has very ancient roots that reach back to the beginning of the process of canonization, in which John was evidently a relative late-comer.

There was no New Testament canon that did not include the Fourth Gospel. At least, we do not have any such canonical list. Yet the very resistance to that Gospel, as represented by Gaius of Rome, and perhaps others, at the end of the second century implies that a gospel canon, consisting of the Synoptics but not John, was establishing itself, however informally. If Matthew and Luke independently used Mark, or even if Luke used Mark and Matthew, such usage implies a nascent canon of the Gospels. There was evolving a "standard" way of treating the mission and message of Jesus that the Fourth Gospel put under severe strain. Polycarp in the 130s and Justin Martyr in the 150s attest the

---

[12] C. H. Dodd, *The Interpretation of the Fourth Gospel* (Cambridge: Cambridge University Press, 1953) and *Historical Tradition in the Fourth Gospel* (Cambridge: Cambridge University Press, 1963).

[13] What might be called the canonical dominance of John is reflected in the fact that the Gospel or the Johannine writings are often treated last in books dealing with New Testament theology of interpretation, a practice implying that John represents the perspective from which the whole is to be viewed. See H. Conzelmann, *An Outline of the Theology of the New Testament* (trans. J. Bowden; New York: Harper & Row, 1969); W. G. Kümmel, *The Theology of the New Testament According to Its Major Witnesses: Jesus-Paul-John* (trans. J. E. Steely; Nashville: Abingdon, 1973); L. T. Johnson, *The Writings of the New Testament: An Interpretation* (Philadelphia: Fortress, 1986). The earlier editions of R. A. Spivey and D. M. Smith, *Anatomy of the New Testament: A Guide to Its Structure and Meaning* (New York: Macmillan, 1969 and 1974) followed the same pattern, treating John last. In the third and subsequent editions (1982, 1989, 1995), however, we broke away from this pattern and simply put John in its place in the Gospel canon.

widespread use of the synoptic tradition, probably the Synoptic Gospels, but not the Gospel of John. When Marcion, roughly a contemporary of Justin, formed his canon he chose as his Gospel a version of Luke, not John. (Yet one might have thought Marcion's dualism would have commended the Fourth Gospel to him.) Only with Tatian's *Diatessaron,* probably to be dated about 170, do we arrive at a "canonical" use of the Fourth Gospel. Interestingly enough, Tatian was a former student of Justin Martyr, who used the Gospel of John rarely, if at all.

When Irenaeus argues for the necessity of *four* Gospels, his arguments from the four winds and the four corners of the earth seem flimsy enough to us. It may be that he is really making a case for the Fourth Gospel which was a relative newcomer to the developing Gospel canon. The evidence for the rejection of, or hesitation about, the Fourth Gospel may be slim, but so is contemporaneous evidence for its second-century use in orthodox circles. That John was used by Valentinian Gnostics is clear enough, as the *Gospel of Truth,* Heracleon's commentary on John, and Irenaeus' polemic against Gnostic exegesis of John suggests. That its popularity among Gnostics (and Montanists) slowed its acceptance into the canon cannot be proved, but constitutes a good and informed hypothesis.[14]

The point is that John encounters some resistance because there is already a developing canon with which it is in some respects at variance. It needed to be explained with reference to the Synoptics before it could be used to explain

---

[14] J. N. Sanders, *Gospel in the Early Church: Its Origin and Influence on Christian Theology up to Irenaeus* (Cambridge: Cambridge University Press, 1943). Martin Hengel *(The Johannine Question* [trans. J. Bowden; London and Philadelphia: SCM and Trinity Press International, 1989]) disputes "the view, widespread today, that the Fourth Gospel is a semi-`gnostic' Gospel which was first rescued for the mainstream church by the efforts of Irenaeus" (5). This, however, is not Sanders' view of the Fourth Gospel. He regarded it as the effort of an author with access to ancient traditions to state the (orthodox) gospel in terms that would be intelligible to (Alexandrian) protognostics (85) and granted that it had already gained wide acceptance in Asia Minor when Irenaeus received it: "This use of it marks the final stage in its acceptance as scripture, for he challenged the Gnostic interpretation of the Gospels and vindicated it as the *regula veritatis,* a position it has held in Catholic theology ever since" (86-87). See also C. K. Barrett, *The Gospel According to St. John* (rev. ed.; Philadelphia: Westminster, 1978) 123-25, 131, who basically concurs with Sanders.

them. Thus, Clement explains it as a spiritual Gospel; Eusebius notes that John was composed with knowledge of the others to explain Jesus' early ministry; Origen derides the growing industry with which John was harmonized with the others. Such efforts to explain and justify the Gospel of John bespeak hesitancy or resistance in some quarters. Moreover, modern exegetes from Bultmann to Brown, and latterly Boismard, have seen in the final redaction of the Gospel of John evidence of knowledge of the Synoptic Gospels—an indication of an effort to reconcile the synoptic and Johannine traditions,

Raymond E. Brown has recently made an important suggestion about the relationship of the First Epistle to the Gospel that also bears significantly on the question of canon.[15] He views 1 John as not only subsequent to the Gospel but deliberately designed to guide its interpretation. First John's emphasis upon the audibility, visibility, and palpability of the word of life (1:1) underscores and interprets what the evangelist meant when he wrote, "The word became flesh and dwelt among us." As Hans Conzelmann pointed out, the beginning (*archē*) in 1 John is the beginning of the Christian tradition, not the primordial beginning as in the Gospel. The beginning of the tradition is its defining point. The Epistle was clearly directed against Christian opponents whose Christology verged in a docetic direction (4:1-3). First John cordoned off the road leading to such an erroneous christology. (Ernst Käsemann's suggestion of a naively docetic Gospel was already anticipated and counteracted by the alert author of the Epistle!) Brown's suggestion is ingenious, and is, of course, argued with erudition and in great detail in his commentary on the Epistles. We cannot here do it justice. But if correct, it contributes another important piece in the puzzle of the Fourth Gospel's canonicity. Brown is suggesting that the Epistles, particularly 1 John, are intended to guide or direct the reading of the Fourth Gospel. One might go beyond Brown, but not, I think, Brown's intention to say that the Epistle intends to say what a canonical reading of the Gospel must be like, and before John was customarily read alongside the other, Synoptic, Gospels. In other words, there was already coming into being a Johannine canon that anticipated the fuller canon of early Christian writings.

---

[15] For Brown's position, see his *The Community of the Beloved Disciple* (New York: Paulist, 1979) 93-144, where he sets out basic historical premises upon which his commentary *The Epistles of John*, (AB 30; Garden City, NY: Doubleday, 1982) is based.

Of course, once the four-Gospel canon was widely established and accepted—something that was already happening at the beginning of the third century—John was in the very nature of the case read in concert with the other Gospels. Käsemann reflects upon the way in which John was harmonized with the Synoptic Gospels—and continues to be—as a necessity, but one fraught with ambiguity.[16] Nevertheless, he himself presents an interpretation of John that shows why such a harmonization—dare one say a canonical reading?—of John was a necessity for the emerging universal church. The charismatic, naively docetic, dogmatic Gospel of Käsemann's reading was scarcely the Gospel the emerging catholic church read! It may be an over-simplification to suggest that the naively docetic aspect was dropped. Perhaps it was developed in terms of the doctrine of the two natures. The charismatic aspect was somewhat domesticated, institutionalized, and channeled. Yet it continued to inspire charismatic activity within the church. The dogmatic aspect was fully embraced, developed, and even made normative in the great ecumenical creeds, especially the Nicene creed. Thus, Käsemann's heterodox Gospel became, ironically, the criterion of orthodoxy, but only as it was read in correlation with the Synoptic Gospels.

Conclusion

So should a canonical reading of the Gospel of John place it at the center of the canon and allow all the rest to be read in light of it? Understandably, that has frequently happened. But we are also in urgent need of reading the Gospel of John in light of the other Gospels, not to mention Paul. The early resistance to the Fourth Gospel, the Epistles' attempt to guide its interpretation, even the early efforts to harmonize John with the other Gospels, bespeak a sense of the need for reading the Fourth Gospel not alone, but in concert. That need may explain theologically the attractiveness of the age-old, and now again more widely espoused, view that John presupposes, if he does not use, the other Gospels. It is not enough for the Jesus of the Sermon on the Mount to be subsumed under the Incarnate Logos. Only the Jesus of the Sermon on the Mount adequately justifies or explains why there should be an Incarnate Logos,

---

[16] E. Käsemann, *The Testament of Jesus: A Study of the Gospel of John in the Light of Chapter 17* (trans. G. Krodel; Philadelphia: Fortress Press, 1968) 74-78.

or who the Incarnate Logos is. Such a statement as I have just made—provocative as I hope it will be—is intelligible in a consideration of canonical readings. Canonical readings go back to the beginnings of the New Testament, at least to the gathering of the various documents. To perceive them is a legitimate historical task. To appreciate them may be a task of literary criticism. To propose them is the continuing task of theological exegesis."

---

[17] We have intentionally spoken of canonical reading rather than canonical criticism because canonical reading is, and has been, practiced by Christians who were unaware of canonical—or any other kind of—criticism. Nevertheless, I want to acknowledge the impact and importance of the canon-critical proposal and work of B. S. Childs, best-known to New Testament students through his *The New Testament as Canon: An Invitation* (Philadelphia: Fortress Press, 1985). Also significant is the more historically oriented approach of J. A. Sanders (see, e.g., *Torah and Canon* |Philadelphia: Fortress Press, 1972|). Only after I had delivered this paper at the 1992 SBL Annual Meeting, did I become aware, through the courtesy of the author, of E. E. Lemcio's article, "Father and Son in the Synoptics and John: A Canonical Reading," in *The New Testament as Canon: A Reader in Canonical Criticism,* (ed. Robert W. Wall; Sheffield: Sheffield Academic Press, 1992).

PART II
THE GOSPEL OF JOHN AT THE CLOSE
OF THE TWENTIETH CENTURY

Chapter Nine

Coming Hermeneutical Earthquake
in Johannine Interpretation
ROBERT KYSAR

In the course of the twentieth century, interpreters of the Gospel of John have experienced one earthquake after another—the shaking of the hermeneutical earth under our feet. And the future promises to be no less tumultuous. The "big one" may be yet to come for readers of John. Of course, predictions are risky and cheap, but my reflections on the Gospel of John at the close of this century serve as an invitation to consider the future. I propose that in the twenty-first century, at least in North America, the interpretation of the Gospel of John will be reshaped still more and done so by at least two essential questions. Those two questions, I suggest, are aroused by opposing and sometimes contradictory features of the Fourth Gospel: first, the sectarian, exclusivistic over against the traps-sectarian and inclusivistic themes; second, the ambiguous contrasted with absolute truth-claims. I offer these reflections from within the context of my own Christian concerns and my role as an interpreter for the church.

First Question: Sectarian/Trans-sectarian Themes

The first question has to do with the Fourth Gospel in the context of the changing religious scene in North America and evolves around the sectarian versus the traps-sectarian themes: How will the sectarian nature of Johannine Christianity function for a church that finds itself in a sectarian relationship with its culture?

This question, of course, assumes that in the next century the whole Christian church in North America will be forced to take its place as just one more religious option in a fully pluralized culture. The final remnants of the Constantinian era of the church in North America will fade away, and the church will find itself in a kind of sectarian relationship with its culture. By sectarian I mean that Christians will constitute a social minority in the culture— a marginal group—and will tend to understand themselves over against the world. In such a setting as this, the Gospel of John is likely to sound newly relevant. Its sectarian language and ideas will appeal to a church under siege and offer sanction and even empowerment for that kind of mentality. The outsider-insider distinctions implied in so much of the Gospel may encourage a new other-worldliness.

The essential question is whether the Gospel of John can be interpreted in ways that appropriate the *best* of that sectarian strain (for which it is infamous) without succumbing to what I take to be the *worst* of such a perspective. Can we find empowerment for a mission to the world—a mission that subverts the powers of injustice and oppression, on the one hand, and refuses, on the other hand, to be seduced by a hostility and hatred toward others? Can we think of ourselves as sent into the world that God so loves, and can we say no to the texts that invite us to regard opponents as demonic? But will the church also be able to read and appropriate the Gospel's trans-sectarian motifs? Will the Johannine witness to the Creator's love of the *kosmos* sufficiently qualify the Gospel's sectarian strains? Will the often-muted strains of mission in the Gospel drown out the implicit hostility toward the church's opponents?

Inherent in this first question is a second part that focuses on the exclusive versus inclusive tension of the Gospel's narrative. In a remarkable way, this Gospel often sounds so very exclusive and sectarian (e.g., love *only* one another). But it also witnesses to a radical inclusion of at least some of the socially marginalized (for instance, the Gospel's attention to women and Samaritans). But in this ironic contradiction the Fourth Gospel may provide sanction and empowerment for *either* the church's inclusive stance or exclusive posture toward others. Which will it be?

My first question about this pair of contradictory emphases does little more than suggest the importance of how the Fourth Gospel will be read and understood in a new cultural context. By what process will the church determine which side of these opposing motifs should guide its life, or in what kind of balance will they function as authoritative? That process will need to produce some clearer and bolder distinctions between the "normative" and the "contingent" in the text. A canonical reading of the Gospel will also be required, so that the whole of the canon functions as a corrective to the contingent character of some of the Johannine themes. A courage to stand at times against the text and to practice a kind of hermeneutic of suspicion that challenges the text's contingencies will be needed. At the same time, the hermeneutical process will need to allow the text to shape Christian life and witness in ways consistent with the Word made flesh.

Second Question: Ambiguous/Absolute Truth Claims

My second question is related to another polarity in the Gospel, namely, the ambiguous and the absolutist claims for truth. It may be put simply: Can the language of the Fourth Gospel continue to function in a revelatory way?

In the century ahead of us, the media is likely to become the most decisive factor in shaping human consciousness and reshaping language. The question is then, how will that reformed consciousness read the language and imagery of the Fourth Gospel? Can that language and those images still convey the presence of a transcendent reality? In a curious way, I believe, the very ambiguities and polyvalence of the Gospel of John may become even more relevant than they have been in the past. My belief is rooted, admittedly, in a guess. A guess that in a culture dominated by the visual media, drowning in information, truth will become generally more ambiguous. Has it not already become so?

In such a culture, where truth is experienced as ambiguity, the Fourth Gospel's paradoxes, ironies, and enigmatic declarations may all take on a fresh quality. This Gospel will speak more clearly through its ambiguities than it has been allowed to do in twentieth-century culture. The paradoxical quality of much of the Gospel will have an increasing ring of truth about it, I believe. So, the language and imagery of the Gospel, which has so often stopped us in our tracks, may provide us frames of reference for life in a new culture. But what of those truths for which the Fourth Gospel makes absolute claims with near-dogmatic certainty? How shall that Johannine feature be read and heard in twenty-first century North America?

If the ambiguities of the language and imagery of the Fourth Gospel take on a new power, the absolute claims for truth in the same Gospel may gradually appear more and more problematic, if not anachronistic. At least, I think, this much is true: The way in which the gospel has served as a wellspring from which the great dogmas of the church were dipped out one after the other cannot survive. With no little personal fear and trembling, I suggest that the christological and trinitarian dogmas so decisively formed in the ancient church under the influence of the Johannine Gospel may become threatened. We Christians will no longer be able to document our view of Christ on the basis of the Johannine text—at least not in the way we have done in the past. We will no longer be so comfortable in reducing the Johannine discourse material to creedal statements. That ease with which we once dipped into the flowing waters of the Gospel narrative for rationale on which to crystallize faith statements will be disturbed. What was read as creed will be seen for what it is, namely, polemic poetry.

How, then, will this Gospel function as a resource for Christian theology in the twenty-first century? Johannine language may help us revise our understanding of theological language and method as a whole and may provoke a more profound appreciation for the symbolic nature of all articulations of faith. As Johannine language is recognized as parabolic poetry, fashioned in the midst of controversy, so then will all expressions of religious truth be recognized as metaphorical, pointing but not describing. The authority of scripture for theology, I believe, may come increasingly to be located not in propositions but in images (word pictures) that hint and tease at ultimate reality and that consequently are vulnerable to varieties of responses. We will search, not for grand propositions, but for controlling and fundamental images, or (if one prefers) formative stories.

Still, there will be no such thing as a single authoritative interpretation of John—no such thing as a true reading of the text. Instead, the church will be forced to recognize the validity of a wide variety of interpretations, and truth found in a range of readings arising from a multicultural body of readers. We will be forced to redefine biblical authority in ways that more honestly recognize the tenuous and culturally influenced character of all authority. In such a way we may be able to claim an authority that liberates and empowers rather than oppresses and controls some for the benefit of others.

Concluding Remarks

Whether or not the church and its scholars will succeed in such an ambitious enterprise remains to be seen. The church as we know it today may splinter even more with the splintering of the various readings of biblical texts, including John. The challenge of the interpretation of the Gospel of John in the future century is formidable. But, in summary, I am suggesting that the Fourth Gospel may play a featured role in the drama of the church in the twenty-first century in North America. It may be cast in that leading role for two reasons: its representation of the issues inherent in an early Christian sectarianism and its portrayal of the nature, function, and authority of religious language.

Chapter Ten

The Gospel of John as a Kinder, Gentler Apocalypse for the 20th Century

J. RAMSEY MICHAELS

The appropriateness of our discussion today is evident because, to the extent that John's Gospel can be dated at all, it is most often placed near the close of its own century and at the threshold of what came to be called the post-apostolic age. Then too, the close of our century is also the close of a millennium. Even though John of Patmos is not its author or implied author, the Fourth Gospel does for its readers something akin to what a new millennium is supposed to do. It turns them momentarily away from the present darkness and ushers them into a transcendent realm, a new dimension of existence, where "the light shines in the darkness and the darkness did not overcome it" (John 1:5).

Ushered into a new dimension? In the 1880s there appeared in England a little work of fantasy in the manner of Lewis Carroll, entitled *Flatland: A Romance of Many Dimensions,* by an author identifying himself only as "A Square.[1] The title speaks of itself. *Flatland* describes a two-dimensional world in which women are lines, working-class men are triangles, professional men are squares, and priests are circles. On "the last day of the 1999th year of our era" (p. 65), the hero, "A Square," meets a spherical stranger from "Spaceland" who leads him into "the Land of Three Dimensions":

> An unspeakable horror seized me. There was a darkness; then a dizzy, sickening sensation of sight that was not like seeing; I saw a Line that was no Line; Space that was not Space: I was myself and not myself. When I could find voice, I shrieked aloud in agony, "Either this is madness or it is Hell." "It is

---

[1] Citations are from the sixth edition (New York: Dover Publications, 1952), based on the second edition (London: Seeley & Co., 1884).

neither," calmly replied the voice of the Sphere, "it is Knowledge; it is Three
Dimensions: open your eye once again and try to look steadily" (p. 80).

The real author of *Flatland* was Edwin A. Abbott (1838-1W6), Victorian
polymath, Shakespeare and Bacon scholar extraordinaire, and author of many
important works on the Fourth Gospel: for example, the article in the
Encyclopedia Britannica (1880); the Johannine material in the article on Gospels
for *Encyclopedia Biblica* (1901); *Johannine Vocabulary* (1905); *Johannine
Grammar* (1906); and Book IV (over 150 pages) of his massive but now almost
totally neglected work, *The Son of Man* (1910; perhaps the subtitle,
Contributions to the Study of the Thoughts of Jesus, was what put us off!).

There is no better reference point than Abbott for comparing the end of the
twentieth century with its beginning. His collaboration with P. W. Schmiedel in
the *Encyclopedia Biblica* helped expose a conservative English-speaking
audience to nineteenth-century German critical scholarship on John. The result
was increased skepticism about the Gospel's historical value, a skepticism which
moved even William Sanday away from his earlier commitment to authorship by
an eyewitness. Sanday wrote in 1920, "I'm afraid there is one important point on
which I was probably wrong-the Fourth Gospel."[2] Abbott himself, ironically,
moved in the opposite direction, writing in 1913,

> I find that the Fourth Gospel, in spite of its poetic nature, is closer to history
> than I had supposed. The study of it ....appears to me to throw new light on
> the words, acts, and purposes of Christ, and to give increased weight to His
> claims on our faith and worship.[3]

Whatever their disagreements, both sides at the turn of the century believed
that the dominant issues in the study of John's Gospel were authorship,
background, and historical reliability. Conservative scholarship created
alongside the text a subtext or subplot about the aged Apostle John—or perhaps
John the Presbyter—combatting Gnosticism in Ephesus. Not-so-conservative
scholarship had a similar subtext except that no one named John was involved.
But within this framework, straightforward literary approaches held their own for
a time. Abbott's studies of Johannine vocabulary and grammar supported the

---

[2] Cited in W. F. Howard, *The Fourth Gospel in Recent Criticism* (London: Epworth,
1961) 7.

[3] Also cited in Howard, *Fourth Gospel,* 35.

literary unity of the Gospel, laying a foundation for later defenses of its unity by Eugen Ruckstuhl and others. Yet, at the same time, Abbott and others helped open the door for German higher criticism to have increasing influence on the English-speaking world and thus eventually for an increasing emphasis on sources, redactions, and displacements in the study of John's Gospel. All these find their programmatic expression in Rudolf Bultmann's commentary of 1941.

Mark Stibbe argues that, like the Gospel of John itself, "studies of the fourth gospel during the twentieth century exhibit a kind of *inclusio*," with the literary approach being dominant from about 1900 to 1930, going into eclipse between 1930 and 1970, and enjoying a resurgence since then.[4] I am not so sure it is that simple. I began teaching John's Gospel in the late fifties, profoundly influenced in those early years by C. H. Dodd's chapter called "Argument and Structure" (pp. 289-443) in *The Interpretation of the Fourth Gospel* (1953). Dodd is best remembered for his extensive work on the Gospel's background, but his literary analysis impressed me even more. Dodd is still worth quoting. Surely with Bultmann in mind, he wrote:

> I conceive it to be the duty of the interpreter at least to see what can be done with the document as it has come down to us before attempting to improve on it. This is what I shall try to do. I shall assume as a provisional working hypothesis that the present order is not fortuitous, but deliberately devised by somebody—even if he were only a scribe doing his best—and that the person in question (whether the author or another) had some design in mind, and was not necessarily irresponsible or unintelligent.[5]

In short, Dodd turned our attention from the author (or multiple authors) toward the text. This of course did not prevent him from "mining" the text for earlier traditions about Jesus in his 1963 sequel, *Historical Tradition in the Fourth Gospel.*[6]

Other scholars followed Bultmann in looking for sources behind the Gospel

---

[4] M. W. G. Stibbe, *John's Gospel* (London and New York: Routledge, 1994) 1-3.

[5] C. H. Dodd, *The Interpretation of the Fourth Gospel* (Cambridge: Cambridge University Press, 1953) 290; for Bultmann's answer, see his review translated in *Harvard Divinity Bulletin* 27.2 (1963) 9-22.

[6] C. H. Dodd, *Historical Tradition in the Fourth Gospel* (Cambridge: Cambridge University Press, 1963).

and redactional work beyond that of the "Evangelist" (whoever the "Evangelist" might be. Although Bultmann's "revelation discourse" did not carry the day, his "signs source" eventually grew into a Signs Gospel in the work of Robert Fortna, who went so far as to write a commentary on the Signs Gospel and the Fourth Gospel simultaneously.[7] Bultmann's "ecclesiastical redactor" continued to provoke discussion, onto least 6:51-58 found its niche within the last of Raymond Brown's five stages in the development of the Johannine tradition in an imagined Johannine community.[8] Brown, like Dodd, managed to have it both ways, with a unified Gospel as the product of a long and complicated development in the "community of the beloved disciple."[9]

The work of Brown, along with that of Louis Martyn,[10] led to new subplots to the Fourth Gospel. Now one could read "in, with, and under" the story of Jesus other stories about a Jewish Christian community struggling for survival against "the Jews" in an unidentified synagogue somewhere in the Mediterranean world, with one eye on Gnostic secessionists and another on stray followers of John the Baptist waiting in the wings. Like would-be novelists, Johannine scholars created a "world" behind (or was it in front of?) the text, an imaginative social world that intrigued us all. Brown's *The Community of the Beloved Disciple* had as its subtitle on the cover, although not on the title page, "The Life, Loves, and Hates of an Individual Church in New Testament Times."

Yet our debt to Raymond Brown is enormous—even if all his reconstructions were to crumble. Brown gave us the reference point from which to look again either at the existing text or at the Johannine tradition behind it, and New Testament scholarship will surely continue to do both. But our topic today is "The Gospel of John at the Close of the 20th Century," not "The Johannine

---

[7] R. T. Fortna, *The Fourth Gospel and Its Predecessor: From Narrative Source to Present Gospel* (Philadelphia: Fortress Press, 1988).

[8] R. E. Brown, *The Gospel According to John (i-xii)* (AB 29; Garden City, NY: Doubleday, 1966) xxxvi-xxxix.

[9] See R. E. Brown, *The Community of the Beloved Disciple* (New York: Paulist Press, 1979). Brown developed his reconstruction of the Johannine community still further in *The Epistles of John* (AB 30; Garden City, NY: Doubleday, 1982) 69-115.

[10] J. L. Martyn, *History and Theology in the Fourth Gospel* (New York: Harper and Row, 1968). A revised edition appeared in 1979.

Tradition at the Close of the 20th Century," and I am comfortable with the priorities set by that title. The subtexts and subplots, sources, redactions, and displacements are all very interesting, and the famed ambiguities or *aporias* remain, but for me the task at hand is more or less what Dodd said it was forty years ago.

The problem is that some purely literary approaches to the Fourth Gospel are still driven by source and redaction theories which supposedly were bracketed in the interests of a synchronic approach. Even Dodd, who did not advocate a Signs Source, described chaps. 2-12 as "The Book of Signs,"[11] surely a legitimate option, but one that should not be allowed to close out other options too quickly. There is, for example, a decisive break at the end of chap. 3 marking the end of John the Baptist's testimony to Jesus and preparing for Jesus' own self-revelation to the world. Moreover, the theory that John 1:1-18 either was or contained a distinct hymnic source of some kind tended to lock in the notion that these verses were a unit to be set apart from the narrative portions of the Gospel and given separate treatment as "the Prologue." Consequently, the narrative beginning *within* this so-called "Prologue" (1:6), with its echo a few verses later (1:15), was viewed as no narrative beginning at all, but simply an "interpolation" or "parenthesis." The question of whether the true "Prologue" or "Preamble" is 1:1-18 or (as John Chrysostom thought) 1:1-5 is a reader's decision, not something settled once and for all either by the nature of the text or by its supposed sources. Similarly, even when chap. 21 is no longer separated from the rest of the Gospel as an "appendix," 20:30-31 are still almost invariably read as a literary conclusion to chaps. 1-20, or even in some sense to the Gospel as a whole. Fernando Segovia's reading of these verses rather as a transition to Jesus' "final farewell" in chap. 21 comes as a welcome alternative to this persistent tendency.[12] Such examples suggest that narrative or reader response criticism of John's Gospel does not always have to follow the "tracks" left by source- or redaction-critical theories.

What happens when we as readers try out new tracks through this ancient

---

[11] Dodd, *Interpretation*, 297.

[12] F. F. Segovia, "The Final Farewell of Jesus: A Reading of John 20:30-21:25," in *The Fourth Gospel from a Literary Perspective (Semeia* 53; ed. R. Alan Culpepper and F. F. Segovia; Atlanta: Scholars Press, 1991) 167-90.

Gospel? Is there any less diversity than when some of us literally rewrote the text ourselves (through source, redaction, and displacement theories) and generated subplots that interested us more than the text? Probably not. We can display our clashing ideologies just as well by *figuratively* rewriting the text through reader response criticism and the like, as we did in the older ways. Therefore, any answer to the question of the social or theological concerns about John's Gospel or its relevance at the close of the second millennium must be a highly personal one. I will keep mine simple.

More than ever, John's picture of the world we live in looks like a very realistic one. The world is indeed a place of darkness and danger, just as it is characterized in John's story of Jesus—this in spite of the end of the cord War and of apartheid in South Africa, and in spite of prospects for peace in the Middle East and Northern Ireland. Rightly or wrongly, more and more Christians in America and elsewhere see themselves as a besieged or oppressed minority: "If the world hates you, be aware that it hated me before it hated you" (15:18). Although not an apocalyptic work, the Gospel of John speaks to the same impulses that push us toward apocalypticism at the turn of the millennium.

Yet there is a difference. The Gospel of John points us toward a resolution that is not simply beyond or after the present world order, but planted within it by the coming of the light. Jesus brings a revelation to his own, not to the world (14:19, 22), and yet his goal is to "prove the world wrong" (16:8), so that the world will "believe" (17:21) and "know" (17:23) that Jesus is from God. Whether this is a judgment or a transformation of the world as we know it is a matter for definition and ongoing debate. Perhaps it is after all a bit like Edwin Abbott's harrowing journey from Flatland to the Land of Three Dimensions set to take place on December 31, 1999.

As it happens, I have a contract for a commentary on John's Gospel that is due just about then, but I doubt that either my work or that of my academic colleagues will affect very much the continuing impact of John's Gospel on the church or on the American public. Abraham Lincoln was wrong when he said, "The world will little note nor long remember what we say here," but the words may be more applicable in our case. Scholars have never controlled the interpretation of John's Gospel and never will. This ancient book, which gave us the redundant but profoundly significant phrase, "born again Christian," has proved through the centuries to have a life of its own, entirely apart from the fashions of academia. As Christians in America become a smaller and smaller minority, not only in self-perception but in actual fact, there is the possibility that the Gospel of John may draw them closer to each other and, at the same time, separate them more and more from the prevailing values of the culture. In this way the Gospel of John could become a "kinder, gentler apocalypse" for the twenty-first century.

Chapter Eleven

Johannine Theology as Sectarian Theology

GAIL R. O'DAY

In addressing the topic of the Gospel of John at the close of the twentieth century, I would like to focus on the place of the Gospel of John in New Testament theology in particular and the Christian constructive theological task in general. It strikes me that there are two areas in which the label "sectarian" impinges on Johannine scholarship. One relates to the historical and social circumstances that contributed to the particular theological expression of the Fourth Gospel. The second, which is my primary interest here, is the later isolation of this particular theological vision in theological conversations. In New Testament theological work, and in Christian theological work more broadly, the Johannine theological vision is often ignored, restricted, or reshaped to fit other theological perspectives. Some of this is the result of Fourth Gospel scholarship itself, because we are often so fascinated by the puzzles, intricacy, and genius of this Gospel that we tend to treat it as a world unto itself. We worry about things Johannine without always placing "the beloved Gospel" into the broader theological conversation.

Yet, the more far-reaching cause of the isolation of the Johannine theological voice lies in the hold of the Pauline theological vision—with a little Synoptic Gospels thrown in—on the determination of "normative" New Testament theological categories. In particular, the power of the Pauline-Augustinian synthesis in Western theology has shaped the way the Fourth Gospel is available for theological conversation. With the significant exception of Rudolf Bultmann, most New Testament theologians are not versed in both Paul and John, but tend to hear John only as a side voice.

Post-modernist critique of Christian tradition has pointed to some of the limits of the Western theological synthesis (cast largely in Pauline categories),[1] and there is an urgency "at the close of the twentieth century" to identify different theological voices and models that more closely approximate the diversity within the New Testament theological witness. The Gospel of John is a powerful voice *within* the biblical tradition that offers resources to deal with the current theological crisis. My suggestion is that the Fourth Gospel's theological voice needs to be made available for the broader theological conversation.

I offer one illustration of the theological possibilities when the Gospel of John is taken as a central voice—and not a secondary voice—in the theological conversation. In the remainder of the paper, I will review the death of Jesus from the Johannine perspective and suggest how including that voice in contemporary conversations might alter the theological landscape.

John 12:20-36 is the most concentrated Collection of sayings on the death of Jesus in John and therefore provides the appropriate vantage point from which to reflect on the meaning of the death of Jesus in John.[2] Before looking at the Johannine understanding of the death of Jesus, however, it will be helpful to review the theologies of atonement that have shaped and continue to shape theological conversations.[3] It is conventional to speak of three atonement theologies that have had the most influence on Christian understanding of the death of Jesus. These three models are commonly identified as: (1) the ransom or "classical" theory, in which Jesus' death is understood as the act or ransom (payment) that bought the world its freedom from sin and death;[4] (2) the

---

[1] See, for example, M. C. Taylor, *Erring: A Post-Modern A/theology* (Chicago: University of Chicago Press, 1984).

[2] A fuller discussion of the issues addressed in this section can be found in my commentary on the Gospel of John, *The New Interpreter's Bible,* vol. 9 (Nashville: Abingdon Press, 1995).

[3] This review of the three theologies of atonement follows the pattern suggested by D. J. Hall in his thorough review of theologies of the atonement in *Professing the Faith: Christian Theology in a North American Context* (Minneapolis: Fortress Press, 1993) 413-434, 463-480.

[4] The most influential statement of this view of the atonement for the contemporary church is that of Gustaf Aulen, *Christus Victor: An Historical Study of the Three Main Types of the Idea of the Atonement* (trans. A. G. Herbert; London: S.P.C.K., 1953).

substitutionary or sacrificial victim model, in which Christ's death is understood as a sacrifice necessary to atone for human guilt and sin:[5] and (3) the "moral influence" theory, in which Jesus' death is understood as a model of moral behavior because it reveals to humanity how much God loves them.[6]

None of the traditional atonement theologies presents a soteriology that accords with that offered in the Fourth Gospel. Theologies of ransom or substitution are wholly absent from this Gospel's understanding of the cross. For example, John 10:17-18 makes quite clear that Jesus is not a victim at his death in John, but is in complete control (see also 12:27-28). Abelard's theology of Jesus' death on the cross as the demonstration of God's love captures part of the Fourth Gospel's soteriology, but as the discussion below will suggest, overlooks the demand for human response and decision that is an essential part of Jesus' "glorification" in John.

In reflecting on the Johannine understanding of the death of Jesus, it is important to begin by remembering that theologies of atonement are in actuality theologies of reconciliation: they attempt to explain how God and humanity were reconciled to one another in Jesus' death. There is a disheartening tendency in theological conversations in the contemporary North American church to subsume all models of reconciliation under the umbrella of "sacrifice." Sacrifice is one way of understanding reconciliation, but not the only way. The resistance to feminist critiques of the substitutionary model of atonement is a disturbing example of the hold that this model has on popular Christian imagination. Feminist suggestions of alternative models are labeled as a distortion of "the tradition"—heretical or worse.[7] Jesus' sayings in John 12:23-36 suggest an alternative model of reconciliation, one that is built around the *restoration of relationship*.

---

[5] The most influential expressions of this theology of atonement may be found in the works of Anselm and Calvin.

[6] The original proponent of this understanding of the atonement was Abelard, but this theory achieved its popularity in the liberal North American churches through the works of the Social Gospel theologians and others who looked to Jesus as a source for moral inspiration.

[7] The response to the suggestions of an alternative model of atonement by Delores Williams (Sisters *in the Wilderness. The Challenge of Womanist God-Talk* [Maryknoll: Orbis Books, 1993]) is a case in point.

In John 12:24 Jesus' death is described as both necessary and life-giving because, as a result of it, community is formed ("much fruit"). The discipleship teachings, vv. 25-26, which in the Synoptic traditions define discipleship exclusively as taking up one's cross, instead define discipleship as serving Jesus and make clear that the goal of such service is restored relationship with God and Jesus. The passion prediction in 12:32 also focuses on relationship, that through Jesus' death all people will be drawn to him. Finally, in the concluding teaching of vv. 35-36, community is described as "becoming children of light."

Throughout the Gospel, this new relationship to God and one's fellow human beings is described in the metaphors of new birth and new or eternal life (e.g., John 1:12-13; 3:3; 7; 6:51; 12:50). Jesus' glorification is the final step in the offer of this new life, because through Jesus' death, resurrection, and ascension God's relationship to the world itself is irrevocably changed. The world that lives in opposition to Jesus ("this world") is judged by Jesus' death, and its power is obliterated (vv. 25, 31). Jesus' death has this effect, not because it is a sacrifice that atones for human sin, but because it reveals the power and promise of God and God's love decisively to the world.

What is striking about John 12:23-36 is that the connection between Jesus' death and the life of the believing community is repeatedly stressed. The faith community consists of those who redefine the meaning of life on the basis of Jesus' death (vv. 24-26). The faith community is the fruit of Jesus' death for those who believe that leads to the repeated expressions of temporal urgency in 12:23-36 (note, for example, the frequent use of "now" in these verses). It is critical to believe in Jesus so that one can share in the gift of his life, the gift that leads to eternal life, to the confident assurance of God's and Jesus' abiding presence.

For Jesus' death to effect reconciliation with God, then, one must make the decision to believe in Jesus. That is, Jesus' death offers reconciliation to all people, but one must decide to accept this offer. This element of tension between the divine initiative and human response is lacking in all the dominant theologies of atonement, and, as a result, the relationship between the human and the divine is skewed. That is, there is a tendency for discussions of atonement to favor either the side of divine initiative (ransom, sacrifice) or of human embrace of God's love (moral influence), but in the Fourth Gospel the focus remains steadfastly on the inseparable interrelationship that is most fully expressed in the Incarnation.

At the heart of the Johannine understanding of the death of Jesus is the recognition that the death of tells is of a piece with the life of tells. Jesus' death is an expression of Jesus' relationship with God that began "at the beginning." For the Fourth Gospel, then, a theology of reconciliation does not focus exclusively on the death of Jesus, but on the Incarnation itself, the life, death, and resurrection of Jesus, and on the interrelationship of God and Jesus in love that the Incarnation reveals.

The Fourth Gospel, then, makes two important contributions to the ongoing conversation about reconciliation. First, it suggests a way of understanding reconciliation that takes *relationship* as a serious theological category. Jesus' death is the ultimate expression of his relationship to God and to his own (10:16-18). The decision to believe is the decision to become a partner in that relationship, to become a member of a community which is bound to God and tells as they are bound to one another, and whose relationship to one another is an extension of the God/Jesus relationship. Second, the Fourth Gospel insists on *the Incarnation* as the starting point for any conversation about atonement and reconciliation and does not isolate Jesus' death on the cross as the sole agent of reconciliation. Jesus' glorification, the events of his "hour," complete what began in the Incarnation (see 12:28), but the Incarnation itself is the locus of reconciliation.

Chapter Twelve

Important Aspects of the Gospel for the Future

LUISE SCHOTTROFF

I identify myself as a feminist theologian of liberation in the context of Germany or, more broadly, western Europe. I have participated consciously and actively as a Christian woman and theologian in my context through the second half of the twentieth century. In these remarks I should like to address three aspects of the Gospel of John that appear to me to be important for the future: (1) the question of anti-Judaism; (2) the character of Johannine messianism; and (3) the relationship between women and political resistance.

Question of Anti-Judaism

First, then, how can we deal, in future, with anti-Judaism in the Gospel of John, or, to put it another way, with those texts in the Fourth Gospel that can be read as anti-Jewish?

I read the Gospel of John as a document stemming from Christian communities after the year 70 C.E. The Johannine communities consist, for the most part, of people of Jewish origin but contain other people who are not of Jewish origin. The historical context of these communities is sharply defined by conflicts with other Jewish groups and social institutions, with respect to which the Christian communities find themselves in the minority. The Christian communities feel themselves threatened by the Jewish majority. They are clearly aware that the majority Jewish population, in turn, is solidly controlled and intensely threatened by the Roman empire. Thus, the conflict between the Jewish majority and the Jewish Christian minority can only be called tragic, because in the situation between the two Jewish-Roman wars the struggle centering on the Torah as the center of Jewish life and the quest for solidarity against Rome was a matter of life and death for everyone.

Even if I do not locate the Gospel of John in Jerusalem, I would like to describe the situation of Jewish and Jewish Christian people in Jerusalem in the year 135 C.E. as an illustration of the harsh reality within which both sides found themselves at an earlier period in the life of the Johannine communities. Eusebius reports that until the Roman overthrow of the Jewish resistance led by Bar Kochba in the year 135 C.E. there were circumcised Jewish Christian bishops in Jerusalem *(Eccl. Hist.* 4.5). Thus, there were communities made up of a majority of Jewish Christians, under Jewish Christian leadership, that did not reject male circumcision. Some of these communities, along with the rest of the Jewish population of Jerusalem, were viciously slaughtered, while others were driven into exile. After this Roman conquest, it was the will of the conquerors that there should no longer be a Jewish population in Jerusalem. That also meant the definitive end of the Jewish Christian communities in Jerusalem. We can most certainly relate the internal Jewish conflict over the messiahship of Jesus reflected in the Gospel of John with the conflict over Jesus the Messiah that Justin Martyr mentions in connection with the Bar Kochba revolt *(Apol.* 1.31). Justin states that Bar Kochba punished Jewish Christians (even with death; see Eusebius's Chronicle of the 17th year of Hadrian = 133 C.E.) if they refused to deny Jesus. Thus, from the point of view of Jewish Christians, this controversy meant the rejection of the messiahship of Bar Kochba in favor of the messiahship of Jesus and thus the refusal to fight on Bar Kochba's side (Eusebius, Chronicle of the 17th year of Hadrian). This did **not** mean that the Jewish Christian communities **sided with Rome.** Those communities, at least the ones in Jerusalem, were just as much victims of the Roman genocide in the second Jewish-Roman war as were the adherents of Bar Kochba.

The Gospel of John was probably written some decades before those events and not in Jerusalem. But it is rooted in this historical situation of the Jewish people before the second Jewish-Roman war. The internal Jewish conflict that is evident at every point in the Gospel of John also meant, from the Christian point of view, the actual weakening of an endangered people by the rigorism of their own Christian position. The dualism of the Gospel of John, which is very close to that of the Gnostic movement, was an obstacle to what I would call, from our present perspective, the necessary solidarity with the majority Jewish population.

However, Johannine talk about "the Jews" and their consignment to the darkness if they do not acknowledge Jesus as Messiah only became anti-Judaism in the period after 135 C.E., when the Gentile Christian church regarded the Jewish Christian communities as merely an insignificant sect. There was no longer a Jewish Christian church with which it needed to contend. The resulting anti-Judaism in the Gospel of John is immediately apparent today, in my own context, whenever the corresponding texts in the Gospel of John are read in worship without any critical commentary. In my context it is particularly brutal because most German congregations have no need to confront any newish people just as was the case for the Gentile Christian church after 135 C.E. and the Roman genocide of the Jewish people. The mass destruction of taws by Germans during the third Reich and the revival of German anti-Semitism have made the Gospel of John a dangerous book in my context. By its mere existence it legitimates Christian and German anti-Semitism today. From my perspective, and in my context, the only option is to use the Gospel of John to maintain awareness of the murderous injustice of Christian antisemitism and to criticize it and thereby to walk the long road to solidarity with Jewish and Jewish Christian people then and now.

Character of Johannine Messianism

Second, how can we give clear expression to the liberating power of Johannine messianism?

Johannine messianism differs from the messianism of the people (*ochlos*) as represented in the Gospel of John. The people long for a liberating messianic struggle against Roman oppression (see 6:15) . The Jewish leadership suppresses both the messianism of the people and that of Jesus' adherents in order not to subject the very existence of the people to Roman genocide (11:48). Jesus says to Pilate: "My kingdom is not of this world" (18:36). This statement, together with Johannine dualism as a whole, is often interpreted in the sense of an a-political Christianity. A distinction is drawn between a Jewish political messianism and a "higher" Christian messianism, so that the religious truth of the latter is kept separate and distinct from any political consequences. "Not of this world" then means, for example, Christian praxis within a small group or conventicle which is shut off from the outside world, which will have nothing to do with the real struggles of the people, and whose God corresponds to a religious praxis that is deliberately withdrawn from politics.

This view of the praxis that corresponds to Johannine messianism does not fit the Gospel of John. In it people who do not openly confess Jesus as Messiah are sharply criticized (see 12:42-43). Jesus, in turn, does not separate himself from the political messianism of the people. It is true that he is "king of the Jews" in a different sense from that desired by the people, but he is the king of the Jews. In particular, Jesus' road to his passion shows how Christian praxis is to be understood in the thought of the Gospel of John: while not coming "from the world," it is active on behalf of the world and the Jewish people (see also 3:16; 4:42). Moreover, according to the Gospel of John, Jesus' death is not a political misunderstanding; it is a martyrdom on behalf of the whole people. Like the other Gospels, the Gospel of John stands within the Jewish tradition of martyrdom as the way to a political liberation of the people. The difference between it and the messianism of the people can be described as a choice between liberation through armed rebellion against Rome or through martyrdom and a lived faith in the God of Israel. Also from a Christian perspective, there is no avoiding the conflict with the Roman government and the Roman army.

Biblical scholarship often emphasizes the central importance of the passion story in the Gospel of John. However, western reception of John contains a strong tradition of interpretation of the Gospel of John as the text of an a-political conventicle and/or an otherworldly Christianity. Under the influence of Rudolf Bultmann's interpretation of John, which dominated in Germany for such a long time, I adopted this interpretation of John in my first scholarly encounter with it, even though I offered a theological critique of an otherworldly Christianity. Today, I am attempting to understand the text in the context of its historical situation, from a political and social point of view; consequently, I read the passion story as a story of resistance, including that of the Johannine communities.

In western Christianity the history of Jewish and Christian martyrdom is almost universally interpreted as an alienating tale of masochism. For me, access to a different understanding of the story of the passion and the history of martyrdom has been opened by Latin American liberation theology and the Fourth Book of Maccabees. The martyred women and men murdered by the military dictatorships in Latin America are risen and living in the hope of their suffering people. The Fourth Book of Maccabees interprets the death of the martyred women and men as a *hilasterion,* an expiation for the soul of the people stained by sin. Through their death, the tyrant and his army lose their power over the people (4 Macc 17-21). The people for whom Jesus died, according to John, consist of the Jewish people and the world, the humanity that rejects God, whom God judges and toward whom God graciously turns.

Women and Political Resistance

Finally, what is the connection between the fascinating traditions of the women in the Gospel of John and that Gospel's tradition of political resistance?

I call many of the women's traditions in the Gospel of John fascinating, even though on closer inspection the picture also contains some dark spots. Let me make this explicit by using John 4 as an example. What is fascinating here is the narrative of a theological dialogue between a nameless Samaritan woman and Jesus. Fascinating are the deeds told of this woman—of which more in a moment. The dark spots I see mainly in the history of interpretation of John 4:16-18: male exegetes (and a few female interpreters as well) read the biography of the Samaritan woman as a story of sexual lust and unbridled passion. These dark spots can be expunged by social-historical inquiry.

A widow or divorced woman had to make sure that she found another patriarchal owner (husband), because her social and economic opportunities were very restricted if she remained unmarried. Babatha, a Jewish woman we encounter in the materials from Nahal Hever, found it necessary, as a young widow with a baby, to marry a man who already had a wife. Apparently, in spite of the fact that she had some kind of economic basis of her own, she saw no alternative to life as the second wife of a man who was evidently much older than she and who died soon afterward. The Samaritan woman probably had a thoroughly typical woman's biography in patriarchy behind her.

Thus, this dark spot can be eliminated through some social-historical reflection. She was a victim or, at most, a cooperator—she understands herself as an agent (4:29, 39) in a patriarchal system that oppressed women. It is more difficult to eliminate the dark spot represented by the way in which Jesus' Samaritan followers despised this woman (4:42). Nevertheless, her actions are fascinating: she allows a Jew to drink from her water jar; she questions him in detail; she dismisses the man (4:17) with whom she lives, who did not even marry her; and she abandons the water jar that she undoubtedly carried several times a day back and forth between the well and the village. Her hard work—many women developed twisted backs by carrying water—is a yoke that she casts from her. She acknowledges her past as a woman married many times, and she becomes the messenger of Jesus, the Messiah, spreading the word in Samaria that he is the savior of the world.

A woman's story like this is often read as a story happening in a place outside political reality: in the house, in the world of family and personal care—far from Roman politics and the history of Jewish resistance. But there is no such unreal place. Babatha was ultimately murdered in a cave where she had hidden, like many other Jewish people, seeking refuge from the Roman army. The Samaritan woman lived not many miles from that cave. Through her actions, she called into question the system of patriarchal oppression of women. In the eyes of the Roman authorities and Roman law, she was therefore deserving of death. Rejection of marriage and subjection to men was regarded as a crime against the state—as we know from the book of Esther, the Acts of Thecla, and other sources. The Samaritan woman went even further. She stood in solidarity with a Jewish Messiah in a world in which the slightest suspicion of Jewish messianism was punished with death, on order of the emperor. The Samaritan temple on Mount Gerizim, like the temple in Jerusalem, was destroyed both by Titus and by Hadrian (Eusebius, *Theophany* 4.23).[1] When the Johannine communities told the story of this woman, they walked with uplifted heads—a perspective for the twenty-first century.

---

[1] Eusebius, *Theophany* 4.23; H. G. Kippenberg, *Garizim and Synagoge* (Religionsgeschichtliche Versuche and Vorarbeiten 30; Berlin and New York: de Gruyter, 1971).

Chapter Thirteen

The Gospel at the Close of the Century:
Engagement from the Diaspora
FERNANDO F. SEGOVIA

The question regarding the significance and relevance of the Gospel of John at the close of the twentieth century demands of the critic an open and frank dialogue with the text. Such dialogue calls for the ground rules of the conversation to be established from the outset, especially since one of the partners in the conversation—indeed the focal partner—is altogether absent from the table, the real author of the Gospel. All one has, in effect, is the implied author or, more accurately still, the implied author as constructed by the various readers and critics, including oneself.

I come to the dialogue at this point in my life with a reading strategy of intercultural criticism, ultimately grounded in what I call a hermeneutics of the diaspora.[1] Before turning to the conversation itself, I should like to begin with a few comments regarding the overall contours and ramifications of such a hermeneutics and reading strategy, so that the character and tone of my conversation with John is clear from the beginning.

---

[1] For the hermeneutics of the diaspora, see "Toward a Hermeneutics of the Diaspora: A Hermeneutics of Otherness and Engagement," in *Reading from This Place*. Volume 1: *Social Location and Biblical Interpretation in the United States* (ed. F. F. Segovia and M. A. Tolbert; Minneapolis: Fortress Press, 1994) 57-73. For the reading strategy of intercultural criticism, see "Toward Intercultural Criticism: A Reading Strategy from the Diaspora," in *Reading from This Place*. Volume 2: *Social Location and Biblical Interpretation in the United States* (ed. F. F. Segovia and M. A. Tolbert; Minneapolis: Fortress Press, 1995) 303-30. For the theology of the diaspora, see "In the World but Not of It: Exile as Locus for a Theology of the Diaspora," in *Latino-Hispanic American Theology: Promise and Challenge* (ed. A. M. Isasi-Diaz and F. F. Segovia; Minneapolis: Fortress Press, 1996) forthcoming.

Character of Dialogue

To begin with, the hermeneutics of the diaspora is rooted in and addresses my own reality and experience in and of the diaspora. At its core lie the concepts of otherness and engagement.

The first concept, that of otherness, is grounded in and reflects the reality and experience of otherness on the part cc individuals from non-Western civilizations who reside, for whatever reason, on a permanent basis in the West. It is a concept with a negative side to it, specifically conveyed by its placement in quotation marks ("otherness"): such otherness implies a biculturalism with no home, no voice, and no face. From this point of view, we find ourselves, following the dynamics of colonial discourse and practice, in the position of permanent aliens and strangers in the world: as imposed and defined "others"—home-less; face-less; voice-less.

The second concept, that of engagement, similarly rooted in and reflects the experience of the non-Western immigrant or refugee in the nest, represents the positive side of otherness, best conveyed perhaps by its placement in a different font, whether italics *(otherness),* my actual preference, or bold **(otherness).** Such otherness embraces biculturalism as its very home, voice, and face: it rejoices in having two homes, two voices, and two faces. Such otherness also holds that all reality—all homes, all voices, and all faces—is construction and, as such, has both perspective and contextuality; that there are many such realities or worlds; and that these worlds or realities, as constructions, can be critically analyzed, questioned, and altered. From this point of view, we find ourselves, following the dynamics of decolonization and liberation, in a position of critical engagement in the world: as self-affirming and self-defining others, not only creating our own home, voice, and face in light of our own reality and experience but also engaged in critical dialogue with all other voices and faces.

Such a hermeneutics involves a corresponding reading strategy, which I call intercultural criticism. Such criticism calls for an approach to the text as an *other* rather than an "other"—as a reality to be acknowledged, respected, and engaged in its very otherness rather than overwhelmed or overridden. To be sure, the task envisioned is not at all an easy one. Indeed, if in contemporary life, as the diaspora well teaches us, it is negative "otherness" that prevails, even as such others struggle to defend and define themselves, how can positive *otherness* be expected in a situation where the others in question lie long silent and can no longer define or defend themselves? In fact, it is a highly utopian task in which one has to resist at all times, against incredible odds, a reading of others as "others" in the light of one's own social location and agenda.

It is with such a formidable task in mind that I pursue intercultural criticism:

-First, intercultural criticism remains embedded in modernism, insofar as it approaches the text as something which is both historically distant and culturally remote. As such, the text is seen in terms of poetics, rhetoric, and ideology: a literary or esthetic, strategic or practical, and cultural or political construction.

-Second, intercultural criticism is also embedded in postmodernism, however, insofar as it is fully aware that a text is not something out there, a reality preceding and guiding interpretation, but rather something that is always read and interpreted, a "text." As such, it is highly conscious of the fact that, even when attempting to treat the text as an *other,* the resulting reading or interpretation is in itself a construction on the part of a reader: a poetic, rhetorical, and ideological product in its own right.

-Third, intercultural criticism is embedded as well in Liberation Theology. Such an attempt to dis-cover and re-create the otherness of the text is undertaken not for the sake of historical or antiquarian interest—a questionable proposition in and of itself within any view of historical research as inextricably contextualized and interested—but rather for the purpose of critical engagement with the text. The operative attitude, therefore, is not one of reverence for the text but rather one of dialogue and struggle with the text in the light of one's own reality and experience.

In the dialogue with the Gospel of John that follows, two points should be made quite clear: first, it is with my own reading and interpretation of the text— my own "text"—that I find myself in dialogue—not with any sort of objective and universal meaning; second, it is from my own social location and agenda in the diaspora that I undertake the dialogue—not from any sort of ideal or universal perspective. Consequently, just as I am perfectly content to admit that there are many possible interpretations of the text, so am I quite glad to admit that there are many possible evaluations regarding its significance and relevance for our context at the turn of the century.

Dialogue with John

With the ground rules properly set forth, I proceed to the conversation itself. I limit myself to three positions that I see as fundamental to the work: (1) its characterization of the world; (2) its ideology of chosenness; and (3) its view of life in the world.

Characterization of the World. Despite certain positive elements in the Gospel's depiction of the world (for example: its creation by the Word of God; the love of God for the world; the human journey of the Word of God; the assigned mission of the children of God in and to the world), the prevailing picture of the world in the Gospel is profoundly negative. Thus, prior to the coming of the Word, the world is said to be in darkness; despite its creation by the Word, the world is described as in the power of supra-human evil spirits; with the coming of the Word, hatred of God emerges as its overriding and distinguishing characteristic; before the departure of the Word, the world is altogether excluded from the prayer of petition and intercession on the part of the Word.

From the perspective of the diaspora, the world of everyday life emerges as deeply divided: overridingly hostile, but calling forth struggle and resistance; fateful and inescapable, yet constantly arousing hopes of and strategies for change; a world of ultimate resignation and endless defiance. On the one hand, therefore, there is much in John that resonates with the reality and experience of the diaspora: the world as fundamentally evil and unjust. It is very difficult for anyone who has had to live through the experience of colonialism and dictatorship, domination and repression, exploitation and civil strife, to put aside the brutal reality of the world. It is very difficult as well for anyone who has undergone the experience of emigration and exile, loss and dislocation, separation from one's home and resettlement in somebody else's land, to forget the bitter reality of the world. For anyone who has found himself or herself thrown into both sorts of experiences and discourses, it is extremely hard to think of the world in terms of wellbeing and justice. On the other hand, there is also something missing in John. From the diaspora, such a stark view of the world is counterbalanced throughout by a clear and irrepressible thirst for justice and wellbeing, a desire to make the world a more pleasant and righteous place in which to dwell. And this, I must confess, I do not find in the Gospel.

Ideology of Chosenness. This characterization of the world is accompanied by a self-characterization of the followers of the Word in the world in terms of an ideology of chosenness, an ideology of over/against: we are the light of the world, the children of God, the ones whom had loves, the ones in whom the Spirit of God dwells, the abode of God in the world—in short, the chosen ones of God. In other words, the Gospel presents human beings in terms of binary oppositions: world versus those not of the world; children of the evil one vis-à-vis children of the Father; those in darkness versus the enlightened ones.

From the perspective of the diaspora, there is, to be sure, a perception of one's voice and face as not of the world, as somehow set apart and specially enlightened: in possession of that insight into the world as construction that only someone in the margins can truly possess. In this regard there is much from the harper that resonates: the utter otherness of the Word of had in the world. At the same time, however, there is, on the basis of hard experience, a profound suspicion of all engulfing narratives, over/against hermeneutics, and totalizing ideologies: in the end, with any ideology of chosenness, one is never too far from a *Herrenvolk* concept, a concept of imperial manifest destiny. In this regard, I am afraid, there is much in the Gospel that repels.

View of Life. Given such characterization of the world and such self-characterization on the part of those who regard themselves as not of the world, it is not surprising to find in the Gospel no basic charter for change in the world and transformation of the world. The call in the end is for patient and strategic abiding and endurance in the face of oppression, for eyes to be fixed on the real home, the real world, of the chosen ones: the house of the Father, where rooms have already been prepared for their use and enjoyment. In the meantime, one continues, under the harshest of circumstances, to attempt to bring light to the world, to attract people to the circle of loved ones, and to engage in love for and service of one another.[2]

From the perspective of the diaspora, there is much here that attracts: given our position in the world, the call for patient and strategic abiding and enduring

---

[2] Such is the message, for example, of the all-important farewell discourse of Jesus in chaps. 1317, in which a vision of the status and role of the children of God in the world is drawn by the implied reader through the eyes of the departing Word; see my *The Farewell of the Word: The Johannine Call to Abide* (Minneapolis: Fortress Press, 1991).

again finds resonance. It is, after all, a call for a face, a voice, a home—a call with which we can readily identify. At the same time, there is much here that disappoints: it is not on an other-world that we want to fix our eyes but on this-world. We remain very much in this world; we know that it is not the way it is solely by the will of God; and we wish to change it, alter it, transform it, with wellbeing and justice in mind. We look for a worldly face, a worldly voice, and a worldly home as well.

Conclusion

In the end, I find myself both nodding and shaking my head as I read the Gospel. Out of my own praxis, I find myself in great sympathy with the point of view of the implied author: how can one speak of the presence of God, of justice and wellbeing, in the world? Out of my own praxis, I also find myself in profound disagreement with such a point of view: speak one must, over and over again, against all odds, for change and transformation, for wellbeing and justice, and for a God who needs to be very much present everywhere. From my diaspora, then, the significance of the Gospel, in terms of its assessment of the problem, remains unquestionable; its relevance, in terms of its proposed solution, must, however, be radically questioned and actively resisted. At the turn of the century, I can only go so far with it.

Chapter Fourteen

What Have I Learned about the Gospel of John?
D. MOODY SMITH

As we approach the end of the twentieth century, and the second millennium, can we confidently assert that we now understand the Gospel of John better than ever before? Or did Irenaeus at the end of the second century already understand it better than we do? The latter is perhaps a moot question, because if he did we presumably wouldn't know it. (It belongs to not knowing not to know that one does not know!) Nevertheless, there are some significant things that we do understand better than Irenaeus, if only because our interests and questions are different. I want to take this opportunity to say what these things are. To put the question in another, more personal way, "What have I learned about the Fourth Gospel in now nearly forty years of marinating in this Gospel and its problems?

The first serious biblical, exegetical books I purchased as a theological student were C. H. Dodd's *Interpretation of the Fourth Gospel*[1] and C. K. Barrett's commentary.[2] As I recall, each cost $7.50, expensive books, but well worth it. These were followed a year or so later by Rudolf Bultmann's *Theology of the New Testament*,[3] and then his *Das Evangelium des Johannes*,[4] over which

---

[1] C. H. Dodd, *The Interpretation of the Fourth Gospel* (Cambridge: Cambridge University Press, 1953).

[2] C. K. Barrett, *The Gospel according to St. John: An Introduction with Commentary and Notes on the Greek Text* (London: S.P.C.K., 1955).

[3] R. Bultmann, *Theology of the New Testament* (trans. K. Grobel; 2 vols.; New York: Scribner's, 1951, 1955), esp. 2:3-92.

[4] R. Bultmann, *Das Evangeliums des Johannes* (Kritisch-exegetische Kommentar über das Neue Testament 2, 15; Göttingen: Vandenhoeck & Ruprecht, 1957). English translation by G. R. Beasley-Murray, R. W. N. Hoare, and J. K. Riches, as *The Gospel of John: A Commentary* (Philadelphia: Westminster Press, 1971).

I was to labor tirelessly—and I hope not tiresomely. All of these were not only important but good purchases, and they have informed my reading of the Fourth Gospel in salutary ways. What have I learned? Nothing that no one else knows, and a few things that some colleagues of great erudition are determined not to know. Notwithstanding a lack of consensus on some crucial issues, however, I make bold to lay out the most significant things I know.

I should say at the outset that I do not know who wrote the Gospel of John and believe that the author, who has none too humble an estimate of the value of his work, has purposefully and successfully concealed his identity. Dodd left the door open to the tradition of Johannine authorship. Barrett became morally certain John the Apostle did not write this Gospel: Bultmann, who doubtless shared the latter view, showed no interest in the question. In the very nature of the case, it would be extremely hazardous to predicate exegesis upon a view of Johannine authorship, traditional or other. It is not a matter of insignificance, however, that the Gospel claims that it is based on an eyewitness, or eyewitness testimony. Although historical criticism does not take this claim at face value, it must nevertheless be conjured with seriously. Now to the things I know.

What I Do Know About the Gospel

HISTORICAL SETTING IN THE GOSPEL

This Gospel invites historical questions, and cries out to be understood historically, that is, in its original historical setting, which is importantly related to Judaism. As a divinity student I heard Professor W. D. Davies say that he believed Paul kept the law all his life. I rushed up after class to protest, politely of course, in the name of the doctrine of justification by faith alone. Professor Davies reminded me, equally politely but firmly, that Paul must be read in his own setting rather than that of the Protestant Reformation.

Seeing John in its historical setting has until recently meant seeing it as a sort of culmination of the development of New Testament theology, or of theology within the New Testament. To see John in that way has seemed reasonable to a host of exegetes, particularly, but not only, in the modern period. After all, Clement of Alexandria thought that John wrote his spiritual Gospel in light of the other three, which set forth the bodily facts. Calvin saw in John the christological key to the other Gospels. Against this background Bultmann,

Dodd, Kümmel[5] and others seem quite reasonable, indeed, traditional, as they treat John as in some sense the culmination of the development of New Testament theology.

Yet there is something at least questionable about this view of John, historically speaking, as Bultmann already saw. It is not entirely obvious that John intentionally builds on earlier Christian witnesses and writings. Did John know the Synoptics? Opinion remains divided, as it was in Bultmann's day. Bultmann thought not. If he knew them, did he have a positive view of them or write with them in view? As Hans Windisch showed, it is possible to grant John's knowledge of the other Gospels without conceding that he approved them or wrote as he did with them in view.[6] Did John know and build upon Paul? Bultmann saw a fundamental theological kinship, but did not think it possible to interpret John as a development of, or on the basis of, Paul.[7] That John reads well as the culmination of New Testament theology does not mean that John wrote with that purpose. To maintain that position may, in fact, make it difficult to grasp John's actual historical (and theological) setting and purpose. For Dodd, who saw the Gospel addressed to an educated Hellenistic readership (with perhaps some familiarity with Judaism), or for Bultmann, who saw in its Gnostic roots a means of exposing a profound understanding of human existence, the historical setting and purpose of the Fourth Gospel were general, if not universal. Among those who have seen in the frequent references to "the Jews" as the enemies of Jesus an indispensable clue to the Fourth Gospel's origins, J. Louis Martyn and Raymond E. Brown have made the most

---

[5] W.-G. Kümmel, *The Theology of the New Testament According to its Major Witnesses: Jesus—Paul—John* (trans. J. E. Steely; Nashville: Abingdon Press, 1973).

[6] H. Windisch, *Johannes and die Synoptiker: Wollte der vierte Evangelist die älteren Evangelien ergänzer oder ersetzen?* (Untersuchungen zum Neuen Testament 12; Leipzig: J. C. Hinriches'sche Buchhandlung, 1926).

[7] Bultmann, *Theology of the New Testament,* 2:9:

Clearly, then, John is not of the Pauline school and is not influenced by Paul; he is, instead, a figure with his own originality and stands in an atmosphere of theological thinking different from that of Paul ....and this independence of John emerges all the more clearly as one perceives *the deep relatedness in substance that exists between John and Paul* in spite of differences in their mode of thought and terminology.

noteworthy contributions.[8] Bultmann's view that "the Jews" of John symbolize unbelief may well contain its grain of truth. Yet the widely held assumption, rooted in antiquity, that John is the latest of the canonical Gospels tended to exclude the possibility that these references to "the Jews" were actually a clue to its original setting. It seemed unlikely that these were "real" Jews. John was assumed to be a generation or so beyond the point of the rupture between the parent, Judaism, and its child, Christianity, a point marked by the work of the Apostle Paul. Yet this view assumed, without sufficient justification, that the so-called rupture with Judaism occurred early, uniformly, and universally. It also assumed that a Gospel written toward the end of the first century would no longer reflect this rupture. Both assumptions are dubious.

It is now generally believed that the Gospel of John is a document that reflects in significant and revealing ways the early relations and rupture between synagogue and church, whether or not the reconstructions of Martyn or Brown are in every detail tenable. Quite possibly John intends to encourage believers in Jesus in his own time and place to identify themselves, and, if they are still within the synagogue, to come out. On the other hand, it is unlikely that John portrayed a controversy with "the Jews" in the time of Jesus, when there was little or no tension in his own time, to encourage Christians living peaceably in synagogues to break with them—that is, that the Gospel suggests a conflict that actually non-existent at the time of its composition. (There is ample evidence in New Testament times of tension between Christians and Jews.) Thus it is widely held that the Martyn-Brown hypothesis captures something essential about the Gospel of John.[9] The Gospel is a controversy document, not

---

[8] Martyn first set forth his view in *History and Theology in the Fourth Gospel* (New York: Harper & Row, 1968; revised and enlarged edition, Nashville: Abingdon Press, 1979). Brown's view was first suggested in his commentary, *The Gospel According to John: Introduction, Translation, and Notes* (2 vole.; AB 29, 29A; Garden City, NY: Doubleday, 1966, 1970) and elaborated in *The Community of the Beloved Disciple* (New York: Paulist Press, 1979).

[9] See my assessment in "The Contribution of J. Louis Martyn to the Understanding of the Gospel of John," in *The Conversation Continues: Studies in Paul and John* (ed. R. T. Fortna and B. R. Gaventa; Nashville: Abingdon Press, 1990) 275-294, esp. 285-291, and the statement of Wayne A. Meeks quoted on 288. Since the publication of my article, the *magnum opus* of John Ashton, *Understanding the Fourth Gospel* (Oxford: Clarendon Press,

a synthesizing document, although it may, in fact, bring together and express essential elements of Christian belief in ways that have become enduring.

The historical setting of the Fourth Gospel also has something significant to say about its alleged anti-Semitism. There is no doubt that "the Jews," or, more correctly, some Jews, are the villains in the Fourth Gospel. The presentation of them reflects, however, a specific historical situation of conflict. We   do not hear directly from the other side, the Jews, in their own documents, although it is not quite correct to say that we know nothing of them. In fact, the Jews are represented as defending monotheism, the law, and their status as children of Abraham. Of course, John does not present them in a favorable light, but his presentation is not an unrecognizable caricature. To take John's negative references to "the Jews" and apply them to Jews in every time and place is to make an identification and application the Fourth Evangelist would have never imagined. Yet the fit between "the Jews'" rejection of Jesus and Judaism's historic positions is recognizable, so that the view that "the Jews" represent historical Judaism and unbelief seems a reasonable one.

An historical view of Johannine origins thus defuses anti-Semitism, but the key issue is how and for what purpose John is read: to condemn the opponents of Jesus or to affirm the salvation and life that believers find in him? Certainly the latter accords more closely with the Gospel's purpose. Yet the other is also present. The community of interpretation remains crucial for understanding the meaning of "the Jews" in the Fourth Gospel. Thus in some circumstances John has been read as an anti-Jewish book. Perhaps more basic conceptually than the portrayal of the Jews in John, however, is the underlying dualism, found also in other documents such as the Johannine Matters and the Dead Sea Scrolls, particularly the Community Rule. (The opponents of the Qumran community are, of course, not called "Jews," but the level of hostility is no less acute.) Tellingly, "the Jews" are nowhere to be found in the letters of John, but the dualism remains and the intensity of hostility is undiminished. The enemies now are not Jews but other, heterodox Christians. In all probability Meeks was profoundly correct to see in John's dualism not so much conceptual borrowing from other sources, whether Jewish or Hellenistic, as a reflection of a social and

---

1991), offers further confirmation of the importance of Martyn's work.

religious situation of alienation and hostility.[10] the roots and effects of such dualism are crucially important, not only for understanding John, but for understanding something about ourselves and the human condition.

JOHN AS AN INDEPENDENT GOSPEL

If John is in some significant sense a Jewish Gospel, it is also an independent Gospel. To say this does not in principle exclude the possibility that John knew other Gospels. Yet John cannot be adequately understood as a supplementation or interpretation of the other canonical Gospels or of any other Gospel that we know or possess.

In my own study of John's relationships with the Synoptics, the commentary of Edwyn Hoskyns was at first enormously important.[11] Hoskyns' view, that John wrote in order to put a proper theological interpretation upon the narratives) of the Synoptics, or something essentially similar to them, to prevent them from being misinterpreted, is initially quite attractive.

John may reasonably be taken to clarify the Synoptics or to make explicit what they imply. Yet such a reading runs into difficulty because at important points, or in significant ways, John contradicts the Synoptic narrative or departs from the Synoptic portrayal of Jesus.

Thus Hans Windisch could maintain that John knew the Synoptics (certainly Mark, probably Luke, possibly Matthew), but departed from them quite deliberately to go his own way. This remains a viable view in my judgment. Indeed, if John conjured seriously, and basically, with the Synoptics, it is more plausible to think his purpose was to displace them rather than to affirm or supplement them. John seems to have gone out of his way to ignore, if not contradict, the other canonical Gospels. John does not accommodate his account to them in any way. When Percival Gardner-Smith proposed that John was simply ignorant of the Synoptics,[12] however, that seemed a more likely

---

[10] W. A. Meeks, "The Man from Heaven in Johannine Sectarianism," *JBL* 91 (1972) 44-72.

[11] E. C. Hoskyns, *The Fourth Gospel* (ed. F. N. Davey; rev. ed.; London: Faber and Faber, 1947).

[12] P. Gardner-Smith, *Saint John and the Synoptic Gospels* (Cambridge: Cambridge University Press, 1938).

possibility to many exegetes, including C. H. Dodd, who made the case exhaustively in his monumental *Historical Tradition in the Fourth Gospel*.[13]

Moreover, the contacts between John and the Synoptics, while real, seem to lie at the fringes or later stages rather than at the center or core of the tradition, even where the accounts run parallel. The works of Bultmann, Brown, and Robert Fortna[14] suggest that where John and the Synoptics are obviously dealing with the same event (e.g., the Triumphal Entry, the Arrest, the Trial before Pilate, the Death of Jesus), John's narratives—while showing points of contact— are not readily explained as having been derived from Mark or any of the Synoptic accounts. John's account does not depart from the Marcan, or synoptic, in ways that may be described as typically Johannine.

Of course, John's total structure or plan, while bearing the broadest similarity to the Synoptics, differs from it in major respects: the three-year ministry, the predominance of Jerusalem and Galilee, the dating of Passover, etc. In the public ministry, the points of contact with Mark or the Synoptics appear haphazard or difficult to comprehend. Thus scholars such as Bultmann, Brown, Fortna, Rudolf Schnackenburg, and Ernst Haenchen—whose approaches, methods, and results often differ in principle and detail—agree that John's contacts with the other canonical Gospels lie at the periphery, and presumably at the later stages of development, rather than at the core or center of the traditions employed.[15]

One inevitably encounters the question of what sources or traditions John

---

[13] C. H. Dodd, *Historical Tradition in the Fourth Gospel* (Cambridge: Cambridge University Press, 1963).

[14] The commentaries of Brown and Bultmann have already been noted (see nn. 8 and 4 above). See Fortna's most recent *The Fourth Gospel and its Predecessor* (Philadelphia: Fortress Press, 1988) *passim*.

[15] The works of Bultmann, Brown, and Fortna are noted above (see nn. 4, 8, and 14). See also R. Schnackenburg, *The Gospel According to St. John* (3 vols.; Herder's Theological Commentary on the New Testament; trans. K. Smyth, C. Hastings, D. Smith, and G. A. Kon; New York: Herder and Herder; Seabury, 1968-82); and E. Haenchen, *John 1/2: A Commentary on the Gospel of John* (2 vols.; ed. U. Busse; ed. and trans. R. W. Funk; Hermeneia; Philadelphia: Fortress Press, 1984).

used, if not the Synoptics. Here critics from R. P. Casey[16] to Frans Neirynck[17] have protested that it is better to work with known sources than with hypothetical ones. In principle this seems an unimpeachable preference. Yet the question of whether the Synoptics actually are the sources of the Gospel of John cannot be begged on the basis of even this good principle; that is, in the name of Ockham's Razor. On the one hand, possible sources other than the Synoptics do not present themselves; at best, they are no longer extant. On the other, efforts to explain the Johannine passion narratives or other parallel accounts as the rewriting of the Marcan (or Synoptic) narratives face significant difficulties, as we have noted. Of course, efforts to uncover the narrative source(s) of the Fourth Gospel, in the passion narrative or elsewhere, often agree on some points, but diverge on others. For example, the attempt to delineate or excavate a sign source (or gospel) from beneath the narrative surface of the Gospel has met with some agreement, and mixed success, among a number of scholars (e.g., Bultmann and Fortna), but has met strong resistance in other quarters.[18] It is perhaps not surprising that agreement is far from complete, even among exegetes who believe John relied on sources other than the Synoptics. Probably John had a miracle source(s) or traditions and an independent passion narrative, very likely written. Our inability to agree on the nature and extent of such a source does not imply it never existed. (Analogously, our inability to reach consensus on any number of historical-critical issues does not mean that they do not exist or that they are, so to speak, out of bounds to inquiry.)

There is, of course, always the possibility that John's use of the Synoptics finds its closest parallel in the way the authors of the apocryphal Gospels used

---

[16] R. P. Casey, "Professor Goodenough and the Fourth Gospel," *JBL* 64 (1945) 535-542.

[17] Frans Neirynck's position has been set forth in a number of works, perhaps most extensively in his debate with M.-É. Boismard, *Jean et les Synoptiques: Examen critique de l'exegese de M.-E. Boismard* (with the collaboration of J. Delobel et al.; BETL 49; Louvain: Louvain University Press, 1979). See also his "John and the Synoptics 1975-1990," in *John and the Synoptics* (ed. A. Denaux; BETL 101; Leuven: Leuven University Press, 1992) 3-62.

[18] Not surprising in the Louvain school, of which Frans Neirynck is the leading voice, but not only there. See now G. Van Belle, *The Signs Source in the Fourth Gospel: Historical Survey and Critical Evaluation of the Semeia Hypothesis* (BETL 116; Leuven: Leuven University Press, 1994).

the Synoptics, or all the canonical Gospels, for that matter.[19] Because of the conventional dating of the apocryphal Gospels in the second century or later, their knowledge of the canonical Gospels becomes a foregone conclusion. (Obviously the late dating and presumption of knowledge of the canonical Gospels are interrelated.) Yet it has recently been argued that certain apocryphal Gospels are actually not later than their canonical counterparts.[20] If not, then they need not presuppose them. On the other hand, if they are later, they obviously do not regard the canonical accounts as canonical in the sense of fixed or immutable forms of narrative. Rather they are still subject to change or midrashic elaboration (as in the case of certain Old Testament books or narratives: cf., for example, the canonical books of Chronicles and the pseudepigraphical Testaments of the Twelve Patriarchs and the Book of Jubilees). In either case, the apocryphal Gospels are not controlled or constrained by the canonical, much less the Synoptic Gospels, in the same way that even Mark controls, or constrains, Matthew and Luke.

It is not necessary to prolong consideration of these intriguing possibilities. Basically the apocryphal Gospels offer two, alternative parallels to John's use, or disuse, of the Synoptics. If John, like a few of the apocryphal Gospels, simply did not have access to the Synoptics, the Gardner-Smith position is affirmed. On the other hand, even if all the apocryphal Gospels' authors had access to the canonical Gospels, there could be an interesting parallel to the case of John and the Synoptics. In neither instance would the Synoptic Gospels exercise control over the Johannine or apocryphal narratives. Both of the latter would have to be seen as exercising remarkable freedom over against their antecedents. It could be maintained that this later position fits the observation that John, like most apocryphal Gospels (insofar as we know them), seems to presuppose on the part of the reader knowledge of the Gospel story. This may be true, but if so, that only raises the further question of whether the Gospel story itself was the sheer invention of, let us say, Mark—so that knowledge of that story means knowledge of Mark—or, alternatively, whether Mark availed himself of a prior

---

[19] See D. M. Smith, "The Problem of John and the Synoptics in Light of the Relation between Apocrypahl and Canonical Gospels," *John and the Synoptics,* 147-162.

[20] For a full statement of this position, see J. D. Crossan, *Four Other Gospels: Shadows on the Contours of the Canon* (Minneapolis: Winston, 1985).

tradition concerning the necessary order and content of any narrative of Jesus' ministry. In the latter case knowledge of the story would not necessarily imply a literary relationship, at least not within (or to) the canonical Gospels.

JOHANNINE COMMUNITY AS DISTINCTIVE

Independent traditions behind the Fourth Gospel, as well as the synagogue conflict, bespeak the existence of a distinctive Johannine community. If John embodies independent traditions, their existence implies a traditioning community. And even if John somehow presupposes the Synoptics, the departures from the Synoptic narratives do not give the impression of self-conscious and purposive literary redaction, but look more like what might happen in a traditioning community.

Of course, the very existence of the Johannine Epistles means that there was a Johannine circle of churches if not a Johannine school. I think both. The Johannine circle is a certainty, even if the letter writer is the same as the evangelist, as tradition holds. But I think it more likely that the letter writer is not the same as the evangelist. Indeed, it is far from certain one author wrote all the letters.[21] If not, then the evidence of a Johannine school increases. All these authors talk, or write, the same. They employ the same theological vocabulary, and even their syntax is similar. Moreover, issues cast up by the Fourth Gospel are dealt with in the Epistles, especially 1 John, as Brown has amply shown.[22] For example, the generous promise of the Spirit-Paraclete, who would lead the community into all truth (16:13), may well have led to competing claims of Spirit possession on behalf of divergent doctrinal positions (1 John 4:13), thus creating a severe problem, not only of doctrine, but of authority within the community. That the latter sort of problem existed is amply clear from 2 and 3 John as well.

----

[21] Judith M. Lieu *(The Theology of the Johannine Epistles* [New Testament Theology; Cambridge: Cambridge University Press, 1991]) demonstrates the relationship but also the complexity of the relations among the Epistles, and hence the difficulty of simply assuming common authorship. See also her *The Second and Third Epistles of John: History and Background* (Edinburgh; T. & T. Clark, 1986).

[22] See R. E. Brown, *The Epistles of John* (AB 30; Garden City, NY: Doubleday, 1982) *passim*, esp. 69-115.

QUESTION OF EDITING

If the Gospel of John is the product of a community or school, within which a great deal of theological and related debate has gone on, it will not surprise us to discover that this fundamental document *(Grundschrift)* of the community has been edited, perhaps repeatedly.

Quite apart from this consideration, the evidence for the redaction of john is stronger than in the case of any other Gospel, or, for that matter, in any other New Testament book. Chapter 21 is unquestionably a later addition, whether by the original author or a later hand. Probably the latter. If 14:31 were followed by 18:1, no one would ever miss chapters 15-17. In fact, 14:31 anticipates 18:1, not the immediately following chapters: "Arise, let us go hence ....Having said these things, Jesus went out with his disciples across the Brook Kidron." Chapter 6 with its Galilean locale, fits after John 4 better than chap. 5, which is set in Jerusalem. Were they transposed at some point in the Gospel's redaction history? Although the matter of whether 6:52-58 is a later addition, and to what purpose, is still debated, it certainly marks a shift in terminology and focus that warrants such a view. Possibly, some of the statements that seem to be editorial corrections, or at least emendations, were in fact added by a later hand (e.g., 3:24; 4:2;18:9). Occasionally the redaction may have been intended to bring the Johannine account into line with the Synoptic (e.g., 3:24; 4:2; 21:15-23; 21:24-25), but this is not always the case. Seemingly, the redaction would have missed many opportunities to make the Fourth Gospel account accord with the others.

In any event, the view of Brown that the redaction took place in a Johannine milieu, or community, and was not a means of bringing this idiosyncratic Gospel into line with a developing orthodoxy (Bultmann) seems on the face of it plausible and probably true.[23] It may be, as Brown suggests, that chap. 21 intentionally reconciles Johannine Christianity with other, apostolic Christians, but his conception of this as an inside job rather than an imposition from without fits the character of the redactional changes, as well as their nature and tone. The redactional elements, insofar as they can be identified, do not reveal a divergent style or vocabulary. Whether they really manifest a different

---

[23] Ibid., 108-112. Bultmann *(The Gospel of John: A Commentary,* 700-706) emphasizes the difference between chap. 21 and the rest of the Gospel by way of showing its divergent character and purpose.

theological perspective—in the sense of an incongenial one—is a matter of debate. At least it is not obvious to all exegetes that they do.

It is a curious fact, as John Ashton points out,[24] that Bultmann never paid attention to the question of the historical, generative milieu of the Fourth Gospel within a Christian community or communities, as much as he dealt with, and endeavored to explain, its *religionsgeschichtliche* background, and even its relation to the putative Baptist sect. Thus it is perhaps not surprising that he seems not to set the composition of the Gospel and the redactional process within a common community. As far as I can see, in principle nothing stood in the way of such an attempt, which one might have expected, given Bultmann's meticulous effort to understand the synoptic tradition in its historical context.

THE GOSPEL IN THE CONTEXT OF THE NEW TESTAMENT

Having first said that John cries out to be understood in its originative historical context, I must now maintain with equal seriousness that John cries out to be interpreted in the context of the New Testament.

Exegetes as diverse as Clement of Alexandria, Calvin, and Bultmann have maintained or implied that John is, theologically speaking, the culmination or keystone of the canon. John brings to expression and emphasizes what is distinctly Christian. This is particularly true with respect to theology, indeed, dogma. Ernst Käsemann's reading of John as dogma accurately strikes an indispensable historical, exegetical, and theological note.[25] John intended to say what Christians—initially his own community—believed in the face of contradiction and opposition, initially from Jews who had once shared the same community. The value of his accomplishment has long been apparent to Christians, but there is also a dark side (an appropriate metaphor in view of the light-darkness dualism of the Johannine literature).

This dark side is ultimately related to the polemical character of the Johannine books (including Revelation, if it be included). The polemical character of the Gospel—for convenience let us confine ourselves to it—is in turn intimately related to what seems an inevitable aspect of human existence,

---

[24] Ashton, *Understanding the Fourth Gospel*, 101-11.

[25] E. Käsemann, *The Testament of Jesus: A Study of the Gospel of John in the Light of Chapter 17* (trans. G. Krodel; Philadelphia: Fortress Press, 1968).

namely, alienation and hostility within individuals, between individuals, within communities, and among communities. In such a crucible of alienation and hostility Christianity was born. In fact, this dimension or aspect of existence is finally caught up in a definitive way in the crucifixion of Jesus himself. The one who teaches and exemplifies love is caught up in the contrarieties of human existence and succumbs to them, or so it seems. Resurrection faith is, among other things, belief that this is not the last word, but rather that God has yet another word.

The Johannine Jesus is then the supreme expression of that divine love that calls human beings to respond by loving God and loving one another. He teaches and exemplifies that love in a definitive way (13:34; 15:12). Thus he is the true light who enlightens every human being (1:9). Yet because the light is so pure, true, and powerful, the darkness is all the more incomprehensible, and those who choose darkness rather than light can only be condemned, because their deeds are evil (3:17ff.). Historically, these people are first "the Jews," but very quickly they become heterodox Christians (1 John 4:1-3; 2 John 7). Paradoxically, the Gospel that contains the purest portrayal and distillation of God's love in Jesus at the same time contains the harshest condemnation of those who have rejected that love and now seemingly stand over against it and outside it.

A great deal more could be said, but I confine myself to a few comparisons of the Gospel of John with other New Testament books or traditions that helpfully put John in a broader perspective.

1. Both John and Matthew present Jesus against a Jewish background, after all his proper historical milieu. It has frequently been suggested that Matthew is the most Jewish of the Gospels, probably because Matthew presents the most Jewish Jesus. If John has sometimes been depicted as the least Jewish Gospel, that is because his Jesus seems not to be Jewish at all, but the Jews' opposite number. Yet John knows well that Jesus was Jewish (4:9, 22). Nevertheless, it is hard to imagine a more anti-Jewish depiction of Jesus' fellow Jews than that found in Matthew 27:25 ("His blood be on us and on our children.") There is obviously also something going on between Matthew's community and the synagogue. On the other hand, Matthew's Jesus himself takes a quite positive position toward biblical, and even Jewish, tradition (5:17-20, for example). He debates not about the "whether" but about the "how" of scriptural interpretation

and certainly would not have spoken of the law as "your law" (cf. John 8:17). There is little doubt that Matthew presents a more accurate picture of Jesus' teaching, the issues he addressed and the positions he took, than does John, who concentrates in a narrow and, strictly speaking, unhistorical manner on Jesus as a teacher of christology who argues about his own status and dignity with Jewish opponents. The Matthean Jesus stands within Judaism, albeit as a figure of unprecedented authority, and addresses issues of common concern. Exactly these issues, which concern human expressions of piety, care for others, and obedience to God, are matters which have a broad appeal and interest to people generally. They are not related to the particularly Jewish-Christian issues and debates about Jesus' claims and role that dominate the Gospel of John. Put briefly, we may need the Gospel of John to interpret adequately who Jesus is, but we also need the Gospel of Matthew (and Mark and Luke) to make intelligible and humane the claims made for Jesus in the Gospel of John.

2. Paul, on the other hand, is similar to John in his unremitting concentration on issues of christology and faith. Like John, Paul does not purvey the actual concrete context of Jesus' ethical teaching, although he may know something about it and on occasion seems to allude to it. For example, in his two citations of Lev 19:18 (Rom 13:9; Gal 5:14), Paul may reflect knowledge of Jesus' love command, although he does not attribute it directly to Jesus. Nevertheless, Paul's interest seems to be elsewhere, on what God is effecting for humanity through Jesus. Yet just at this juncture, Paul obviously differs from John at several points, which are crucially important. For one thing, Paul sets the salvation event within the framework of God's covenant relationship with his people Israel. In doing so, he makes it quite clear that he intends to interpret the sending of the Son (Gal 4:4) as a culminating event within that history, but not as the cataclysmic abolition of it. Moreover, he refuses to announce the abolition of God's promises to Israel, his people, because they have refused his offer of salvation. Christians tend to interpret Paul's "All Israel will be saved" (Rom 11:26) to mean they will accept Jesus as Messiah as a response to the (Gentile) Church's preaching. Paul, however, seems not to want to put the matter in these terms.

As to the Christ event itself, Paul, as is commonly and correctly said, sees the significance concentrated in the death of Jesus. Usually, Paul speaks of the effect of this death in cultic or juridical terms. Yet Paul clearly views it as an act of God's love and compassion (Rom 5:6ff.) in which Jesus actively participated. While the death of Jesus was a murderous act, it was carried out by men who did not understand what they were doing (1 Cor 2:8), not by men who saw the issues plainly and yet decided against Jesus (John 19:14-16). Thus in Paul's thought, the death of Jesus effects not division and further alienation and hostility but peace and reconciliation, as he states in 2 Cor 5:16-21, where God's action in Christ clearly means his action in Jesus' death. Paul never tires of emphasizing the regenerative power of Jesus' death (Rom 6:1-4), that it brings into being a new situation (Rom 7:1-6). The interpretation of Christ's work as making peace and bringing unity among peoples set forth in Eph 2, while perhaps going beyond what tact wrote, understands and interprets Paul's theology of the cross correctly. There are then essential dimensions of a theology of the cross that are lacking in John and need to be supplied from Paul. Yet in John Jesus' death is the revelation of the glory, the glory of God, and owe does have Jesus say, " I, when I am lifted up from the earth, will draw all people to myself" (12:32). There is a universal, missionary thrust in John (17:20-23) that stands in some tension with the characteristic sharp dualism. For the most part, however, Jesus' death in John is the fulfillment of the world's, or the Jews', enmity. He dies in defense of his own. His death underscores the gulf that separates Jesus from his enemies.

3. Hebrews, like John, portrays the revelation, and covenant, established by God, through Jesus, as superseding the old (Heb 8:13). In Hebrews, as in John, the pre-existent Son was God's agent in creation. The Jesus of Hebrews is for the most part the exalted high priest, the heavenly Christ, as in John. Yet for Hebrews as for owe the incarnation is indispensable and its reality unequivocally stated (cf. John 1:14 and Heb 4:14; 5:1-4, 7-10). Christian theologians have, I believe, tended to interpret the laconic assertion of John 1:14 in light of Hebrews' eloquent testimony to what it means to be human, and to suffer. Here Hebrews fills up what is lacking in the Gospel of John, as does the First Epistle (especially 1:1-4 and 4:1-3).

While both John and Hebrews take what might be described as a negative attitude to the Judaism contemporary with them, there is a significant difference. John seems to urge believers in Jesus to come out, separate themselves, from the synagogue. Hebrews, if interpreted along traditional lines, urges Christians not to revert to the synagogue. (I am aware that this interpretation of the purpose of

Hebrews is no longer so widely held as it once was.) The point is that the Gospel of John seems much nearer to the historical point of genuine hostility and breach. Hebrews appears farther removed. There is remoteness rather than hostility. Whatever persecution may be coming (12:9) is not anticipated from Judaism or Jews. The heroes of Israel are examples of faith for the community, and Jesus assumes his place as the pioneer and perfecter of their (and our, the Christians') faith (12:2). He endured hostility from sinners (12:3), not Jews specifically. Supersession for Hebrews seems a more technically theological, and religious, matter, than a point of still-heated debate and conflict. There is a sense in which Christian theology is in the very nature of the case supersessionist in its view of and relationship to Judaism.

At least it was so viewed by ancient Jews. Otherwise, there might have been no Christianity. Yet on this point we have something to learn from the Letter to the Hebrews, which takes a somewhat longer and calmer view of these matters than does John. My point, in conclusion, is very simple. John does bring into clear focus important issues of Christian theology. For good reason John has seemed to represent the essence of distinctive Christian doctrine, especially christological doctrine. There is nothing wrong with that. In fact, it is helpful, not only for Christians, but for others who want to know what Christianity is about. Yet when the Gospel of John is taken out of the context of the other canonical Gospels, and the New Testament generally, it conveys a truncated view of what early Christianity, much less Jesus of Nazareth, was about. To put matters succinctly, only the Jesus of the Sermon on the Mount warrants the claims made by, or for, the Johannine Christ. So John needs now to be read in a canonical context. Apart from that context its claim to authority is strident, shrill, and even dangerous. Only within that context do the claims of the Johannine Jesus carry authentically Christian significance and conviction.

Postscript

This essay began as a lecture, delivered from brief notes, in which I put aside all considerations of balance and bibliography and simply asked, "What have I learned?" More than half a year later I have, in good tradition-historical fashion, moved from the oral to the written stage and have tried to reconstruct, style, and state a bit more carefully what was said on that occasion.

As I now contemplate what I said, I am struck by how old-fashioned and conservative it must appear to those now working on the forefront of Johannine research, who may get the impression that the author has not read much, or been much affected by what he has read, in the last twenty-five or so years. To the reader as to myself, it will become apparent how traditional in the sense of historical and theological my own interests and commitments are.

My fundamental assumption is that we are presented with a given, the Gospel, which we are trying to perceive for what it was in order to understand and assess its meaning, which is aptly described as revelatory, as it models and invites theological reflection. Moreover, I have come to realize that the discernment of a given in the Gospel is not necessarily grounded upon foundationalist philosophical presuppositions, but may itself be a perception of faith. Not of faith as commitment to established doctrine, but faith as the expectation of hearing what one would not otherwise know or could not otherwise believe. Historical research and reflection stand in the service of such hearing.

Naturally, much recent work on the Fourth Gospel bears upon this interest and concern. One rightly asks about the literary character of the Gospel,[26] about how it is to be read,[27] or how it functions as revelation.[28] The question of what is presupposed by the Gospel now moves from *religionsgeschichtliche* investigations of a century ago to contemporary sociological and anthropological theory, for which such research is by no means irrelevant.[29] Yet my own assessment of the usefulness of such research cannot be divorced from a perhaps inchoate, yet fundamental, determination to hear the text and to learn from it about God and myself. Quite possibly the proof of the possibility of such hearing then lies within myself. But, of course, not within myself only, for then

---

[26] R. A. Culpepper, *Anatomy of the Fourth Gospel: A Study in Literary Design* (Philadelphia: Fortress Press, 1983).

[27] F. F. Segovia, *The Farewell of the Word: The Johannine Call to Abide* (Minneapolis: Fortress Press, 1991).

[28] G. R. O'Day, *Revelation in the Fourth Gospel: Narrative Mode and Theological Claim* (Philadelphia: Fortress Press, 1986).

[29] J. H. Neyrey, *An Ideology of Revolt: John's Christology in Social Science Perspective* (Philadelphia: Fortress Press, 1988). Note the earlier work of Wayne A. Meeks; see n. 10 above.

the danger of autism or solipsism would be unavoidable. One inevitably reads and hears the Gospel of John within the context of a community of hearers and readers who strive to understand the text and interpret it among themselves.

On the one hand, this can mean—but does not necessarily mean—that one reads, hears, understands, and interprets the Gospel, like the Bible generally, within the Christian church. (This churchly text of interpretation is intimately connected with the call to read John within the canon.) In that case, historical work is by no means irrelevant, as it takes account of past interpretations going all the way back to, and including, the origins of the text. The Christian interpreter has an important interest in knowing what the text has meant, and even what the author intended, even if those putative meanings are not to be identified with the revelation of God through the text, which is always a present, and ongoing, event.

On the other hand, however, the Gospel of John, as a part of a corpus of ancient literature, may also be read and interpreted in other communities, with other interests. Preeminent among these is the Society of Biblical Literature, whose interests, constituency, and expectations have become quite different, even in the several decades in which I have been a member. Perhaps in order to put this sort of difference quite simply, Krister Stendahl coined his now proverbial distinction between what the text meant and what the text means. The former might then be regarded as the province of SBL and the latter of the church, or churches. But things presently appear more complex. Professional members of SBL now conjure with the question of what the text means in relative independence of what it meant. While Christian theologians and theological exegetes obviously engage the question of the present meaning of biblical texts, they have, as we have noted, an interest in establishing that those present meanings all importantly relate to what the text meant. Thus there may be a fruitful overlap and interpretation with the still lively historical and literary interests of the professional society. (One might, however, ponder the significance of the change of the Society's name several decades ago when "Exegesis" was dropped, so that SBLE became SBL.)

If I were to offer an alternative to Stendahl's distinction, it would have to do with control rather than past and present (i.e., "meant" and "means"). Who is in control and what is the purpose of control? Professional exegetes as interpreters of biblical texts in the scholarly or academic community have as their proper purpose and goal to control the text, that is, to explain it, whether as a phenomenon of ancient or modern culture. The presumption is scientific: that we shall master the object of investigation. The theological or churchly exegete seeks to understand the text in order to be controlled by it. Such exegesis has a great deal in common with preaching, properly understood. The goal is not to stand outside or above the text in order to explain it, but to stand within or under the text in order to be explained by it. Whether there is any common interest or ground between such attitudes and approaches is not an insignificant question. Obviously, I think there is, but this is far too large and important a subject to be aired fully here. Certainly it deserves continuing discussion from either side.

Conclusion

Reading Readers of the Fourth Gospel and Their Readings:
An Exercise in Intercultural Criticism
FERNANDO F. SEGOVIA

In a study such as this one, concerned as it is with reading and how different readers of the same text, in this case the Gospel of John, approach and interpret that text, it is appropriate if not imperative for me as reader to outline my own approach to the reading of these readers and their respective readings of the Gospel. In so doing, both the rationale and contours for the mapping of these readings will become clearer. In what follows, therefore, I begin with a number of preliminary comments about reading, its constructs and strategies; then turn to an analysis of the various reading constructs and strategies employed by these different interpreters of John and the results of such strategies and constructs; and conclude with some reflections on the exercise as a whole. In the process, not only will the enormous diversity of contemporary approaches to the Fourth Gospel become quite obvious but also the enormous range of opinion regarding its interpretation, significance, and relevance.

Reading—Strategies and Constructs

I begin, then, with some remarks on reading as such, first from the point of view of my own reading strategy and construct and then from the point of view of reading constructs and strategies in general.

READING FROM THE DIASPORA: INTERCULTURAL CRITICISM

I have described my strategy for reading in terms of intercultural criticism and its underlying theoretical orientation and élan as a hermeneutics of the diaspora, a hermeneutics of otherness and engagement.[1] Both are grounded in

---

[1] For intercultural criticism, see "Toward Intercultural Criticism: A Reading Strategy from the Diaspora," in *Reading from This Place*. Volume 2: *Social Location and Biblical*

my own reality and experience of the diaspora, with its corresponding theology of mixture and otherness, a variation of Liberation Theology, and thus presuppose a social-reader construct—a reader from the diaspora of non-Western civilizations residing in the West and a reader with overriding sociocultural and sociopolitical concerns and commitments.[2] By way of introduction, a few words about the hermeneutics of the diaspora in order.

First, with regard to the element of otherness, I should explain that it is my aim in this regard to look at the text—any text, written or otherwise—as an other to me as much as possible, not as an "other" to be controlled and overwhelmed (signified by its placement in quotation marks) but rather as an *other* to be respected and acknowledged in its own terms (signified by its highlighting in italics). This is an exercise which I regard as highly utopian and ultimately elusive, given what I consider to be a fundamental ethnocentric tendency to read the other in our own being and likeness, yet also essential, given the ever-present need to recognize that one's world is but one version of "reality," with its own perspective and location. Second, with regard to the element of engagement, I should further explain that this search for otherness entails not only acknowledgment of and respect for such *otherness* but also engagement with it, a critical dialogue with liberation in mind. In other words, the purpose of such an exercise in criticism is not simply to survey and describe the other but rather to converse and struggle with the other in the light of one's own context and agenda.

Out of this hermeneutics of the diaspora, there emerges a reading strategy with three basic interrelated and interdependent dimensions in mind. First, a

---

Interpretation in the Global Scene (ed. F. F. Segovia and M. A. Tolbert; Minneapolis: Fortress Press, forthcoming: 1995) 303-30; for the hermeneutics of the diaspora, see "Toward a Hermeneutics of the Diaspora: A Hermeneutics of Otherness and Engagement," in *Reading from This Place*. Volume 1: *Social Location and Biblical Interpretation in the United States* (ed. F. F. Segovia and M. A. Tolbert; Minneapolis: Fortress Press, 1995) 57-73.

[2] See "Two Places and No Place on Which to Stand: Mixture and Otherness in Hispanic American Theology," *Listening. Journal of Religion and Culture* 27 (1992) 26-40; and "In the World but Not of It: Exile as Locus for a Theology of the Diaspora," in *Hispanic American Theology: Promise and Challenge* (ed. A. M. Isasi-Diaz and F. F. Segovia; Minneapolis: Fortress Press, forthcoming).

reading of the text in question as a literary, rhetorical, and ideological construction in its own right. Such a reading constitutes not so much the retrieval and reconstitution of a text but rather the production of a "text" on my own part. Second, a reading of all such "texts," including my own, as literary, rhetorical, and ideological constructions in their own right. Since a text is conceived not as something "out there" but as something that is always read and interpreted, any reading or interpretation of it, including my own, is always a "text," with its own perspective and location. Such inter-"textual" dialogue, I might add, offers a certain measure of protection in the search after *otherness,* insofar as one repeatedly comes across any number of readings of the same text besides one's own. Third, a reading of the readers behind "texts," including myself, as literary, rhetorical, and ideological constructions in their own right. Since a text is regarded as something that is always read and interpreted, the real readers behind such "texts," their constructs and strategies, become as important for analysis as either the texts themselves or their "texts." Indeed, within such a perspective, the reader also functions as a text, with its own location and perspective.

In this particular essay my focus of attention will be not on a reading of the Gospel of John as such, the production of a "text" of the Gospel on my part, although I do carry out such a task as one of the participants in the symposium on the significance and role of the Gospel at the turn of the century; nor on a reading of my-"self" as a reader, as a text, although the present section does provide elements of such a reading; but on a reading of different "texts" of the Gospel—different readings of the Gospel by different readers from different perspectives and social locations, and with different purposes in mind, though also with a common interest on a self-conscious approach to the reading and interpretation of the Gospel.[3] It is, therefore, an attempt on my part to see how

---

[3] I should point out that, given my own participation as both reader and editor in the project, such a reading of "texts" on my part will involve critical analysis only in the sense of a comparative examination of the various reading strategies and constructs used by the different real readers in question. To engage in critical analysis in the sense of dialogue and struggle with these different real readers regarding their respective interpretations of the Gospel would be unseemly as well as unfair, in the light of my twofold position in the project.

the Gospel is read, interpreted, and evaluated in the contemporary scene, at the close of the twentieth century, by readers who not only live in the aftermath of the theoretical and methodological explosion in biblical criticism but who also take into serious and self-conscious consideration the question of reading the Gospel.

READING CONSTRUCTS AND STRATEGIES: A MAPPING

For such an exercise, an overall sense of the different reading constructs and strategies available to readers of the Gospel is in order.[4] Most important among these for my purposes here is what I would call the universal-reader/real-reader axis, which I shall use as the primary axis of analysis. In other words, I am particularly interested in how the real readers represented in these pages address and deal with their own status and role as real readers in the reading, interpretation, and evaluation of the Gospel.

At one end of this spectrum lies the universal-reader construct: uncontextualized or without location, neither historically situated nor culturally conditioned; a perceptor and describer of "reality"; objective and value-free. At the other end, lies the real-reader construct: thoroughly contextualized and located, historically situated and culturally conditioned; a constructor of "reality"; subjective and value-oriented. Both poles, it should be emphasized, are constructs: while a universal reader is patently a construction of real readers, the real reader, howsoever conceived, is also a construction of real readers—that is to say, it is the way that readers choose to construct themselves at any one t ime given their social location and perspective.

In addition to this primary axis of inquiry, a number of other axes, secondary but nevertheless important for my purposes, are not only possible but common.

---

[4] For reader-response criticism in biblical criticism, see: R. M. Fowler, "Who is 'the Reader' in Reader Response Criticism?" in *Reader Response Approaches to Biblical and Secular Texts* (ed. R. Detweiler; *Semeia* 31; Atlanta: Scholars Press, 1985) 5-23; S. D. Moore, *Literary Criticism and the Gospels: The Theoretical Challenge* (New Haven and London: Yale University Press, 1989), esp. chap. 6; R. M. Fowler, "Reader-Response Criticism: Figuring the Reader," in *Mark and Method: New Approaches in Biblical Studies* (ed. J. C. Anderson and S. D. Moore; Minneapolis: Fortress Press, 1992) 50-83; "Reader Response Criticism," in *The Postmodern Bible* (ed. The Bible and Culture Collective; New Haven and London: Yale University Press, 1995) 20-69.

While some intersect naturally with the real-reader pole of the primary axis, others do so with respect to the universal-reader pole.

Real-reader Constructs. Real-reader constructs may be analyzed from two different points of view: the social-reader/individual reader axis and the compliant-reader/resistant-reader axis.

First, real-reader constructs admit of two basic types, the individual reader and the social reader, and thus one can readily speak of a social-reader/individual-reader axis. At the individual-reader pole of the spectrum, the emphasis is on the reader as an individual subject, with the focus on psychological location and the psychological issues of the individual in question. Obviously, the variety of individual-reader constructs is countless, a situation which is further complicated by the options regarding psychological or psychoanalytic theories to be used in analyzing psychological location. At the social-reader end of the spectrum, the emphasis lies on the reader as a social subject, a member of distinct social groupings or communities, with the focus on social location and the social issues of the grouping(s) in question. Again, a wide variety of social-reader constructs is possible, depending on which social dimension(s) of identity is highlighted—socioreligious; sociopolitical; socioeducational; race; gender; sociocultural; and so on.

Second, real-reader constructs can also be classified according to the degree or extent to which they accept or reject the claims of the text, thus giving rise to the compliant-reader/resistant-reader axis. At the former end of the spectrum, there is the reader who readily submits to the claims of the text as an ideological construction; at the latter end, the reader who will have nothing to do with the text and its message.

Universal-reader Constructs. Universal-reader constructs may be examined from a number of different perspectives, such as the process of reading; the knowledge of the reader; and the experience of reading.

First, there is the firsttime-reader/multiple-reader axis with a focus on the process of reading. A firsttime-reader construct approaches the text as a fresh reader altogether (largely paralleling, therefore, the experience of the narratee)—without any previous knowledge of the text; attentive to the details of the narration; reacting to this information (or lack thereof) as it is dispensed (or withheld); having knowledge only of what has transpired in the text up to the point of reading; speculating about future developments in the text. The multiple-reader construct approaches the text as a seasoned reader—with previous and extensive knowledge of the text; attentive to the whole of the narration and aware of patterns and cycles in the text; reacting to the text as a whole; having knowledge of the text from beginning to end. While the firsttime-reader pole places a high value on temporal sequence and slow-motion reading, the multiple-reader pole favors spatial arrangement and fast-motion reading.

Second, there is the historical-reader/textual-reader axis with a focus onto knowledge of the reader. A historical-reader construct approaches the text as if living in a different time or culture, usually pretending to match those of the text in question; the textual-reader construct approaches the text as if it were the reader that the implied author had in mind into composition of the text. While the former construct tends to rely on information external to the text, the latter construct is put together from the information provided by the text itself.

Third, there is the naive-reader/informed-reader construct with a focus on the experience of reading. A naive-reader construct approaches the text with no information about the subject matter whatsoever—whether from a literary, historical, or social point of view—while an informed-reader construct comes to the text with a claim to considerable expertise in such matters. While the former construct emphasizes innocence, the latter values sophistication.

I would conclude by emphasizing that in all of these reader-construct axes there is a broad central section or middle range; in other words, the choices presented within each axis of approach and inquiry are by no means binomials or alternatives but multiple or options. The reading constructs and strategies available to readers of the Fourth Gospel are thus numerous and far-ranging. In what follows, I should like to examine both the position papers regarding the Gospel and the reflection papers on the Gospel in the light of these various axes, but again with special attention to the that of the universal-reader/real-reader.

What is John?

With the rationale and contours for this exercise in intercultural criticism on my part properly set forth, I turn to a critical analysis of the reading constructs and strategies adopted and actual readings produced by a variety of academic, professional readers of the Gospel. There are two different kinds of readings. The first type has to do with self-conscious approaches, from a number of different perspectives, to the question of reading the Fourth Gospel and consists of eight extended position papers in all, gathered together in a first part entitled, "Readers and Readings of the Fourth Gospel." The second involves comments by real readers on the significance and relevance of the Gospel at the turn of the century and brings together six brief reflection papers in all, brought together in a second part entitled, "The Gospel at the Close of the Twentieth Century." The result is a kaleidoscopic overview of approaches to the Gospel as well as of interpretations and evaluations of the Gospel in the contemporary scene and hence an excellent barometer of biblical criticism today as seen through the focus of Johannine scholarship.

READERS AND READINGS OF THE FOURTH GOSPEL

Although the position papers have been divided, for heuristic purposes, into the two categories of "Literary Approaches" and "Theological Approaches," I much prefer to engage these papers on a strictly alphabetical basis, given not only the porousness of the distinction itself but also the character of the proposed analysis.

Ethical Challenges to the Gospel (R. Alan Culpepper). with regard to the primary universal-reader/real-reader axis, the only such axis actually invoked, Culpepper opts entirely for a real-reader construct in his approach to the Gospel. This real reader is of the social-reader type and reveals a variety of layers, all ultimately interrelated and interdependent—a real reader with socioreligious, socioeducational, and sociocultural dimensions.

First and foremost, Culpepper presents himself as a Christian, with the following points in mind: within the Protestant tradition; a member of the Southern Baptist church; and a child of foreign missionaries, who grew up in the southern cone of the Americas. From this socioreligious perspective, Culpepper is specifically interested in the Gospel as a *document of faith*—a "text that shapes the character and content of one's religious beliefs"—and points to a fundamental shift, a "pilgrimage," in his own attitude toward the Gospel as a document of faith. This pilgrimage is presented in terms of a binomial opposition. On the one hand, in keeping with the Protestant principle of the centrality of Scripture, Culpepper points out how, for most of his life, he never questioned the character of the Gospel as a document of faith—a text that conveyed the essence of the Christian gospel to all peoples at all times. On the other hand, he reveals how, in the light of the increasing pluralization of U.S.

culture, he has begun to wonder about its relevance as a document of faith for Christians in contemporary culture. Such considerations provide the driving force behind this first essay.

In addition, Culpepper also comes across as a highly-trained academic reader, thoroughly acquainted with the Gospel's history of interpretation. Such a history he unfolds in terms of recurring challenges to its status as a document of faith: first, in terms of theological orthodoxy, involving its early use by Valentinians and Montanists alike; second, in terms of historical accuracy, having to do with the rise of historical criticism in the 19th century and its challenge to traditional approaches to biblical interpretation; more recently, in terms of ethical relevance. In other words, this is a document of faith with a history of interpretative crises— a text that has survived a number of earlier challenges and is now faced with a third and very different challenge, a text once again in danger of losing its authority for believers.

Finally, Culpepper describes the present crisis affecting the Gospel in terms of three broad sociocultural concerns. His findings are mixed, ranging from very pessimistic to thoroughly optimistic. First, working out of a post-Holocaust context and prompted by comments and reflections on the part of Jewish scholars regarding the hostility of the Gospel toward Jews, Culpepper agrees that the anti-Jewish character of the Gospel is quite profound and cannot be at all circumvented. His response is quite pessimistic in this regard: aside from paying closer attention to the actual translation of the Greek term *hoi Ioudaioi*, Culpepper can only argue for aggressive awareness of the Gospel's anti-Judaism.[5] Second, faced with recent questions on the part of commentators from marginalized social groups whether the Bible, including the Fourth Gospel, has anything to say to such groups, Culpepper answers much more positively: a number of recent studies do indeed indicate that such is the case; consequently,

---

[5] At the same time, it is Culpepper's position that, from a strictly historical point of view, the Gospel is not anti-Jewish as such, insofar as (a) it reflects conflict within the synagogue itself and thus comes from a period in which Christians and Jews are not clearly distinct; (b) the first Christians were for the most part Jews; and (c) what the Gospel opposes is unbelief not Jewishness as such. The problem is thus not with the Gospel as such but with the reception and use of the Gospel. Similar positions, with certain variations, will be adopted by both Schottroff and Smith.

there is need for traditional critics—male, Western interpreters—to exercise a hermeneutics of suspicion with regard to their own contexts and agendas in the face of such voices, a hermeneutics that deals openly with issues of power and privilege.[6] Third, in the light of dialogue with individuals of other religious traditions and the concerns of non-Western Christians, Culpepper adopts a middle-of-the-road position regarding religious exclusivism in the Gospel, with a view of the Gospel as contradictory in this regard: while undeniably presenting salvation in terms of confession in Jesus as Christ, the Gospel also projects the figure of the cosmic Christ as the light that enlightens every human being, undercutting thereby any claims to Christian monopoly on God's revelation.[7]

In the end, therefore, Culpepper's pilgrimage remains open: the firm certitude of earlier years has given way to a position of cautious ambiguity. In effect, the Gospel can still function as a document of faith for Christians in a pluralistic society, but it all depends on how the Gospel is interpreted, how Christian believers respond to the new ethical concerns coming to the fore. For Culpepper, therefore, the real reader must also be a resistant reader. As such, Culpepper calls for a hermeneutics of ethical accountability—for critical methods that are forthcoming about location and interests, aware of the text's own ambiguities and open to the voices of the marginalized, and attuned to the effects and implications of criticism. Only then, he concludes, can the Fourth Gospel remain a document of faith for Christians in a pluralistic society.

Anti-Judaism and the Gospel (Werner H. Kelber). As in the case of Culpepper, Kelber not only has recourse to a real-reader construct but also works exclusively within the primary axis of the universal-reader/real-reader. Such a construct is more intensely social than that of Culpepper. In other words, Kelber reveals little of himself as a reader in this essay, portraying himself

---

[6] From the point of view of women as a marginalized social group, both Schneiders and Schottroff will agree with such a position: while interpreters of the Gospel leave a great deal to be desired, the Gospel itself does not.

[7] This issue of exclusivism is also the issue of sectarianism, and Culpepper's position comes close to that of Kysar: the Gospel itself offers conflicting directions in this regard. Both Michaels and I adopt a more somber view of exclusivism/sectarianism in the Gospel: while Michaels sees it as a positive dimension, I regard it as negative and dangerous.

instead as a member of a collective readership of Christian theologians and interpreters—a real reader within a socioreligious and socioeducational community of interpretation. This collective readership is further constituted on the basis of certain sociohistorical and critical developments: first and foremost, a post-Holocaust context in which Christian theologians and interpreters have no choice but to deal with the anti-Judaism present in their foundational texts; second, a contemporary critical scene in which interpreters are called upon to deal with the ideological allegiances of such texts. As such, Kelber, like Culpepper, is similarly concerned with the ethical dimensions and ramifications of the Gospel, but only with respect to the question of the Jews and anti-Judaism.

With regard to anti-Judaism in the Gospel, Kelber draws a stark picture indeed. While invariably portrayed, even today, from a theological point of view as a text of profound spirituality, grounded in a high conception of the Spirit, and as a document of love and truth, as manifested by the sending of the Son and the fullness of metaphysical presence respectively, Kelber argues that the Gospel possesses as well a profound sense of anti-Judaism and that such anti-Judaism is by no means incidental or secondary to the text but rather fundamental to and inherent in the metaphysics and theology of the Gospel. As such, it is a dimension of the Gospel that cannot be readily excised or bypassed but remains intrinsically tied to its theological and metaphysical programme.[8] The purpose of the study, therefore, is to bring to the surface this underlying connection between the spirituality and the anti-Judaism of the Gospel.

In so doing, Kelber engages in what one may call ideological criticism, with specific recourse to the concepts of identity and otherness, both with regard to

---

[8] On this point Kelber is far more radical than Culpepper. Although Culpepper does ultimately argue that there is no way to ignore or bypass the anti-Jewish character of the Gospel and recommends an aggressive awareness of this dimension of the Gospel on the part of readers and interpreters, he does nevertheless argue, on the one hand, that the Gospel does not preach hatred of the Jews as such and, on the other, that its anti-Jewish hostility can be somewhat mollified by paying particular attention to the question of translation, particularly with regard to the expression *hoi Ioudaioi*. Kelber speaks outright about hatred for the Jews and sees all attempts to deal with the anti-Judaism of the Gospel that fail to see it as fundamentally interconnected with its theological and metaphysical ambitions as circumventing the issue.

the metaphysics (the Logos; the descent of the Logos into the world; the mission of the Logos in the world) and the ethics (the representation of believers and non-believers alike) of the Gospel and with a special focus on the characterization of the Jews and its relationship to the Gospel's agenda.[9] In effect, grounded in a complex metaphysical and linguistic framework, the Gospel draws a distinction between insiders and outsiders, between love as self-giving as the standard for intra-Christian conduct and repudiation of the other as demonic as the standard for extra-Christian relations, with the Jews as the embodiment of such others. In so doing, Kelber argues, the longing of the Gospel for identity ends up by trampling upon any concept of difference.

In the end, unlike Culpepper, Kelber stops as a real trader at this crucial junction: having pointed out the problem in full force, he does not go on to explain what he as a real reader, whether individual or social, would or should do with such a foundation text. In other words, having exposed the agenda of anti-Judaism in John at its most fundamental level, he provides no reading strategy for the theologian or interpreter to address the problem, to interpret the Gospel in a post-Holocaust context, to deal with issues of identity and otherness in the contemporary world.[10] Thus, while the real reader emerges as very much of a resistant reader, the ramifications of such critique and struggle are not pursued.

---

[9] In effect, as he points out in the Epilogue, Kelber argues for a criticism that goes beyond historical, literary, and reader concerns to analyze, along the lines of feminist criticism with respect to gender, the way in which positions of dominance and submission are constructed in the text, especially with regard to questions of identity (the "us") and difference (the "them"). If anything, Kelber argues, historical, literary, and reader concerns have only served to continue and reinforce the traditional interpretation of the Gospel as a document of the Spirit, of love, and of truth. It is a position similar to the one I take.

[10] In this regard the end result is not unlike his own description of what happens in a historical critical study of anti-Judaism in the Gospel. Just as historical criticism leaves one at the end with a keen sense of the origins of the conflict—a sense of the distant past but no more, so does this type of ideological criticism leave one with a sense of the radicality of the anti-Jewish agenda from both a literary and theological point of view—a keen sense of its ethical ramifications but no sense of how to proceed vis-à-vis a foundational text in the present. On this point, I would disagree: the critic must take a position.

The Many Readers and Meanings of the Gospel (Craig R. Koester). From the point of view of the dominant axis of the universal-reader/real-reader, Koester is—in contrast to not only Kelber and Culpepper but also all other readers as well—rather firmly lodged within the universal-reader pole of the spectrum, although he does refer occasionally to contemporary real readers. In fact, such readers, encompassing both "popular" and "scholarly" readers, constitute the point of departure for the study: while many find the Gospel meaningful and engaging, they do so in a myriad of ways, with almost as many readings in existence as there are readers. At the same time, Koester continues, most such readers would argue *against* the validity of all readings (and corollaries thereof: all readers as equally competent and a text means whatever a reader wants it to mean) and *for* the need to distinguish between incorrect readings and adequate readings. Thus, it is the problematic of multiplicity in interpretation that provides the basic élan for this study, with a response sought in a different kind of reader altogether. In other words, Koester not only reveals nothing about himself as a real reader but also, finding contemporary readings of the Gospel to be all over the interpretive map, assumes a universal-reader construct as he begins to look for some sort of controlling reader-construct.

In search of this construct, he has recourse to the secondary axis of the historical-reader/textual-reader, where, while readily acknowledging the value of ancient-reader constructs as advanced by historical criticism, he opts for a variation of the textual reader proposed by literary criticism, namely, the implied reader a la Wolfgang Iser.[11] This reader Koester depicts as follows: a

---

[11] The argument against historical-reader constructs is really an argument of degree rather than an either/or argument. To wit: While it is the aim of ancient-reader constructs to establish interpretive parameters for a proper reading of the text by enabling contemporary readers to enter into the world of the first century, to understand the evangelist in his own terms, and to look for the discrete readers addressed by the evangelist (the "intended" readers), the fact remains that our ability to do so is always limited. Consequently, while historical research must play a key role in searching for an adequate meaning of the text, in the end it can never completely guarantee the meaning of the text. By way of contrast, the implied-reader construct is tied to the text as such and thus greater control can be exercised by contemporary readers in its delineation and characterization. Nevertheless, its formulation is impossible without proper knowledge of the sociohistorical context and thus without a proper exercise of historical research.

reader who responds to the network of structures within the text; who thus possesses what is necessary for the text to exercise its effect; and who can be identified at a basic level by observing what the text assumes the reader to know and takes the trouble to explain. While textually based and hence more immediate,[12] such a reader remains nonetheless a stranger to contemporary readers, insofar as what "it" knows presupposes a particular social and historical context and hence historical research.

In the case of the Fourth Gospel, Koester goes on, literary and historical studies make it imperative to speak not of one implied reader but of several such implied readers. In other words, the Gospel appears to have been written for readers with different perspectives. This position is then further elaborated as follows: First, the Gospel presupposes different kinds of ethnic readers (Jewish; Samaritan; Greek) as well as different kinds of geographical readers (not only readers belonging to different communities within the same area but also readers residing in different geographical areas). As such, the Gospel addresses a variety of Christians from different backgrounds. Second, the Gospel also presupposes a variety of readers from the point of view of knowledge: from the maximally informed to the minimally informed. In this regard, the Gospel offers not only the possibility of adequate meaning at various levels of understanding but also the possibility of growth in understanding, with a belief in the divinity of Jesus as seemingly the apex of the scale. At this point, Koester clearly invokes as well the secondary axis of the naive-reader/informed reader, with a corresponding classification of the different implied readers along this spectrum. Third, the Gospel offers as well recurring examples of incorrect understanding. Thus, while a scale of adequate understanding is clearly presupposed, a range of incorrect interpretation is also offered throughout.

---

[12] The position adopted here is quite objectivist in orientation, as confirmed by his approving reference to Jeffrey Staley to the effect that implied readers die only when the texts in which they are contained are destroyed; in other words, the implied reader "lives" in the text, a creation of the author and in no way a creation or co-creation of any real reader. The implied reader is "out there"—a fact or datum to be recovered. Of course, it is precisely because of such an objectivist foundation that the construct of the implied reader is presented as a controlling device in interpretation. For a thoroughly subjectivist interpretation of the implied reader, see Newheart.

For Koester, therefore, the construct of the implied reader, with its literary and historical dimensions, provides a sound and proper way of adjudicating readings of the Gospel within the maze of contemporary interpretation. At the same time, given the particular character of the implied-reader construct in John, with its spectrum of readers and scale of understanding, a range of adequate interpretation is granted. In other words, within certain interpretative parameters, a plurality of interpretations is possible. In the end, to be sure, this spectrum of readers and scale of meanings have been identified in the text and outlined by the universal-reader posture adopted by Koester—an informed reader well acquainted with historical and literary methodologies as well as a Christian reader, a reader with profound socioreligious and socioeducational concerns.[13] When compared to the readings of the Gospel advanced by Culpepper and Kelber, Koester's reading offers quite a different conception of he Fourth Gospel: a Gospel that calls for ever greater understanding on the part of its readers so that they can ascend from minimal to maximal levels of understanding and a Gospel that seemingly requires no resistant reading of any sort from its readers. Koester's vision is one of greater reflection and comprehension, not of dialogue and critique.

The Metaphoric Power of the Gospel (Robert Kysar). In contradistinction to the three previous readings, Kysar takes up a position at the center of the universal-reader/real-reader axis. In his attempt to focus on the strategy of the author, the use of metaphors in that strategy, and the experience of the reader in the light of this strategy—what he characterizes as a non-formal reader-response

---

[13] Although not mentioned as such, there can be little doubt that for Koester authorial intention plays a major role in interpretation. What else could be responsible for addressing such a variety of readers at the same time, for offering such a progressive scale of adequate meaning, and for ruling out certain kinds of meanings and interpretations throughout? Only the author, it would seem, whether real or implied, could exercise such control in composition and interpretation. At the same time, of course, the text itself becomes a sort of super-text: faithfully preserving and conveying such boundaries for proper interpretation; allowing for a degree of variation in interpretation, of a vertical sort, that is to say, from lower to greater understanding; and open to ever greater clarity and comprehension.

approach—Kysar proposes the following reader construct: an innocent contemporary reader, reading the Gospel for the very first time.[14]

This is a construct, as he himself explains, with a double footing. On the one hand, the construct is the product of a real reader, an alter ego of Kysar himself. As a real reader, Kysar describes himself from a variety of social perspectives: affluent and empowered; white and male; in the academy and in the church. Of these it is the latter pair—the socioeducational and socioreligious dimensions-that comes across as the most important by far. Thus, from the point of view of a Christian academic in the Lutheran tradition, the Gospel represents a source of authority in the community, with academic inquiry undertaken in the service of the church. On the other hand, though a product and reflection of this real reader, the construct is also a type of universal reader. Its contours are circumscribed as follows: particularly interested in questions of faith; having knowledge of and recourse to the gospel narrative up to the point of reading; careful and sensitive to the nuances of the text; vulnerable to the text and its influence. Although risky, given the real reader's extensive knowledge of the Gospel and its history of interpretation, the construct is nonetheless envisioned as a fruitful device, opening up a fresh reading of the Gospel.

Such a reading, focused here on what he calls the dialogue-discourse of John 3:1-15 involving Nicodemus and Jesus, may be characterized as a reading in slow motion, recording in detail the sequential and shifting reactions, both cognitive and affective, of the firsttime reader to the narrative strategy of the author.[15] The result is a reading of the unit that leaves the firsttime reader

---

[14] In effect, Kysar situates himself within the middle range of the universal-reader/real-reader axis by having recourse to the firsttime-reader/multiple-reader axis. The reader he concocts is thus a contemporary real reader (himself) who proceeds to read as if he were reading the text for the very first time, a universal reader.

[15] This procedure may also be described as taking place at the narrator/narratee level of narration, with the latter as a present-day though fictive narratee following for the first time the step-by-step narration of the narrator. Such a narratee is quite involved as well in following the point-by-point interaction at the level of narration involving the characters in the story, Jesus and Nicodemus, as recounted by the narrator. In so doing, Kysar does indeed dispense, as he claims, with the level of the implied author/implied reader, except, in my opinion, for the concluding section on the making of metaphor within the Gospel. In fact, given the line of argumentation, with its close attention to linguistic and literary detail as well

disconcerted and frustrated, without understanding—a reading without closure, yet hooked and determined to read on and reread the passage in the light of all that follows, seeking understanding—a reading in search of closure, convinced of the vital importance of the passage. This reading experience is said to come about as a direct result of the many metaphors employed in the course of the passage—metaphors whose full meaning remains beyond grasp, given their ambiguity and polyvalence, but whose significance is without question, given the focus on the kingdom of God and eternal life. At the end, therefore, the firsttime reader, despite a keen sense of disappointment and alienation, continues to read, because he wishes to understand what is required in order to enter into and see the kingdom of God and have eternal life.

For Kysar, this metaphorical quality and experience of the passage applies to the whole of the Gospel. In effect, the author is said to create a metaphorical "ecosystem" in which earthly phenomena are aligned with transcendent realities, thereby disrupting the reader's worldview (defamiliarization) but at the same time opening the way for a possible transformation of this worldview (transfamiliarization). Within this ecosystem, the author is also said to arrange the metaphors in a stacked or progressive manner, culminating with that of the cross as crucifixion-enthronement. As a result, a sense of direction is offered to the reader, insofar as all metaphors—including those of John 3:1-15: kingdom of God and eternal life—are to be read in the light of the cross. Yet, a sense of ambiguity persists as well, insofar as with each metaphor comes both clarification and obfuscation. In the end, therefore, there is advancement in understanding, shedding light on the whole of the narrative and its metaphorical ecosystem, but no final resolution or closure.

Thus, for Kysar, as for Koester, there appears to be no room or need for any type of resistant or critical reading of the Gospel.[16] Both are convinced of the

---

as narrative strategy, a very high notion of the "author"—the implied author, really—is presupposed: someone seemingly in control of the metaphorical ecosystem of the Gospel, its creation, its deployment, and its effects.

[16] There seems to be a shift in position in this regard with the reflections on the Gospel to follow in his reflection paper of the second part. There Kysar argues that the Gospel presents (at least) two sets of conflicting directions to the readers, the first having to do with relationship to the world and the second with regard to the nature of truth. While the presentation at this point seems to be in terms of comprehension/ ambiguity, the formulation

vital importance of its message, and both call for a fuller understanding of this message. The form of the message, however, is conceived in rather different ways: seemingly straightforward in Koester, but baffling and beckoning for Kysar. Instead of a scale of meaning devised by the author with a variety of readers in mind, with progression along this scale seen as not only a possibility but a desideratum, Kysar speaks of a metaphorical world elaborated by the author with understanding and ambiguity, direction and polyvalence, at its core. The result is progression in understanding, even with n certain apex in mind (the cross), but without complete resolution in the end. Consequently, this is a text that grips and baffles the reader, orienting and disorienting, a text that—to anticipate his later reflections on the role of the Gospel in the contemporary world—conveys truth-claims along with a good measure of ambiguity. Although implicit, it seems clear from such a reading that an interpreter in the service of the faith-community, such as Kysar himself, cannot but keep both dimensions of the Gospel in mind—striving for resolution, and finding some, yet having to settle at the same time for persistent and inescapable ambiguity.

The Gospel and Feminist Spirituality (Sandra M. Schneiders). With Schneiders there is a full and explicit return to the real-reader pole of the universal-reader/real-reader axis. From the beginning she portrays herself as particularly concerned with issues of spirituality and feminism—a real reader with explicit socioreligious as well as sociocultural preoccupations and commitments with regard to issues of gender. First, as a believing critic, she looks upon the biblical text as potentially revelatory and regards such a revelatory experience as personally transformative. Second, as a feminist critic, she is concerned with androcentric and patriarchal bias wherever it occurs, whether at the level of the text or its history of interpretation. Thus, from her position as a believing critic, her goal is to interpret the text in such a way as to bring out its transformative power for readers; at the same time, from her stance as a feminist critic, her objective is to counteract patriarchal and androcentric bias wherever it exists. This twofold approach she describes in terms of

---

there appears to be in terms of comprehension along different lines, both grounded in the Gospel itself.

"feminist spirituality" and its reading strategy as a "transformative feminist reading."[17]

Two general principles govern this reading strategy. The first is to seek a complete or integrated reading of the text in question, not only in terms of its individual units or passages but also in terms of their narrative contexts as well as of the text as a whole. The second is to be faithful to the text while interacting with contemporary religious concerns. Both principles can be seen readily at work in this study of John 20:11-18, the resurrection appearance of Jesus to Mary Magdalene.

Its focus is clearly on a female character, Mary Magdalene, as well as on the androcentric and patriarchal bias evident in the interpretation of this character at the hands of male biblical critics—informed male real readers. Thus, until quite recently, the traditional interpretation of this unit would look upon this first resurrection appearance of Jesus as a minor and private appearance, an attempt to offer consolation to a distraught female disciple before making his official and public appearances to the male disciples in order to commission them to carry on his work in the world. However, through a literary analysis of the passage—an integrated analysis with a focus on narrative structure, character development, and theological content—Schneiders sets out to counteract such rampant bias by showing that the text itself calls for a radically different reading: in effect, through this first appearance, Mary Magdalene is presented as the official apostolic witness to the Johannine community, the one who proclaims the Easter kerygma entrusted to her by Jesus and the one upon whom the pascal faith of the community is based. In this particular case, therefore, Schneiders shows that the bias is not in the text as such but in the interpretation of the text by a virtual monopoly of interested male critics,[18] so

---

[17] Such an approach is further characterized as highly interdisciplinary in nature, open to a variety of methodological and theoretical orientations (historical, literary, and theological)—all in the service of transformation.

[18] An unspoken corollary of this line of argumentation would seem to be that there is a key to the text and its meaning, a key that male interpreters have not possessed and a key that a consciously feminist approach readily provides. In other words, Schneiders comes close here to a rather objectivist view of the text with a meaning "out there," but a meaning which may or may not be properly retrieved. At the same time, she comes close as well to arguing for her own approach as non-ideological, insofar as it is said to recapture "the plain content

much so that an official apostolic witness of the early church, qua woman, has boon completely overwhelmed in the process.

For Schneiders, the Easter kerygma entrusted to and proclaimed by Mary Magdalene as a result of this appearance is that Jesus is not dead but alive, glorified and risen, with God but also present from now on in the community of disciples, the children of God in the world. In keeping with her goal of producing an integrated reading of the text at all levels, Schneiders further points out how such a message fits both within the immediate context of the passage, the resurrection narrative of John 20, as well as the Gospel as a whole: the unit responds to a basic question posed by the narrative context, "Where is the Lord?"—he is both with God and the children of God; in so doing, the unit is in accord with the basic aim of the resurrection narrative in the Gospel—not to announce the fate of Jesus after death but to explore the meaning and effects of Jesus' glorification for his disciples in and through his resurrection appearances.

The reading is transformative in two ways. It is transformative from a feminist point of view, insofar as it rehabilitates the word of a woman bearing witness, official and apostolic witness, with clear ramifications for contemporary church order. Second, it is transformative from a spiritual point of view, insofar as it shows how the Johannine kerygma proclaims a Jesus that is both glorified and present within and among his disciples of all generations, including our own. In other words, what was true of the first generation is also true of ours: as glorified, Jesus is present within and among us as well. We too are the children of God in the world.

For Schneiders, therefore, as for Culpepper and Kelber, there is need for a critical and resistant reading of the Gospel. Such a reading, however, is focused not on the question of anti-Judaism, marginalized social groups, or religious

---

and intent of the johannine text." How such a position accords with her own description of her task as offering *a* rather than *the* complete and integrated reading of the text is not clear. While all the readings of the Gospel thus far by and large tend to objectify the text and its meaning—though both Culpepper and Kysar express caution in this regard—the issue comes particularly to the fore in this study, given Schneiders' explicit challenge to a long-standing tradition of interpretation on the basis of her own access to the plain content and intent of the text.

exclusivism, but on the issue of gender and, more specifically, on women as a marginalized group within the Christian church, faced with androcentric and patriarchal bias either in the text or in its interpretation.[19] As such, resistance may be directed, as is the case here, not so much at the text itself but at the way in which it has been interpreted. At the same time, for Schneiders there is need as well for a spiritual reading of the text, a reading which looks upon the text as revelatory and transformative, as conveying kerygma and thus affecting the lives of Christian believers of all generations. Indeed, the resistant reading is ultimately in the service of the transformative: how could the presence of bias against women be considered revelatory and transformative? how could the glorified Jesus be present in a community where female disciples are marginalized by the male disciples? That is why the reading strategy proposed is described as both spiritual and feminist, given the character of the texts in some cases and the character of their interpretation in most cases.

The Gospel and the Canon (D. Moody Smith). Like Kysar, Smith takes up a position within the central range of the universal-reader/real-reader axis, but of a very different sort altogether. On the one hand, he does have recourse to contemporary real readers. In so doing, however, he discloses little of himself as a reader but speaks rather in terms of a social-reader construct—a corporate readership of Christian believers, within which he clearly situates himself. On the other hand, he also has recourse to a variety of historical readers of the

---

[19] It is interesting to note in this regard how much emphasis Schneiders places on the status and role of the disciples in the world as those in whom God and Jesus dwell, the children of God. Indeed, it is for their sake, for the sake of both the female and the male disciples of Jesus, the Christian readers of the Gospel, that a feminist, spiritual reading is undertaken, so that all may be transformed. Yet, it is precisely at this point that other ramifications of such a message come to the fore: not only the question of anti-Judaism (New Israel; New Covenant; New Moses), whose specter she does acknowledge in passing, but also the issue of religious exclusivism (New Creation; the Children of God; the Teacher), which remains dormant. In other words, within this framework, what is the status and role of those who do not believe, in whom Jesus does not dwell, and who are not members of the children of God? Is a resistant reading in order? Is a spiritual and transformative reading possible? These are questions that a transformative, feminist reading, engaged as it is in the proper and much-needed rescue of women as full members of the community of disciples, does not pursue or incorporate.

Gospel, both ancient (its original or intended readers as well as subsequent readers in the early centuries of the church) and recent (modern as well as contemporary Johannine scholars). In so doing, he speaks as a professional, academic reader, a critic well-informed in the history of the interpretation of the Gospel. As such, Smith operates with both a real-reader construct and an universal-reader construct. Thus, by bringing the secondary axis of the historical-reader/implied-reader, where he takes up a solid position at the former end of the spectrum, to bear on the primary axis of the universal-reader/real-reader, he ends up at the center of this axis—a real reader with clear socioreligious and socioeducational concerns.

What brings these two concerns together is his argument for what he calls a canonical reading of the biblical texts, a reading in the light of the New Testament as a whole, with particular reference in this study, of course, to the Fourth Gospel. In effect, Smith draws a close parallel between the way contemporary Christian readers approach the Gospel today and the way in which historical (Christian) readers approached it in the past. In both cases, the Gospel is read in the light of the other books of the canon, especially the Synoptic Gospels: as both the key to the canon (and the other gospels) and supplemented by it (and by them). This is a reading that Smith ultimately describes as not only natural and time-honored but also as quite proper and commendable, in direct contradistinction to the way of reading introduced by historical criticism, with its emphasis on an independent reading of the text in question (except, of course, with regard to questions of a literary-historical nature).

At the contemporary level, therefore, Smith points out how believers in general instinctively read the Fourth Gospel: on the one hand, as the hermeneutical key to the rest of the canon and the other gospels in particular, insofar as the Gospel is believed to give expression to the highest portrayal of Jesus and his message in the New Testament; on the other hand, as presupposing other Christian traditions, especially that of the Synoptic Gospels.[20] At the

---

[20] Such a popular way of reading, he points out, is in rather good company. Not only does it actually follow the apparent position of the Gospel itself and its author, with its many references to other early Christian traditions, but also the dominant position in critical scholarship as well, whereby the Gospel of John is seen as coming after and presupposing

historical level, then, Smith finds a similar phenomenon at work: on the one hand, a Gospel that meets with resistance at first, because of its challenge to the standard portrayal of Jesus and his message in the Christian tradition at large; on the other hand, a Gospel that, once accepted as part of the canon, emerges as the hermeneutical key to the canon and the Christian tradition, given its lofty presentation of Jesus and his message.

Such a way of reading the Gospel, Smith argues, is a valid and necessary reading, but with a twist. The canonical reading he envisions is not a reading that privileges the Fourth Gospel as such, as has invariably been the case, but a reading that approaches the Gospel as both influencing and being influenced by, enlightening and being enlightened by, the rest of the canon, particularly but not exclusively with regard to the Synoptic Gospels. As he puts it, it is a reading that does not subsume the Jesus of the Sermon on the Mount to the Jesus of the Incarnate Logos, but a reading that sees these two characterizations in tandem, with the Jesus of the Sermon on the Mount both providing the justification for and explaining the Jesus of the Incarnate Logos. Such a reading, Smith concludes, constitutes the continuing task of theological exegesis.

For Smith, therefore, there is no perceived need for a resistant reading of the Gospel. The need rather is for what he calls a canonical reading of it: a thoroughly intertextual reading within the framework of the Christian canon, a reading that approaches the relationship between the Gospel and the rest of the canon in bidirectional terms. To be sure, such a reading does have an inherent element of resistance, insofar as it goes against the grain of an isolated or independent reading of the Gospel, or any text for that matter, emerging as a result of modern biblical criticism. I would further characterize it as a reading with the church and its practice firmly in mind; a highly theological reading in the traditional sense of the term, with a heavy focus on christology; and a reading that presupposes a very high conception of the Christian Scriptures.

---

either the Synoptic Gospels themselves or an earlier stage of the synoptic tradition. What the Christian readers of today instinctively do, therefore, on the basis of the juxtaposition of the books and stories in the canon and the natural merging of the narratives, is what academic scholarship by and large holds as well as what the author of the Gospel would have welcomed.

The Gospel and the Many-sided Reader (Jeffrey L. Staley). Staley's position within the universal-reader/real-reader axis is very much toward the latter pole. Indeed, the entire first section of the study sets out to show why he opts for such a position: he begins by detailing his initial moorings in reader-response criticism of the formalist kind, well within the universal-reader pole, where he basically followed a firsttime-reader strategy; then, he outlines the various criticisms directed at this type of reader-response criticism, from a liberationist, poststructuralist, and social-science perspective; finally, taking such criticisms to heart, he argues for the need on the part of reader-response critics to own up to their reading constructs and strategies. In other words, Staley argues, it is time for real readers, such as himself, to come to the fore.

For his own real-reader construct, then, Staley has recourse to two different but related facets of his life—a real reader with profound sociocultural and socioeducational roots. The sociocultural dimension involves a bicultural experience and goes back to his early years as a child of Christian missionary parents.[21] This real reader hails from a Plymouth Brethren family, thoroughly steeped in an authoritarian and anti-intellectual religious tradition, but grows up in a Navajo Indian Reservation—a reader confronted with two very different worlds, out of which develops a natural curiosity about different ways of perceiving the world. The socioeducational dimension has to do with his later academic training as a biblical critic. This real reader comes from a fundamentalist background, quite at home in a dispensationalist and devotional reading of the Scriptures and with a view of the Fourth Gospel as closed and authoritarian, but is exposed at university to the methods of literary criticism and a corresponding view of the Gospel as playing tricks on and undermining the reader—a reader confronted once again with very different worlds, from

---

[21] The beginning experience is thus not unlike that of Alan Culpepper, except that the mission is not overseas but at home, among Native Americans in the Southwest. Staley, however, unlike Culpepper, goes on to speak of his later rejection of this authoritarian and fundamentalist background. Not unexpectedly, therefore, he comes across much more critical of what he calls the "what" of the Gospel—its content or ideology—than Culpepper. Thus, while Culpepper phrases the question in terms of the Gospel as a document of faith, Staley dispenses altogether with such terminology and focuses on the cultural and historical distance of the Gospel for contemporary readers.

which emerges a natural curiosity about narrative worlds, about stories and their effects upon readers. The result of such autobiographical experiences is a real reader who is committed not only to imaginative and dramatic readings of biblical texts but also to bringing across the "differentness" of biblical texts, and John in particular, by exploring the presentation (narrative poetics) and persuasive power (narrative pragmatics) of such difference. It is a reading strategy ultimately grounded in a sense of curiosity and openness.

The present study on the narrative of Jesus' death in the Gospel represents a concrete example of how Staley goes about reading the Gospel from such a real-reader perspective. In effect, what he does is to admit the presence in him of various voices and to give expression to these voices in terms of a dramatic scenario involving three characters—three individuals who have been crucified and are at the point of death. From the course of the dialogue, it becomes clear that these three individuals represent critical types: reader-response, social-scientific, and poststructuralist interpreters engaged in an analysis of the crucifixion scene. Each argues on behalf of his position and against those of the other two, with no final resolution in sight. The result is a view of biblical criticism as multidimensional and diffuse, even within himself as an individual critic—it is also a sign of his commitment to imaginative and dramatic readings, his interest in stories and how they work their effects upon readers, and his keen awareness of different worlds and different ways of perceiving the world.[22]

One could say that the strategy offered has resistance at its very core, insofar as each point of view resists the other points of view and argues against them, with no final resolution, no definitive closure, no unity or coherence in sight.[23] As such, it is not so much resistance to "what" the Gospel has to say, as for

---

[22] Staley may be described as a real reader who employs three informed or learned reading strategies, each based on a different theoretical orientation. However, in employing each strategy, what one finds is the real reader, Staley, speaking, not a universal-reader construct. In other words, this is the way he reads, and such reading happens to have multiple venues or channels.

[23] While such a position would certainly take to heart the critique of poststructuralist criticism and would clearly incorporate but also relativize the critique of sociocultural criticism, it would only meet halfway the critique of liberation criticism: true, it does shed light on the real reader and his social location, but in the end it takes no position or, to put it another way, the position it takes is too open-ended.

example in the case of Kelber, but resistance to the way in which the Gospel can be read. It is a resistance that emerges not only out of his curiosity about other cultural worlds but also out of his interest in narrative worlds—a resistance in favor of multiple voices and multiple readings.

The Gospel and the Individual Reader (Michael Willett Newheart). As with Culpepper, Kelber, Schneiders, and Staley, Newheart also takes a firm position within the real-reader pole of the universal-reader/real-reader axis. Unlike the others, however, all of whom opt instinctively for a social-reader construct in the social-reader/individual-reader axis, Willet's focus is on the individual reader. This is so not because he dismisses or bypasses the socialization of readers, their social location, but rather because he feels that the individuality of readers, their psychological location, has not been properly examined in biblical criticism. Yet, he argues, two developments within literary criticism clearly point the way in this regard: first, the emphasis of formalist reader response on the affective or emotional response of readers, widely acknowledged but not actually pursued; second, the emphasis of cultural reader response on the social location of real readers, since social context ultimately shapes the individual psyche as well, a fact that has been neither much acknowledged nor pursued. Willet's call, therefore, is for a "psycho-literary" reading of the Fourth Gospel—a psychological analysis of the reader's experience.[24] As the label indicates, this reading strategy involves two distinct theoretical components: literary criticism, with a focus on reader response and the interaction between text and reader; psychological theory, with recourse to the analytic psychology of Carl Gustav Jung.

From the point of view of literary criticism, psycho-literary interpretation can proceed at two different levels of experience, given the broad spectrum within reader response itself: that of the implied reader and that of the real reader. For Newheart, however, these two levels are highly interrelated and interdependent, insofar as the implied reader is said to be a projection of the real

---

[24] Given the close relationship posited between social location and psychological location, with a view of psychological issues as certainly unique to the individual subject but also as effectively circumscribed by the interpretive communities of which the individual subject forms part, Newheart also refers to this strategy in terms of "psycho-social" literary criticism.

reader onto the text, with different real readers giving rise to different implied readers. On either level the primary interest is on the individual subject and the psychological issues at play, although again, to be sure, such issues are said to be in part the result of membership in certain interpretative communities. For Newheart, therefore, the implied-reader construct is clearly not a universal-reader construct but the construct of a real reader, an individual anchored in community.

From the point of view of psychological criticism, psycho-literary interpretation highlights the emotional response of the reader to the narrative. On the one hand, the text provokes an inner image or archetype in the reader, a flow of psychic energy in the unconscious. On the other hand, the reader projects this image onto the narrative, establishing thereby an emotional bond with the narrative; in so doing, the reader searches for wholeness, for resolution of unconscious issues. Consequently, the narrative compensates or corrects some conscious attitude in the reader's psyche, while the reader attempts to resolve his or her complexes through reading. Once again, for Newheart, the emotional response in question is both social and unique: social context does shape response to narrative—social groups have different experiences with inner images and project different images onto the narrative; however, within such social groups, individuals also have different experiences with inner images and project different images onto the narrative. It is this latter response with which Newheart is particularly concerned.

Newheart concludes with a psycho-literary reading of John, with special emphasis on the reader's emotional reaction to the characters of the narrative, both from the perspective of the implied reader and of himself as real reader (the creator of the implied reader). From the former perspective, the narrative presents Jesus as a symbol of the Self, which works toward wholeness in the psyche; the implied reader then projects this image onto Jesus and establishes thereby both a cognitive (Jesus as Son of God and Mysterious Other) and an emotional bond (love; peace; joy). From the latter perspective, Newheart describes a twofold bond on his part with this Jesus: while Jesus' intimacy with God meets his own longing for parental connection, given certain emotional issues involving Mother/Father Complexes, Jesus' status as Other further connects with his own sense of alienation from his religious tradition and society at large.[25] Such a reading remains, to be sure, a highly personal one, since other readers would respond in other ways to and establish different bonds with the narrative.[26]

One such reading—a reading which he himself does not produce in this study—is the reading of resistance.[27] Thus, while he himself accepts the claims of the implied author and functions as a compliant reader, other readers from different psycho-social locations may very well end up rejecting such claims, becoming resistant readers in the process. Moreover, just as his acceptance of these claims is grounded in his own psycho-social location, so would their rejection on the part of other readers be similarly grounded in their own psycho-social locations. In other words, for Newheart the Gospel and its rhetoric is personally attractive and satisfying, but this is no guarantee that it will prove so

---

[25] This emotional bond with the character Jesus has certain ramifications with regard to the other characters in the narrative: while the implied reader and the real reader behind the construct identify with those who believe in Jesus, "they" become alienated from those who reject Jesus, above all the character of "the Jews." The issue of anti-Semitism thus comes, as Newheart himself realizes, very much to the fore. He himself, however, does not pursue this particular angle of inquiry, in part because he associates such a response to the Gospel with its Jewish readers. The position taken, however, seems to be much closer to that of Kelber than to that of Culpepper and Smith: insofar as "the Jews" function in such a way in the narrative—though they are not alone in this regard, as the figures of Judas and Pilate readily demonstrate—anti-Judaism is intrinsic not only to the rhetoric of the narrative but also to the emotional response of the implied reader.

[26] Although personal, his response is further identified socioculturally in terms of race (white), socioeconomic class (middle-class), sexual orientation (heterosexual), socioeducational status (highly educated/academic), gender (male), and socioreligious status (Christian). However, the focus of inquiry remains throughout on the psychological dimensions of his reading, not on the social dimensions nor on the relationship between these two dimensions.

[27] To be sure, Newheart claims that a psycho-literary reading is always a critical reading, insofar as the real reader in question is forced to ask a number of fundamental questions regarding his or her own emotional response to the narrative. It is not always critical in the sense of resisting, however, since the real reader may respond, as he himself does in this case, by accepting the claims of the implied author as conveyed through the rhetoric of the narrative.

for others. To put it another way, while resistance is in principle at the core if his strategy, such resistance will not always emerge from all readers with respect to the same text or even the same features if the text; it all depends in the end on the psycho-social location of the readers in question.

Concluding Comments. A number of comparative comments can be readily made with regard to these different readings and interpretations of the Gospel on the part of real readers self-conscious and forthcoming about reading constructs and strategies.

1. One finds different attitudes on the part of these readers toward their own status as real readers. Most do approach the text as full and explicit real readers: Culpepper; Kelber; Schneiders; Staley; Newheart. Kysar and Smith stand at the center of the spectrum, quite aware of themselves as real readers, yet having recourse as well to an operative universal-reader construct—for Kysar, a firsttime-reader construct; for Smith, a variety of historical-reader constructs. Koester takes his point of departure from the realm of real readers but then proceeds to situate himself firmly within the universal-reader pole of the spectrum by recourse to a variety of implied-reader constructs.

2. Among those who do read self-consciously as real readers, whether in full or in part, there are different attitudes toward the real-reader construct in question. Thus, with respect to the amount of information disclosed, the spectrum runs from the quite forthcoming (Staley; Newheart), to the forthcoming but not as expansive (Culpepper; Kysar), to the rather reserved (Schneiders; Smith), to the quite reserved (Kelber). In his own comments regarding real readers, Koester comes across as forthcoming but not expansive: real readers are basically portrayed as offering a myriad of interpretations, while arguing against any critical position to the effect that all interpretations are valid and for a sense of criteria in interpretation.

3. With respect to the social-reader/individual-reader axis, the character of the real-reader construct in question also varies. At its most fundamental level, all of these readers opt for a social-reader construct, except one, Newheart, who argues strongly in favor of the individual-reader construct. In addition, the former stress a variety of social factors: the socioreligious (Culpepper; Kelber; Kysar; Schneiders; Smith); the socioeducational (Culpepper; Kelber; Kysar; Smith; Staley); and the sociocultural (Culpepper; Schneiders; Staley). The

portrayal of the real readers given by Koester would seem to favor the socioreligious dimension.

4. With respect to the compliant-reader/resistant-reader axis, the shape of the real-reader construct varies once again. At the resistant-reader end of the spectrum lies Kelber; at the compliant-reader end, the following can be readily situated: Kysar, Smith, Schneiders, and Newheart (although the last two include resistance in principle within their strategies). In the middle one finds Culpepper and Staley. Were one to extrapolate from the portrayal of the implied readers provided by Koester, one would have to situate Koester well at the compliant-reader pole.

5. In terms of universal-reader constructs, one finds an appeal to a firsttime-reader construct (Kysar); appeals to both historical-reader (Smith) and textual-reader (Koester) constructs; and an appeal to a variety of constructs along the naive-reader/informed-reader axis (Koester).

6. Finally, from the overall discussion a number of important issues can be readily discerned:

-First and foremost, there is the question of the Gospel and the Christian church, that is to say, the role of the Gospel as Scripture and Word of God for Christian believers. This issue comes across in a number of ways: its character as a document of faith (Culpepper); a foundational text within the post-Holocaust context (Kelber); a progressive document of faith (Koester); a metaphorical document of faith (Kysar); a revelatory and transformative text (Schneiders); a canonical text (Smith). The range of opinion varies: from the very positive (Koester; Smith); to the positive but possibly problematic (Culpepper; Kysar; Schneiders); to the thoroughly problematic (Kelber).

-Second, very prominent as well is the question of anti-Judaism in the Gospel, ranging from the quite explicit (Culpepper; Kelber) to the mostly implicit (Schneiders; Smith; Newheart). The range here is quite broad as well: from a view of the Gospel as fundamentally anti-Jewish (Kelber; Newheart) to a view of it as anti-Jewish not in itself but as a result of later interpretation (Culpepper; Smith).

-Finally, a number of other issues come to the fore as well, such as: (a) the question of multiplicity in interpretation, ranging from a more positive (Kysar; Staley) to a more negative (Koester) evaluation of such multiplicity; (b) the relevance of the Gospel for marginalized social groups, in general (Culpepper)

or with respect to a specific group (Schneiders); (c) the question of exclusivism
or sectarianism (Culpepper); and (d) the question of cognitive/emotional bonding
and the wholeness of the self (Newheart).

THE GOSPEL AT THE CLOSE OF THE TWENTIETH CENTURY

The Gospel as Hermeneutical Earthquake (Robert Kysar). Kysar identifies
himself forthwith as both a Christian and an interpreter for the church—a real
reader with predominant socioreligious commitments and goals. From this
perspective he offers a dramatic scenario for the church of North America in the
twenty-first century, with a corresponding view of the Fourth Gospel as playing
a key role within such a drama. This scenario has two sides to it. First, the church
will come to represent not only one religious option among many in a thoroughly
pluralized culture but also a social minority within such a culture; as a result,
Christians will tend to see themselves increasingly as a marginal group in
opposition to the world. Second, given the fundamental role of the media in
shaping human consciousness and language, truth will become increasingly
ambiguous as well. On both counts, Kysar argues, the Gospel of John is likely to
emerge as quite influential in the church. However, given the presence of
conflicting positions within the Gospel itself regarding both world and truth, the
basic question will be how the Gospel will be interpreted, that is to say, in what
direction it will be interpreted.

Thus, for example, the sectarian nature of the Gospel may readily appeal to a
newly sectarian church; similarly, the ambiguous character of John's language
may prove attractive in such a pluralist context. The problem, however, is that the
Gospel contains both sectarian and trans-sectarian themes, ambiguity as well as
absolute claims to truth. Consequently, certain basic questions regarding
interpretation will come to the fore. On the one hand, will the church opt for the
best rather than the worst elements of sectarianism and make use of the trans-
sectarian themes of the Gospel? On the other hand, will the church turn to the
ambiguity of the Gospel rather than to its absolute truth claims?

For Kysar, the answers to these questions may provoke a hermeneutical
earthquake of heretofore unseen proportions. In effect, the Gospel may well be
read in terms of a twofold imperative: (a) a mission against the powers of
injustice and oppression, a mission of radical inclusion, in a world loved by
God; (b) a view of Christian theology in terms of metaphor, of fundamental

images or formative stories. Such an earthquake, however, will take place only if certain choices are made over others in a reading of the Gospel, with both alternatives grounded in the text. In the end, therefore, Kysar himself calls for a resistant reading of the Gospel, a reading that favors certain ideological dimensions of the Gospel over others, a reading that is open rather than closed to those elements of plurality and ambiguity that will mark the church and the world of the twenty-first century.

The Gospel as Kinder, Gentler Apocalypse (J. Ramsey Michaels). Michaels presents himself, much more indirectly than Kysar, as both a Christian believer and a professional biblical critic—a real reader with pronounced socioeducational and socioreligious ties. From this twofold perspective he argues, like Kysar, for a major role for the Gospel in the world of the next century.

From the point of view of the academy, Michaels provides a history of Johannine scholarship in the twentieth century in four basic movements, centered around scholarly attitudes toward the integrity of the present text of the Gospel: (1) at the beginning of the century, a focus on the text as such, with questions of authorship, background, and historicity as paramount; (2) with the introduction of German critical scholarship, an increasing preoccupation with sources, redactions, and displacements behind the text; (3) a return to the text as such in the United States by way of a reconstruction of the history of the community behind the text; (4) presently, at the end of the century, increasing concern with the character of the text as text on account of literary criticism. From this perspective, Michaels situates himself within the last movement and calls for a sustained and thoroughgoing analysis of the text as presently configured. At the same time, he acknowledges that such a critical orientation will in no way alter the range of interpretations regarding the Gospel. Consequently, he argues, any answer to the question of its role at the turn of the century will have to be highly personal in nature.

His own he provides from the point of view of the church. In effect, he posits a basic analogy between (1) the world at the time of the Gospel and the world at present, and (2) the message of the Gospel then and its message now. On the one hand, both worlds—similarly situated at the end of a century and indeed of an era (the apostolic age/the millennium)—are described in terms of "darkness." On the other hand, for both worlds the Gospel offers a "light" in the darkness, a new dimension of existence. In our own case, Michaels describes such "darkness" not only in sociopolitical but also, and above all, in socioreligious terms—like Kysar, he argues that Christians in America and elsewhere will increasingly see themselves as besieged and oppressed. Under such conditions, the Gospel may once again offer a "light" of hope, a resolution in and for the world, not along the lines of apocalypticism but rather by drawing Christians closer to one another and putting distance between them and the values of the world.

In the end, unlike Kysar, Michaels does not see the Gospel as presenting conflicting directions vis-à-vis the world, with a fundamental option open to believers. Rather, the conflict is between apocalypticism and "johannine light," with the latter as the preferred alternative—a sort of kinder, gentler apocalypse.

The Gospel as Sectarian Theology (Gail R. O'Day). As in the case of both Kysar and Michaels, O'Day comes across in these reflections as a professional biblical critic but with a particular concern for the state of contemporary constructive theology—a real reader at home in the Christian Western theological tradition and thus with paramount socioreligious concerns. Within such a context, O'Day sees the Fourth Gospel as playing a very important role, indeed a saving role, at the turn of the century on account of its particular theological vision, a vision described as sectarian not only from the point of view of the New Testament itself but also, and above all, of the theological tradition of the West.

Such a tradition, O'Day points out, has largely followed a Pauline framework. The problem, however, is that at present this consensus in in crisis, under challenge from postmodernism and faced with calls for other and different voices more in keeping with the diversity present in early Christianity itself. One such voice, O'Day suggests, should be that of the Fourth Gospel—unique not only within the context of early Christianity but also in a theological consensus that has either bypassed it altogether or shaped it to its own ends. For O'Day a specific contribution of John at this point would be to offer a very different interpretation of the death of Jesus, a death presented not according to the standard theologies of atonement or reconciliation (ransom; sacrifice; moral example) but rather in terms of a restoration of relationships—a new relationship between humanity and God as well as a new relationship among human beings themselves. In effect, by revealing God's love for the world and breaking the power of the world, Jesus' death not only restores relationship with God but also creates community. Moreover, this theology of reconciliation places, unlike the others, as much emphasis on the divine element as on the human element: it is through faith in Jesus that human beings enter into community with God and one another. Finally, this theology, unlike the others as well, also looks at the death of Jesus not by itself but within the context of and climax of his life and ministry: it is the incarnation itself that is the locus of reconciliation.

For O'Day this Johannine focus on relationship and community, very much of a sectarian focus in the Western tradition, provides a way out of the present crisis in theology. Consequently, for O'Day the role of the Gospel at the turn of the century could be crucial, even redeeming. As with Michaels, therefore, the Fourth Gospel presents for O'Day no conflicts or problems but rather a splendid and much-needed theological option for the contemporary world, not so much because of the growing sectarian character of the Christian church, both in terms of numbers and influence, but rather because of its emphasis on restoring relationship and community with God and one another.

The Gospel and Liberation (Luise Schottroff). From the start Schottroff draws an explicit portrait of herself as a feminist theologian of liberation in a European and, above all, German context—a real reader with a variety of socioreligious, sociopolitical, and sociocultural concerns. From this multiple perspective, she weighs the role of the Fourth Gospel at the turn of the century: given her German context, she addresses the question of anti-Judaism in the Gospel; in the light of her theological moorings in Liberation, she deals with the question of messianism; given her grounding in feminism, she turns to the role of women in the Gospel. Her position regarding the meaning and significance of the Gospel for the future is mixed: quite negative with respect to anti-Judaism, yet quite positive regarding both messianism and feminism.

To begin with, Schottroff argues that, from a historical point of view, the Gospel is not anti-Jewish but rather reflects the intra-Jewish conflict between a Jewish majority and a Jewish Christian minority present in the period between the first Jewish-Roman War of 66-70 C.E. and the second Jewish-Roman War of 132-135 C.E. It is only with the decimation of Jews as well as Jewish Christians in Palestine that the Gospel becomes anti-Jewish at the hands of the

Gentile Christian churches.[28] From then on, however, its use in the Christian tradition—and above all in her own recent German context—at the service of anti-Judaism is undeniable. Consequently, and especially in the light of the resurgence of anti-Semitism in Germany, the Gospel is a dangerous book, and the interpreter has no choice but to keep this anti-Judaism ever in mind and to engage in constant denunciation of it. From this socioreligious point of view, therefore, there is need for a radical reading of critique and resistance.

From a sociopolitical point of view, however, the Gospel is quite valuable, when properly interpreted. In effect, John preaches a messianism that is neither otherworldly nor apolitical, as traditionally conceived, but rather quite worldly and political, not however along the lines of political liberation but rather of martyrdom on behalf of the people, as practiced today in many parts of Latin America. Similarly, from a sociocultural point of view, the Gospel proves quite effective as well, again when properly interpreted. Thus, John for the most part portrays women in a very good light, as individuals in the public and political sphere, and as excellent models for the twenty-first century.[29]

For Schottroff, therefore, unlike both Michaels and O'Day, the Gospel proves both dangerous and useful, not so much because it conveys conflicting directions regarding the same concerns—as Kysar argues—but rather because of the directions offered with respect to different concerns. Thus, while its profound and long-standing association with anti-Judaism calls for repudiation,

---

[28] On this point, Schottroff comes across as much closer to Culpepper than to Kelber: in and of itself the Gospel is not anti-Jewish, given the predominantly Jewish character of the Johannine communities, precisely one of the arguments invoked by Culpepper. In other words, it is historically improper, given the nature of the conflict at work, to speak of anti-Judaism at the time of composition. Thus, from the time of composition up to the outbreak of the second Jewish-Roman war, the sharp dualism of the Gospel was the result of an internal Jewish conflict whose main effect it was to prevent the solidarity of the Jewish people in the face of Roman imperial power.

[29] Schottroff is thus very close to the position adopted by Sandra Schneiders: the "dark spots" concerning women in the Fourth Gospel are not so much "dark spots" in and of the text as "dark spots" of a history of interpretation in the hands of male scholars. When properly examined, through the lens of a feminist optic, both Mary Magdalene and the nameless Samaritan woman emerge as fine examples of female characters in the narrative.

its stance regarding messianism and women, while often misinterpreted, are quite laudable and relevant.

The Gospel and the Diaspora (Fernando F. Segovia). I begin my own remarks with an explicit description of myself as a reader from the diaspora, by which I mean the reality and experience of individuals from non-Western civilizations who reside on a permanent basis in the West, with a corresponding reading strategy of intercultural criticism—a real reader with distinctive sociocultural concerns. The diaspora, I argue, involves otherness and engagement. The concept of otherness points to a situation of biculturalism in which there is no home, no voice, and no face—a position as permanent aliens or strangers in the world. The concept of engagement not only proceeds to embrace such a situation as one's very home, voice, and face, but also leads one to realize that all reality is construction, that there are many such realities, and that such realities can be analyzed, questioned, and altered—a position of critical engagement in the world.

As a reading strategy grounded in the diaspora, therefore, intercultural criticism involves an approach to texts in terms of otherness and engagement— as constructs and realities to be acknowledged, respected, and engaged rather than overwhelmed or overridden. Such an approach, while admittedly utopian, is nonetheless imperative. First, the text is seen as a poetic, rhetorical, and ideological product in its own right; second, the text is always seen as a "text" as well, not as something "out there" but as something that is always read and interpreted by a reader, including oneself; third, both text and "texts" are analyzed with liberation in mind, that is to say, in terms of critical dialogue and struggle in the light of one's own reality and experience.

My reading of John from the diaspora shows both profound agreement and profound disagreement with the Gospel on a number of fundamental points. For example, with regard to the portrayal of "the world" in the Gospel, I find myself in basic agreement with its position to the effect that the world is fundamentally evil and unjust, yet miss that sense of a thirst for justice and wellbeing present in the diaspora. Similarly, with respect to its portrayal of Jesus' followers as "chosen," I readily identify with the idea of a privileged position and optic vis-à-vis the world, but find its sharply dualistic presentation, its metanarrative of chosenness, quite unacceptable and most dangerous. Finally, with regard to its view of life in the world, I fully agree with its call for patient and strategic abiding, but very much miss that sense of urgent need for change in the world so dear to the diaspora. I would summarize such a reading as follows. From the point of view of its assessment of the situation, I find the Gospel to be highly significant—How can anyone speak of justice and wellbeing in the world? However, from the point of its proposed solution, I find the Gospel quite irrelevant—Speak one must, in pursuit of wellbeing and justice.

For me, therefore, a reading of resistance is, in principle, at the very core of my reading strategy of intercultural criticism, insofar as the latter calls for critical engagement with texts and "texts" from the perspective of one's reality and experience and with liberation in mind. From such a perspective, a variety of fundamental positions of the Fourth Gospel are accepted and rejected at one and the same time. In this regard I would differ considerably from both Michaels and O'Day, while also going much beyond Kysar and Schottroff, insofar as the problem lies not—vis-à-vis Kysar—with conflicting directions regarding the same issue but with unacceptable directions on any number of issues and insofar as these issues are—vis-à-vis Schottroff—many, profound, and in the text (or, more accurately, in my "text") rather than in the "texts" of others.

The Gospel and Johannine Scholarship (D. Moody Smith). In his reflections on the Gospel, Smith comes across, very much along the lines of Michaels, as someone who has both the academy and the church in mind—a real reader with clear socioeducational as well as socioreligious concerns. The former perspective he pursues at length by providing a summary of what he has learned about the Gospel after almost four decades of research and scholarship; the latter perspective he brings to the fore in a brief postscript. These two perspectives are not at all unrelated: for Smith academic interpretation is at the service of religious interpretation, the scholarly reading at the service of the theological reading.

With regard to the academic interpretation of the Gospel, Smith addresses five topics in particular. First, the question of historical setting, especially with respect to Judaism. Three basic positions are outlined: (1) the Gospel finds its concrete origins in the early relations and rupture between synagogue and church; (2) the Gospel is not anti-Semitic, insofar as its portrayal of "the Jews," while highly negative, applies only to *some* Jews, reflects a specific historical situation of conflict, and is by no means a historical caricature; (3) such a negative portrayal of "the Jews" forms part of a more fundamental dualism involving followers of Jesus and opponents of Jesus.[30] Second, the question of literary independence: whether it knew other Gospels or not, the Fourth Gospel represents neither a supplementation or interpretation of the other canonical Gospels or any other extant Gospel. Third, the question of an independent community: there was both a distinctive Johannine circle of churches and a Johannine school. Fourth, the question of editing: in all likelihood the fundamental document of the community has been repeatedly edited. Finally, the question of the Gospel's role in the canon: John needs to be read in the light of the other canonical Gospels and the New Testament in general, otherwise it conveys a truncated view of Jesus and early Christianity—strident, shrill, dangerous. Thus, while the Gospel does bring to expression what is distinctly Christian, what Christians believed in the face of contradiction and opposition, it does so in a highly polemical fashion, as a result of such alienation and hostility. Consequently, the proper way to read it is to do so within the context of the New Testament canon.[31]

---

[30] On the question of anti-Judaism in the Gospel, Smith adopts a different position altogether. First, against Kelber, Smith would argue that anti-Judaism is not intrinsic as such to the theology and metaphysics of the Gospel, insofar as only *some* Jews are involved. Second, like Culpepper and Schottroff, he would further argue that, from a strictly historical point of view, the Gospel is not anti-Jewish: aside from the fact that not all Jews are meant, the polemic should also be seen as the result of (intra-Jewish) conflict involving rupture. Besides, what it does have to say about the Jewish position, even if cast in the most uncomplimentary of terms, is essentially correct. Third, such a polemic must be placed within the wider framework of Johannine dualism, which involves a much wider range of villains—the opponents of Jesus. Finally, unlike Culpepper and Schottroff, Smith does not see as much of a need to engage the Gospel in this regard, although he certainly disagrees with any usage of the polemic to apply to all Jews regardless of time or place. In other words, the later use of the Gospel in Christian history and tradition, of which he is very much aware, is a separate question altogether from that of its original situation.

[31] For Smith, therefore, the question of anti-Judaism merges into the wider question of the Gospel's dualistic polemic, which is in turn a variation of the question of religious exclusivism. In effect, the stance of the Gospel is quite problematic: a supreme portrayal of Jesus with both a ringing affirmation of those who believe in him and a devastating condemnation of those who do not—beginning with "the Jews," going on to members of the

With regard to the religious interpretation of the Gospel, Smith has recourse to the question of control—who has it and what is its purpose—to explain his position. While academic interpretation is in the hands of professional exegetes, who have as their goal a mastery of the text, whether from an ancient or modern perspective, theological interpretation is in the hands of churchly exegetes, whose purpose it is to understand the text in order to be controlled by it. For Smith, therefore, theological interpretation regards the Gospel as a given, whose meaning is revelatory but must be perceived for what it was. As such, historical research—academic interpretation—allows one to learn from the text about God and about oneself as member of the Christian church, although in the end the meaning uncovered by historical research is not to be identified with the revelation of God through the text, which is always present and ongoing.

For Smith, therefore, the Gospel does not call so much for a resistant reading but for a corrective reading. It does indeed have the most pointed presentation of Jesus and the early church in the New Testament, but if read by itself, apart from the rest of the New Testament, the downside of such a presentation, its representation of those who oppose Jesus and the early church, proves one-sided and dangerous.[32] A canonical reading is thus very much in order, a reading which at the same time exemplifies the kind of religious or theological interpretation Smith calls for, whereby the text (as revelatory) possesses the reader rather than the reader the text, but always with the help of scholarly interpretation.

Concluding Comments. Again, a number of comparative comments can be readily made with respect to these different reflections on the significance and relevance of the Gospel at the close of the twentieth century on the part of real readers self-conscious and forthcoming about their own status as real readers.

Johannine communities by the time of the Letters, and ultimately encompassing anyone who rejects or opposes Jesus. In order to preserve the former dimension of the Gospel, which is explained as the result of a socioreligious situation of alienation and hostility, and play down the latter, a canonical reading is of the essence.

[32] It is interesting to note in this regard that this is, in a certain sense, the very opposite of what Gail O'Day is calling for: while for her the Johannine interpretation of the death of Jesus proves a much-needed corrective to the standard theories of the atonement, based on Paul and the Synoptics, for Smith it is the non-Johannine portrayal of Jesus that proves a much-needed corrective to the figure of the Logos given expression by John.

1. Different attitudes can be discerned with regard to the fundamental question of significance and relevance of the Gospel at this particular time in history. Three of these readers (Tsar; Michaels; O'Day) see the Gospel of John as (potentially) playing a major if not key role in the early twenty-first century, whether from the point of view of the Christian church (Kysar; Michaels) or of constructive theology (O'Day). The others do not express themselves in such categories but speak instead in terms of an overall role for the Gospel at the turn of the century.

2. While all of these readers approach the Gospel as full and explicit readers, different attitudes may be found toward the real-reader construct in question. Thus, with respect to the amount of self-information disclosed, the spectrum runs from the more expansive (Schottroff; Segovia), to the forthcoming (Tsar; Michaels), to the more reserved (O'Day; Smith).

3. In terms of the social-reader/individual-reader axis, all of these readers opt for a social-reader construct, but the character of this construct varies, with different social dimensions emphasized in the process: (a) socioreligious concerns (Kysar; Michaels; Schottroff; Smith); (b) socioeducational concerns (Michaels; O'Day; Smith); and (c) sociocultural concerns (Schottroff; Segovia).

4. In terms of the compliant-reader/resistant-reader axis, the shape of the real-reader construct varies as well. At one end of the spectrum, there is the view of the Gospel as a rather positive text, a text to be appropriated. Such I would argue is the position represented by Michaels and O'Day. At the other end, there is the view of the Gospel as a text with both positive and negative features, a text to be engaged. That I would argue is my own position, which calls for a rejection of some of the Gospel's most prominent features. Then, there is a middle range with a variety of positions: the Gospel as containing conflicting directions, some positive and some negative, regarding the same issues (Kysar); the Gospel as containing some negative elements, which are to be rejected (Schottroff); the Gospel as containing some dangerous elements, which are to be corrected (Smith). On the whole, therefore, the basic attitude toward the Gospel as a document at the close of the twentieth century is a positive one. At the same time, however, the possibility of critique and resistance is granted in principle by most.

5. Finally, the overall discussion in these reflections gives rise to a number of important issues:

-First and foremost, one finds once again the question of the Gospel and the church—the role of the Gospel as Scripture and Word of God for Christian believers, addressed from a number of perspectives: its importance for a sectarian church and pluralist conception of truth (Kysar); for a growing sectarian church in the world (Michaels); for constructive Christian theology, given its unique portrayal of Jesus' death in terms of restoring relationships (O'Day); for a political and worldly type of Christian messianism (Schottroff); and for the definition of Jesus and his message (Smith). The range of opinion in this regard goes from the very positive (Michaels; O'Day; Schottroff), to the cautious (Smith), to the conflicting (Kysar).

-Second, the question of exclusivism or sectarianism proves rather prominent as well, with the following range of opinion in evidence: from the very positive (Michaels), to the divided (Kysar), to the corrective (Smith), to the very negative (Segovia).

-Third, there is also the question of anti-Judaism (Schottroff; Smith). On the one hand, there is fundamental agreement to the effect that, while the later tradition did without doubt read the Gospel from an anti-Jewish perspective, the Gospel itself is not, from a strictly historical point of view, anti-Jewish (Schottroff; Smith). On the other hand, the attitude to be adopted toward this issue varies: from radical opposition (Schottroff) to consideration of it within the wider issue of dualism (Smith).

-Finally, a couple of other issues are raised as well: (a) the relevance of the Gospel for marginalized social groups, with respect to both minority groups (Segovia) and women (Schottroff); (b) the political ramifications of the Gospel for life in this world, ranging from the quite positive (Schottroff) to the quite negative (Segovia).

Concluding Reflection

This exercise in intercultural criticism, in the analysis of various "texts" of the text of the Gospel of John, has brought out certain important facets of the collection as a whole. It has, for example, highlighted the emergence of real readers in reading and interpretation, as real readers begin to reveal themselves not only with regard to their reading constructs and strategies but also with respect to their social location and perspectives. It has also highlighted the diversity of constructs and strategies appealed to by real readers in reading and interpretation, both with regard to real-reader constructs and universal-reader constructs. It has further highlighted the diversity of interpretations and evaluations of the Gospel produced by real readers at this time: different foci of analyses; different findings; different attitudes toward such findings. In so doing, the collection does indeed serve as a good reflection of and barometer for the present state of biblical criticism as a whole at the close of the twentieth century.

Despite such differences, such multiplicity of interpretation, the Gospel does come across, on the whole, as a highly positive and relevant text for church and world alike at the turn of the century, even when reservations and cautions are raised, as they are in a number of studies. Such findings and results make it certain that, on the one hand, fascination with the Fourth Gospel will continue well into the twenty-first century and that the text of the Gospel will continue to be read, while, on the other hand, such readings will take any number of directions and result in any number of interpretations, in any number of "texts" of the Gospel. These findings and results make it increasingly certain as well that in this reading of the text of the Gospel and this production of countless "texts" of the Gospel, the real readers and constructors of such "texts" will no longer remain silent and dormant but will step forward to claim their readings and "texts" openly and publicly, in the light of their own perspectives and social locations. And this will prove a most positive and healthy step for both Johannine Studies and biblical criticism in general.

Index of Citations

Index of Authors

3 5282 00600 9586

Printed in the United States
38551LVS00003B/56